21st century skills

Rethinking How Students Learn

Solution Tree | Press

a division of
Solution Tree

555 North Morton Street
Bloomington, IN 47404
800.733.6786 (toll free) / 812.336.7700
FAX: 812.336.7790

email: info@solution-tree.com
solution-tree.com

Visit **go.solution-tree.com/21stcenturyskills** to view chapter 6 and 11 graphics in full color and to access live links to tools and materials.

Printed in the United States of America
14 13 12 11 10   2 3 4 5

Library of Congress Cataloging-in-Publication Data

21st century skills : rethinking how students learn / [edited by] James Bellanca, Ron Brandt.
    p. cm. -- (Leading edge)
  Includes bibliograpical references and index.
  ISBN 978-1-935249-90-0
  1. Learning ability. 2. Learning strategies. I. Bellanca, James A., 1937- II. Brandt, Ronald S. III. Title: Twenty-first century skills.
  LB1134.A22 2010
  370.15'23--dc22
                            2010002492

Solution Tree
Jeffrey C. Jones, CEO & President
Solution Tree Press
President: Douglas M. Rife
Publisher: Robert D. Clouse
Vice President of Production: Gretchen Knapp
Managing Production Editor: Caroline Wise
Senior Production Editor: Suzanne Kraszewski
Copy Editor: Rachel Rosolina
Proofreader: Sarah Payne-Mills
Cover Designer: Orlando Angel
Text Designer: Amy Shock

Acknowledgments

Assembling a coherent book from the ideas of a group of highly individualistic and creative thinkers is never easy. Our efforts to develop this volume were facilitated by the cooperative spirit of the contributing authors and the editorial staff at Solution Tree Press. In fact, the book's development has been a model of the skills we seek to promote: collaboration, communication, creative and critical thinking, and lots of problem solving.

Special thanks go to Robb Clouse, Solution Tree Press publisher. Robb became the third musketeer in identifying potential authors, establishing criteria, selecting the articles, and making helpful suggestions. We also appreciate the support and attention to detail of Gretchen Knapp, vice president of production, and Suzanne Kraszewski, senior production editor.

Table of Contents

About the Editors

James Bellanca and Ron Brandt

 James Bellanca, MA, is founder and CEO of International Renewal Institute, Inc., and acting director of the Illinois Consortium for 21st Century Skills. He founded SkyLight Professional Development in 1982. As its president, he mentored more than twenty author-consultants as he led SkyLight in pioneering the use of strategic teaching in comprehensive professional development. Bellanca coauthored more than twenty books that advocated the application of thinking and cooperating across the curriculum with the theme "not just for the test, but for a lifetime of learning." Currently, Bellanca is building on the theories of cognitive psychologist Reuven Feuerstein to develop more effective responses to the learning needs of students whose academic achievement continues to lag. A longtime proponent of teaching that is aligned with the advocated best practices of 21st century skills, Bellanca's most recent publications include *Designing Professional Development for Change: A Guide for Improving Classroom Instruction*; *Enriched Learning Projects: A Practical Pathway to 21st Century Skills*; *Collaboration and Cooperation in 21st Century Schools*; *200+ Active Learning Strategies and Projects for Engaging Students' Multiple Intelligences*; and *A Guide to Graphic Organizers: Helping Students Organize and Process Content for Deeper Learning*.

Ron Brandt, Ed.D., was editor of publications for the Association for Supervision and Curriculum Development (ASCD), Alexandria, Virginia, for almost twenty years before his retirement in 1997. During his career at ASCD, he was best known as executive editor of *Educational Leadership* magazine. In the 1980s, he promoted the teaching of thinking in elementary and secondary schools, collaborating with Robert Marzano and a team of other educators in development of a book, *Dimensions of Thinking*, and a related teacher training program, *Dimensions of Learning*. He is also the author or editor of numerous other publications. Before joining the staff of ASCD, he was a teacher and principal in Racine, Wisconsin; director of staff development in Minneapolis, Minnesota; and for eight years was associate superintendent of the Lincoln Public Schools in Lincoln, Nebraska.

Preface

Ron Brandt

Educators are faced once again with a daunting challenge: this time, it is to equip students with 21st century skills. Critics oppose the idea on the grounds that emphasizing skills such as critical thinking and problem solving will erode the teaching of important content, including history and literature. Their concern may be valid, but their position that "skills can neither be taught nor applied effectively without prior knowledge of a wide array of subjects" (Common Core, 2009) is not. Both knowledge *and* skills are needed, and they are interdependent; advocates and critics agree about that. And the authors of this book know from experience that effective teaching involves students *using* skills to acquire knowledge.

No generation can escape the responsibility of deciding what students should learn by analyzing what adults are called upon to do. When the United States was young, citizens of New England were taught to do simple calculations, write letters, and read the Bible. In the 1900s, as farming grew in complexity, high schools in rural areas began teaching vocational agriculture. With the current blitz of fast-moving developments in technology, schools are beefing up their science and mathematics programs.

The obvious need for education to relate to society's demands was satirized in a delightful little book published seventy years ago that told how, in Paleolithic times, schools supposedly came to teach fish grabbing and saber-toothed tiger scaring (Benjamin, 1939). The book's purpose was not to belittle efforts to match curriculum to societal needs; rather, it used gentle humor to warn how difficult it can be to keep up these efforts. When Paleolithic educators finally decided to add a course in tiger scaring, for example, they could locate only two harmless, moth-eaten old tigers for students to scare.

So trying to foresee students' future needs is not being trendy; it is a necessity. But, of course, it is only the beginning. The hard parts are, first, determining how these new demands fit in relation to the existing curriculum; second, finding ways they can be taught *along with content*; and then, managing the complex process of implementation. This book is intended to help you with these momentous tasks. Like the fictitious Paleolithics in Benjamin's book, we may not be completely successful in these efforts, but we must accept the challenge.

References

Common Core. (2009). *A challenge to the Partnership for 21st Century Skills.* Accessed at www.commoncore.org/p21-challenge.php on November 5, 2009.

Benjamin, H. R. W. (1939). *The saber-tooth curriculum.* New York: McGraw-Hill.

Ken Kay

Ken Kay, JD, has spent the past twenty-five years bringing together the education, business, and policy communities to improve U.S. competitiveness. He is president of the Partnership for 21st Century Skills, the nation's leading advocacy organization focused on infusing 21st century skills into education and preparing every child to succeed in the new global economy. He also serves as the CEO and cofounder of e-Luminate Group, an education consulting firm.

Throughout his career, Kay has been a major voice and premier coalition builder on competitiveness issues in education and industry—particularly policies and practices that support innovation and technology leadership. As executive director of the CEO Forum on Education and Technology, he led the development of the StaR Chart (School Technology & Readiness Guide), used by schools across the country to make better use of technology in K–12 classrooms. A lawyer and nationally recognized coalition builder, Kay has also facilitated initiatives by universities and technology leaders to advance research and development policy and by computer industry CEOs to advance U.S. trade and technology policy.

In his foreword, Kay presents the Framework for 21st Century Learning advocated by his group. He responds to three key questions—(1) Why are the skills listed in the framework needed for learning in the future? (2) Which skills are most important? and (3) What can be done to help schools include these skills in their repertoire so that 21st century learning results?—and argues for realigning the teaching-learning relationship so that it focuses on outcomes.

Foreword

21st Century Skills: Why They Matter, What They Are, and How We Get There

Ken Kay, President, Partnership for 21st Century Skills

The writer Malcolm Gladwell (2000) astutely describes how and why social change happens when we arrive at a "tipping point," the moment when a critical mass of circumstances come together and sets us on a new and unstoppable course. Scientists, economists, and sociologists all use this term to describe moments when significant change occurs and results in a new reality that is markedly different from the old.

I believe we are on the threshold of a tipping point in public education. The moment is at hand for a 21st century model for education that will better prepare students for the demands of citizenship, college, and careers in this millennium.

I am honored that the editors have asked me to introduce this book and set the context with the overarching theme of 21st century skills, using the Framework for 21st Century Learning developed by the Partnership for 21st Century Skills (2009a). This book is a compilation of reflections on the possibilities for 21st century learning by some of the most thoughtful educational minds in the United States. It is gratifying that so many of them are engaged in envisioning and substantiating more robust approaches to educating young people, particularly since those of us in the Partnership have worked since 2001 on the same exciting project.

The vision for 21st Century Learning offers a holistic and systemic view of how we can reconceptualize and reinvigorate public education, bringing together all the elements—21st century student outcomes and 21st century education support systems—into a unified framework.

The vision for 21st century learning developed by the Partnership for 21st Century Skills (2009a), summarized in figure F.1, offers a compelling context for the chapters in this volume. This vision offers a holistic and systemic view of how we can reconceptualize and reinvigorate public education, bringing together all the elements—21st century student outcomes and 21st century education support systems—into a unified framework. For us, the starting point for this framework is actually the end result: the outcomes—in terms of mastery of core academic subjects, 21st century themes, and 21st century skills—that should be expected of students once they leave school to venture successfully into higher education, workplaces, and independent life. It's only when we understand these outcomes that we can then begin building the supporting infrastructure that will lift the education system to commanding heights. The raison d'être for the support systems—standards and assessments, curriculum and instruction, professional development, and learning environments—should be to achieve the results that truly matter for students.

Without a clear and thorough articulation of the outcomes that students need, reshaping the infrastructure is premature. Here's an analogy: if you are building a house, it doesn't make sense to order the plumbing fittings before the architect finishes the design specifications. In education, 21st century student outcomes *are* the design specs for the rest of the system.

The Partnership has crafted an all-encompassing vision for a 21st century education system. We don't have all the answers, however. As the contributions to this book make clear, there are many more wonderful ideas percolating that will strengthen the vision of 21st century learning and help transform every aspect of the system.

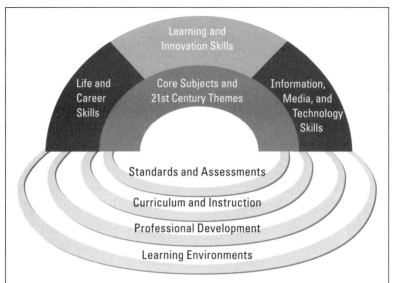

Core Subjects

- English, Reading, or Language Arts
- World Languages
- Arts
- Mathematics
- Economics
- Science
- Geography
- History
- Government and Civics

21st Century Themes

- Global Awareness
- Financial, Economic, Business, and Entrepreneurial Literacy
- Civic Literacy
- Health Literacy
- Environmental Literacy

Learning and Innovation Skills

- Creativity and Innovation
- Critical Thinking and Problem Solving
- Communication and Collaboration

Information, Media, and Technology Skills

- Information Literacy
- Media Literacy
- Information and Communications Technology (ICT) Literacy

Life and Career Skills

- Flexibility and Adaptability
- Initiative and Self-Direction
- Social and Cross-Cultural Skills
- Productivity and Accountability
- Leadership and Responsibility

21st Century Education Support Systems

- 21st Century Standards and Assessments
- 21st Century Curriculum and Instruction
- 21st Century Professional Development
- 21st Century Learning Environments

Source: Partnership for 21st Century Skills, 2009a. Reprinted with permission.

Figure F.1: The Partnership for 21st Century Skills Framework for 21st Century Learning.

We aren't rigid about the language used to describe 21st century skills, either. We say *adaptability*, for instance, while others prefer *resiliency*. We say *critical thinking*; others say *systems thinking*. No matter—we're all talking about the same concepts. On the other hand, the term *21st century skills* is not a vague and squishy catchword that can mean anything. Every element of our model has been defined, developed, and vetted by leading experts, scholars, educators, business people, parents, and community members.

We invite individuals and organizations to use our framework to spark a lively national dialogue about all of the elements required for enriching 21st century minds. It is particularly important to engage educators and representatives of the business community in this dialogue (Wagner, 2008). It's critical for states, districts, and schools to have these conversations and agree on the student outcomes they value—and then to create systems that can deliver.

Why Do We Need a New Model for Education in the 21st Century?

The forces instigating the inevitable changes on the horizon in education have been building for some time:

- **The world is changing**—The global economy, with its emerging industries and occupations, offers tremendous opportunities for everyone who has the skills to take advantage of it. There has been a dramatic acceleration in global competition and collaboration over the past thirty years, spurred by information and communications technology. The service economy, which is driven by information, knowledge, and innovation, has supplanted the industrial economy and reshaped businesses and workplaces. More than three-quarters of all jobs in the United States are now in the service sector. Manual labor and routine tasks have given way to interactive, nonroutine tasks—even in many traditionally blue-collar occupations. Technology has replaced workers who perform routine work, while it complements workers with higher-level skills and empowers them to be more productive and creative (Autor, Levy, & Murnane, 2003). Advanced economies, innovative industries and firms, and high-growth jobs increasingly reward people who can adapt and contribute to organizations, products, and processes with the communications, problem-solving, and critical-thinking skills that enable them to customize their work and respond to organizational expectations (Partnership for 21st Century Skills, 2008).

In this era of rapid change, the social contract prevalent for a good part of the last century doesn't exist anymore. Doing well in school no longer guarantees a lifelong job or career as it did for previous generations of Americans. Today, people can expect to have many jobs in multiple fields during their careers. The average person born in the later years of the baby boom held 10.8 jobs between the ages of eighteen and forty-two, according to the U.S. Bureau of Labor Statistics (Bureau of Labor Statistics, U.S. Department of Labor, 2009). The new social contract is different: only people who have the knowledge and skills to negotiate constant change and reinvent themselves for new situations will succeed. Competency in 21st century skills gives people the ability to keep learning and adjusting to change. Twenty-first-century skills are the ticket to moving up the economic ladder. Without 21st century skills, people are relegated to low-wage, low-skill jobs. Proficiency in 21st century skills is the new civil right for our times.

The forces instigating the inevitable changes on the horizon in education have been building for some time:

- The world is changing.

- U.S. schools and students have not adapted to the changing world.

- The United States has no clear sense of purpose or direction for securing our future economic competitiveness.

- **U.S. schools and students have not adapted to the changing world**—Our current public education system is not preparing all students for the economic, workforce, and citizenship opportunities—and demands—of the 21st century. Many students do not receive the family and societal support they need to stay in school. On top of that, many students are not engaged or motivated in school learning that seems out of step with their lives and irrelevant to their futures. The high school dropout rate has reached crisis proportions, with only 70 percent of students—and only 50 percent of minorities—graduating from high school on time and with a regular diploma (Swanson, 2009).

Alarmingly, we now face two achievement gaps—one national and one international. Nationally, Black, Hispanic, and disadvantaged students perform worse than their peers on national assessments (see, for example, Grigg, Donahue, & Dion, 2007; Lee, Grigg, & Donahue, 2007; National Center for Education Statistics, 2009), dragging down the collective capacity of the future workforce. This is especially troubling as the demographics of the United States are shifting, with minority populations growing at a much faster pace than the rest of the population (U.S. Census Bureau, 2008).

Internationally, American students score lower than the average on the Programme for International Student Assessment (PISA), the benchmark assessment in reading, mathematics, and science for the developed countries of the world (see, for example, Organisation for Economic Co-operation and Development, 2009). PISA results are telling because these assessments measure the applied skills—what we call *21st century skills*—of critical thinking and problem solving. Even the best U.S. students cannot match their peers in other advanced economies on PISA.

Even if all students earned a high school diploma and mastered traditional academic subjects, they *still* would be ill prepared for the expectations of the new economy. Today, a different set of skills—21st century skills—increasingly powers the wealth of nations. Skills that support innovation, including creativity, critical thinking, and problem solving, are in great demand (Casner-Lotto & Barrington, 2006; Conference Board, 2007; Lichtenberg, Woock, & Wright, 2008), yet employers report substantial deficiencies in these and other applied skills among even college-educated entrants into the workforce.

Educational attainment is no longer a guarantee of either academic or skills proficiency (van Ark, Barrington, Fosler, Hulten, & Woock, 2009).

- **The United States has no clear sense of purpose or direction for securing our future economic competitiveness**—The United States remains the most competitive nation on the planet, but "creeping complacency" could erode this dominance (International Institute for Management Development, 2009; Scott, 2009). Science, technology, engineering, and mathematics (STEM) experts in industry and higher education have been warning for years that the United States is losing ground when it comes to preparing an adequate supply of workers for these critical fields. Competitor nations in Asia and Europe have gotten the message that skills matter, and they are catching up. Concerted international efforts—and marked success—at improving education and 21st century skills mean that the United States is no longer unrivaled in producing highly qualified, nimble, and ambitious workers for the new economy. In addition, the substantial economic growth fueled by information technology since the late 1980s and early 1990s is likely to max out without investment in intangible workforce assets, including ideas, knowledge, and talent (van Ark et al., 2009).

What Should a 21st Century Education Look Like?

Meeting the challenges we face requires a new model for education—one in which every aspect of our education system is aligned to prepare Americans to compete.

The Partnership for 21st Century Skills has spent the better part of a decade developing a robust Framework for 21st Century Learning (shown on page xv in figure F.1) that responds to the changing demands young people face today. Sustained and enthusiastic support from leading education organizations, the business community, and policymakers—and reality checks with parents, frontline K–12 and postsecondary educators, and community organizations—have shaped this framework into a comprehensive, intentional, and purposeful vision for 21st century education (Trilling & Fadel, 2009).

The graphic is powerful because it communicates at a glance the integration of core academic subjects, 21st century themes, and 21st century skills, with the educational support systems clearly aligned to these student outcomes. The Framework for 21st Century Learning offers a compelling, responsive, and viable direction for public education—starting now—for a number of reasons.

The Framework Focuses on Results That Matter

A 21st century education must be tied to *outcomes*, in terms of proficiency in core subject knowledge and 21st century skills that are expected and highly valued in school, work, and community settings. It is a national travesty that a majority of U.S. students leave high school without the core competencies that employers and postsecondary educators cite as the most critical for real-world performance and advanced learning. Critical thinking, problem solving, creativity, and the other 21st century skills are the tools people need to move up the economic ladder.

> A 21st century education must be tied to *outcomes*, in terms of proficiency in core subject knowledge and 21st century skills that are expected and highly valued in school, work, and community settings.

With 21st century skills, students will be prepared to think, learn, work, solve problems, communicate, collaborate, and contribute effectively throughout their lives. Some say these kinds of skills are not unique to the 21st century. This is true. We call them out for three reasons.

First, these skills are rarely incorporated deliberately throughout the curriculum, nor are they routinely assessed. This status quo relegates these skills into the "nice to have" rather than the "must have" domain in education, which means they are taught unevenly. It is more likely that young people pick up these skills by chance in everyday living and job experiences and, yes, sometimes in school—if they are lucky enough to have good mentors or are astute enough to recognize and build these skills on their own. We simply can no longer afford to continue this haphazard approach to developing the most critical skills if we are to remain a competitive nation.

Second, these skills are essential for *all* students today, not just an elite few. In bygone economies, Americans lived in a hierarchical world with an assembly-line mentality. Top managers and experts took on the lion's share of the thinking, problem solving, decision making, and communicating for their organizations. They gave orders, and most workers were expected simply to follow directions. This is not so today. Competitive organizations have flattened management structures, increased their use of technology, created more flexible work arrangements, and given greater responsibility to frontline workers and collaborative project teams. Such significant organizational and behavioral shifts have boosted productivity and innovation (Black & Lynch, 2004; Gera & Gu, 2004; Pilat, 2004; Zoghi, Mohr, & Meyer, 2007). With these realities, students who do not master 21st century skills will never fulfill their economic potentials.

In this flattened structure, every worker has more information and tools at his or her disposal—and much greater autonomy in using them. In exchange, workers are expected to be self-directed and responsible for managing their own work. As a manager at Apple told me, any employee who needs to be managed is no longer employable. The same shift of responsibility to individuals applies to personal life. There are fewer authority figures to take care of people or tell them what to do. Today, people have to manage their own health care, arming themselves with information, making choices about coverage, acting as their own advocates, and partnering with health-care providers to manage their health. Likewise, participating in civic life requires people to seek out information to understand issues on their own. The decline of print journalism, for example, means that the latest local news may not be delivered to the doorstep every day.

Third, the skills that employers and postsecondary educators say are required for success have converged. Even entry-level employees now are expected to use 21st century skills to accomplish their work (Casner-Lotto & Barrington, 2006; Conference Board, 2007; Lichtenberg, Woock, & Wright, 2008). Most jobs that pay a living wage today require at least some postsecondary education—and this is particularly the case for the 271 jobs with high-growth potential over the next ten years, according to the U.S. Department of Labor (Bureau of Labor Statistics, U.S. Department of Labor, 2008).

Most students aspire to college because they understand this. Indeed, there has been a significant increase in the proportion of the labor force with at least some level of higher education (Carnevale & Desrochers, 2002). Twenty-first-century skills are equally important for successful transitions to college and workforce training programs. Among the components of college readiness presented by the Bill & Melinda Gates Foundation are "academic behaviors" and "contextual skills and awareness" (Conley, 2005, 2007), which reflect the kinds of skills captured in the Framework for 21st Century Learning. All students should be prepared with the skills they need to do well, whatever route they decide to take in the future.

The Framework for 21st Century Learning also incorporates several new 21st century themes that might not seem familiar. Again, employers and educators—along with parents, policymakers, and community advocates—identified these themes and skills as crucial. Typically, though, they are not emphasized in public education. These themes are grounded in everyday life as people across the United States are living it now. They want schools to integrate these new themes, which blend content and skills, to better prepare young people to thrive in a complex world.

For example, global awareness is a new essential in the global economy. Americans need a secure understanding of global issues that affect them as citizens and workers. They need to be able to learn from and work collaboratively with people from a range of diverse cultures and lifestyles. They need to be able to communicate in languages other than English.

Likewise, financial, economic, business, and entrepreneurial literacy are new imperatives. Guaranteed pensions are a rarity today, so the responsibility for retirement planning, saving, and investment management falls on individuals. Recent crises in the banking, credit, and mortgage industries—and the severe recession—underscore the importance of understanding how economic forces impact people's lives. Failure to make responsible financial choices could adversely affect individuals' quality of life for years. At work, people need to know how they fit in and contribute to a larger organization, and they need to bring an entrepreneurial mindset to their lives. By recognizing opportunities, risks, and rewards, they can enhance their workplace productivity and career options and take changing circumstances in stride.

Finally, the Framework for 21st Century Learning articulates several skills that definitely break new ground, at least in education: creativity and innovation, flexibility and adaptability, leadership and cross-cultural skills—for *all* students. These are the kinds of skills that set people apart. Small leaps of imagination can result in tremendous personal and organizational advances. A willingness to respond positively to change leaves people open to new possibilities and more comfortable with the inevitable vagaries of life. Taking on leadership roles gives people more control over their lives, while cross-cultural skills strengthen their effectiveness in interacting with others they encounter in school, work, and the community.

These new skills also differentiate leading from lagging organizations and nations. They undergird every aspect of competitiveness: ingenuity, agility, and continuous improvement; the capacity to turn bold ideas into innovative products, services, and solutions; and the ability to champion worthwhile endeavors, overcome obstacles, and bridge cultural divides.

Taken together, the combination of core academic subjects, 21st century themes, and 21st century skills redefines rigor for our times. Many Americans have been advocating a more rigorous education to prepare students for college and career readiness—a position that we share.

However, *rigor* traditionally is equated with mastery of content (core subjects) alone, and that's simply not good enough anymore. Knowledge and information change constantly. Students need *both* content knowledge *and* skills to apply and transform their knowledge for useful and creative purposes and to keep learning as content and circumstances change.

I've heard John Bransford, a noted professor of education and psychology at the University of Washington and the coauthor of *How People Learn: Bridging Research and Practice* (2000) and *How Students Learn: Science in the Classroom* (2004), put it this way: In the United States, we tell students the same thing a hundred times.

On the 101st time, we ask them if they remember what we told them the first hundred times. However, in the 21st century, the true test of rigor is for students to be able to look at material they've never seen before and know what to do with it.

Infusing 21st century skills into core subjects actually ratchets up rigor. Recalling facts or terms from a textbook, or performing simple processes or procedures, places a low level of cognitive demand on students. Demonstrating deeper understanding through planning, using evidence, and abstract reasoning, for example, is more demanding. Making connections among related ideas within the content or among content areas, or devising an approach to solving a complex problem, requires extended thinking and even higher cognitive demand (Webb, 1997).

The connection between skills and rigor shows up on international assessments such as PISA. Students who can apply critical thinking and problem solving to math and science content perform better than those who cannot. In a 21st century education system, rigor must refer to mastery of content *and* skills.

As I see it, then, there are plenty of convincing indicators that proficiency in 21st century skills is the right result for our time. Enriching minds for the 21st century requires organizing the public education system around this goal.

The Framework Recognizes That Educational Support Systems—Especially Professional Learning Experiences—Are Vital

The vision for 21st century learning is situated in reality: producing the results that matter in terms of student outcomes in 21st century skills requires every aspect of the education system to be aligned toward this goal.

The vision for 21st century learning is situated in reality: producing the results that matter in terms of student outcomes in 21st century skills requires every aspect of the education system to be aligned toward this goal.

While this might seem to be a monumental aspiration, the evidence suggests that states are prepared—even very willing—to take on this work. By October of 2009, fourteen states (Arizona, Illinois, Iowa, Kansas, Louisiana, Maine, Massachusetts, Nevada, New Jersey, North

Carolina, Ohio, South Dakota, West Virginia, and Wisconsin) had committed to retooling their standards and assessments, curriculum and instruction, professional development, and learning environments to support 21st century skills outcomes. The states and districts that are making real progress are those that take a holistic and systemic approach, articulating the skills they value and aligning every other part of their systems to move in this direction.

Many of these states face daunting challenges. Major industries are restructuring and eliminating jobs. The recent economic downturn has exacerbated this problem, and seriously affected state budgets and schools. Nevertheless, these states have carefully examined the framework and endorsed it as their model for building a 21st century education system. They realize that they must reinvent their education systems to renew their workforces and their economies. West Virginia, for example, is revising and refocusing its standards, assessments, instruction, professional development, teacher preparation, preK, and technology programs around the Partnership's Framework for 21st Century Learning.

Professional development is far and away the most important part of the work. Steve Paine, superintendent of schools in West Virginia, tells me that 80 percent of his efforts are devoted to improving teacher effectiveness in delivering 21st century instruction. He has it right. Articulating the skills that matter is only the first step. States and districts cannot assume that teachers can break out of the 20th-century box without sustained professional development. The West Virginia Department of Education has put a full-court press on this mission, initially training every teacher in the state during in-depth summer sessions on 21st century skills and in follow-up web-based coaching during the school year. The state also has a dynamic, interactive website, Teach 21, with a wealth of resources to assist teachers in their everyday classroom practices.

At the Partnership, we've developed detailed content maps and online resources that add layers of specificity to 21st century learning for teachers. These resources promote the kinds of hands-on, inquiry-based learning and development of higher-level thinking skills that the most effective teachers employ (Darling-Hammond et al., 2008). Indeed, many classroom teachers and educators who work closely with students in schools are leading the way in delivering this kind of instruction. All of the teaching resources are available at a dedicated website: Route 21 (www.21stcenturyskills.org/route21/).

The entire supporting infrastructure of education must be modernized to establish the conditions for 21st century teaching, learning, and outcomes. And, as we have learned from previous standards-setting initiatives, ignoring the infrastructure puts an undue burden on students. It is unfair and unproductive to expect students to meet new and higher expectations if the supporting infrastructure does not exist. To help states, districts, and schools move forward, we have developed and updated our MILE guide with implementation guidance and self-assessment tools (Partnership for 21st Century Skills, 2009b).

All of the critical elements of an education system contribute to 21st century skills outcomes, and they cannot be left to chance.

The Framework Resonates With Policymakers, Educators, the Business Community, Community Organizations, and Parents

Plenty of organizations have developed models for improving education. Not many have had the courage to vet their models with thousands of people from every walk of life. Our model of core subjects, 21st century themes, and 21st century skills has been put to this test.

We developed the framework in concert with our nearly forty membership organizations, including the National Education Association and its 3.2 million members. We took the framework on road tours, reaching out to policymakers, educators, business people, community organizations, and parents. We listened to their comments and strengthened the themes and skill sets. We surveyed business people and parents, who strongly agree that 21st century skills are vital for success today (Casner-Lotto & Barrington, 2006; Partnership for 21st Century Skills, 2007). They also believe by overwhelming margins that schools should teach 21st century skills. Their beliefs are based in reality—the expectations of workplaces, the demands of citizenship, and the challenges of life that they face every day. We've been informed by the surveys and reports of other organizations, which confirm our findings.

This is not a small point. A major difference between 21st century skills advocacy and other improvement initiatives, such as the 1980s push to revamp education, is that the leaders of this movement include policymakers, educators, *and* the business community. We are speaking with a united voice. Together, we have taken the time to gauge the interest and attitudes of key stakeholders in public education. And we have strived to build broad-based support for our model from the top down and the bottom up. In many states, governors, leaders in state education agencies and state boards of education, local school boards, business people, community organizations, educators, parents, and the voting public are engaged and energized by our model.

> We are speaking with a united voice. Together, we have taken the time to gauge the interest and attitudes of key stakeholders in public education.

There is much more work to do to build public understanding nationwide—in every district, community, and family. Yet the support we already have, plus the accomplishments of our fourteen leadership states, gives us the opportunity to engage in a vigorous national conversation about new student outcomes for the 21st century—and to bring more supporters on board.

State, district, and school leaders and their communities will want to examine the changes their economies have experienced over the past twenty years. They'll want to think through the new skills students will need for the next twenty years and beyond. And once they articulate these new skills in their own words, they will be ready to align their education systems to make their vision a reality.

The Future of Learning

This book is another telltale sign that we've reached a tipping point in education. That so many notable minds are thinking hard about the future of learning is a signal that we just might be on the cusp of bold action.

At stake at this moment are the nation's competitiveness and all that goes along with it: a strong democracy, international leadership, lasting prosperity, and better prospects for generations to come. It is as true today as ever in our history that the American people are the engine of economic growth. In this time, for this era, however, they need to be equipped with knowledge and skills to compete in the 21st century.

In meeting rooms and classrooms across the country, I have met thousands of people who are ready to take on this challenge. The broad public support for the Framework for 21st Century Learning suggests the strong potential for building political will for a 21st century education system. It is exciting that the framework has generated this kind of interest, but it is far too early to proclaim victory.

> We need to move from consensus about the *vision* of 21st century learning to a thorough understanding of and commitment to the *outcomes* of 21st century learning.

We need to move from consensus about the *vision* of 21st century learning to a thorough understanding of and commitment to the *outcomes* of 21st century learning. There is a danger, in fact, that a "21st century education" or "21st century skills" could mean anything. Many people equate technology-rich classrooms or modern schools or rigorous core subjects with 21st century learning, regardless of whether students are mastering 21st century skills. In reality, the ability to use digital devices in no way means that students know anything about global awareness or health literacy, learning and innovation skills, life and career skills, or even media literacy skills. Similarly, many educators claim that they already teach 21st century skills, even though these skills are not systemically infused into standards and assessments, curriculum and instruction, or professional development and learning environments.

The most important next step is to agree on outcomes in terms of proficiency in 21st century skills. And it's not enough to want these outcomes—it's essential to plan the entire education system intentionally and transparently around them. A great place to start is to use the lens of 21st century outcomes to aggressively pursue the ideas in this book.

Acknowledgments

Special thanks to the former and current members of the Partnership for 21st Century Skills board and strategic council for their tremendous support of 21st century skills, and to Martha Vockley for her special contributions to the development of this foreword.

References

Autor, D. H., Levy, F., & Murnane, R. J. (2003, November). The skill content of recent technological change: An empirical exploration. *Quarterly Journal of Economics, 118*(4), 1279–1333.

Black, S. E., & Lynch, L. M. (2004, February). What's driving the new economy?: The benefits of workplace innovation. *The Economic Journal, 114*, 97–116.

Bureau of Labor Statistics, U.S. Department of Labor. (2008, June 27). *Number of jobs held, labor market activity, and earnings growth among the youngest baby boomers: Results from a longitudinal survey.* Washington, DC: Author. Accessed at www.bls.gov/news.release/pdf/nlsoy.pdf on December 8, 2009.

Bureau of Labor Statistics, U.S. Department of Labor. (2009). *Occupational projections and training data, 2008–09 edition.* Accessed at www.bls.gov/emp/optd/optdtabi_5.pdf on December 8, 2009.

Carnevale, A. P., & Desrochers, D. M. (2002, Fall). The missing middle: Aligning education and the knowledge economy. *Journal for Vocational and Special Needs Education, 25*(1), 3–23.

Casner-Lotto, J., & Barrington, L. (2006). *Are they really ready to work? Employers' perspectives on the basic knowledge and applied skills of new entrants to the 21st century U.S. workforce.* New York: The Conference Board. Accessed at www.21stcenturyskills.org/documents/FINAL_REPORT_PDF09-29-06 .pdf on June 18, 2009.

Conference Board. (2007). *CEO challenge 2007: Top 10 challenges* (Research Report 1406). New York: Author.

Conley, D. T. (2005). *College knowledge™: What it really takes for students to succeed and what we can do to get them ready.* San Francisco: Jossey-Bass.

Conley, D. T. (2007). *Toward a more comprehensive conception of college readiness.* Eugene, OR: Educational Policy Improvement Center. Accessed at www .gatesfoundation.org/learning/Documents/CollegeReadinessPaper.pdf on June 18, 2009.

Darling-Hammond, L., Barron, B., Pearson, P. D., Schoenfeld, A. H., Stage, E. K., & Zimmerman, T. D., et al. (2008). *Powerful learning: What we know about teaching for understanding.* San Francisco: Jossey-Bass.

Donovan, S., Bransford, J., & Pellegrino, J. W. (Eds.). (2000). *How people learn: Bridging research and practice.* Washington, DC: National Academies Press.

Donovan, S., & Bransford, J. (2004). *How students learn: Science in the classroom.* Washington, DC: National Academies Press.

Gera, S., & Gu, W. (2004, Fall). The effect of organizational innovation and information technology on firm performance. *International Productivity Monitor, 9,* 37–51. Accessed at www.csls.ca/ipm/9/gera_gu-e.pdf on June 18, 2009.

Gladwell, M. (2000). *The tipping point: How little things can make a big difference.* Boston: Little, Brown.

Grigg, W., Donahue, P., & Dion, G. (2007). *The nation's report card: 12th-grade reading and mathematics 2005* (NCES 2007-468). U.S. Department of Education, National Center for Education Statistics. Washington, DC: U.S. Government Printing Office. Accessed at http://nces.ed.gov/nationsreportcard/pdf/main2005/2007468.pdf on December 7, 2009.

International Institute for Management Development. (2009). *IMD world competitiveness yearbook.* Lausanne, Switzerland: Author.

Lee, J., Grigg, W., & Donahue, P. (2007). *The nation's report card: Reading 2007* (NCES 2007-496). Washington, DC: National Center for Education Statistics, Institute of Education Sciences, U.S. Department of Education. Accessed at http://nces.ed.gov/nationsreportcard/pdf/main2007/2007496.pdf on December 7, 2009.

Lichtenberg, J., Woock, C., & Wright, M. (2008). *Ready to innovate: Key findings.* New York: The Conference Board. Accessed at www.artsusa.org/pdf/information_services/research/policy_roundtable/ready_to_innovate.pdf on June 18, 2009.

National Center for Education Statistics (2009). *The nation's report card: Mathematics 2009* (NCES 2009-451). Washington, DC: Institute of Education Sciences, U.S. Department of Education. Accessed at http://nces.ed.gov/nationsreportcard/pdf/main2009/2010451.pdf on December 7, 2009.

Organisation for Economic Co-operation and Development (2009). *Top of the class: High performers in science in PISA 2006.* Paris: Author. Accessed at www.pisa.oecd.org/dataoecd/44/17/42645389.pdf on December 7, 2009.

Partnership for 21st Century Skills. (2007). *Beyond the three Rs: Voter attitudes toward 21st century skills.* Tucson, AZ: Author. Accessed at www.21stcenturyskills.org/documents/P21_pollreport_singlepg.pdf on June 18, 2009.

Partnership for 21st Century Skills. (2008). *21st century skills, education & competitiveness: A resource and policy guide.* Tucson, AZ: Author. Accessed at www.21stcenturyskills.org/documents/21st_century_skills_education_and_competitiveness_guide.pdf on June 18, 2009.

Partnership for 21st Century Skills. (2009a). *Framework for 21st century learning.* Tucson, AZ: Author. Accessed at www.21stcenturyskills.org/documents/framework_flyer_updated_april_2009.pdf on November 1, 2009.

Partnership for 21st Century Skills. (2009b). *The MILE guide: Milestones for improving learning & education*. Tucson, AZ: Author. Accessed at www.21stcenturyskills.org/documents/MILE_Guide_091101.pdf on December 8, 2009.

Pilat, D. (2004, December). *The economic impact of ICT: A European perspective* (IIR Working Paper 05–07). Paper presented to the Conference on IT Innovation, Tokyo. Accessed at www.iir.hit-u.ac.jp/iir-w3/event/WP05–07pilat .pdf on June 18, 2009.

Scott, M. (2009, May 19). Competitiveness: The U.S. and Europe are tops. *Business Week*. Accessed at www.businessweek.com/globalbiz/content/may2009/ gb20090519_222765.htm on June 18, 2009.

Swanson, C. B. (2009, April). *Cities in crisis 2009: Closing the graduation gap*. Bethesda, MD: Editorial Projects in Education. Accessed at www.edweek .org/media/cities_in_crisis_2009.pdf on December 7, 2009.

Trilling, B., & Fadel, C. (2009). *21st century skills: Learning for life in our times*. San Francisco: Jossey-Bass.

U.S. Census Bureau. (2008, August 14). *An older and more diverse nation by midcentury*. Washington, DC: Author. Accessed at www.census.gov/Press-Release/www/releases/archives/population/012496.html on December 7, 2009.

van Ark, B., Barrington, L., Fosler, G., Hulten, C., & Woock, C. (2009). *Innovation and U.S. competitiveness: Reevaluating the contributors to growth*. New York: The Conference Board.

Wagner, T. (2008). *The global achievement gap: Why even our best schools don't teach the new survival skills our children need—and what we can do about it*. New York: Basic Books.

Webb, N. L. (1997, April). *Criteria for alignment of expectations and assessments in mathematics and science education* (Research Monograph 6). Madison, WI: National Institute for Science Education. Accessed at http://hub.mspnet.org/ media/data/WebbCriteria.pdf?media_000000000924.pdf on June 18, 2009.

Zoghi, C., Mohr, R. D., & Meyer, P. B. (2007, May). *Workplace organization and innovation* (Working Paper No. 405). Washington, DC: U.S. Bureau of Labor Statistics.

Introduction

James Bellanca and Ron Brandt

Initiatives for significant change in an important sector of society often come mostly from outsiders. That is the case with the movement known as 21st century skills, spurred by the Partnership for 21st Century Skills. The Partnership includes large corporations, national professional organizations, and state offices of education. These agencies are concerned because they foresee a need for people with skills that go beyond those emphasized in today's schools. Elected leaders, including President Obama and many state governors, agree that this change is essential if U.S. students are to remain competitive in the global job market.

To accomplish its goals, the Partnership has delineated a Framework for 21st Century Learning that it would like to see each state adopt as the preeminent agenda for improving teaching and learning (see figure F.1 on page xv of the foreword by Ken Kay, president of the Partnership for 21st Century Skills). The redesign of policies in partner states is expected to begin with modification of current educational standards. Next, the Partnership wants to see practices aligned with the standards, with the result that students will show that they have developed the necessary skills.

In fact, desired practices that are intended to garner these outcomes are beginning to show. Early adopting teachers, principals, district leaders, and school boards have begun to put the framework into place. There are individual teachers who have changed their classrooms into technology-rich learning places. Their students experiment, do projects, take risks, and solve meaningful problems.

Although the number of whole schools that are attuned to the 21st century skills agenda falls short of those that continue to be mired in the practices and content of the 20th century, pockets of change are emerging. This is especially true in states that are members of the Partnership. In some states, the leaders of schoolwide change are charter schools organized to escape the "same old, same old" model of teaching and learning. In others, they are public schools that are redefining the teaching-learning connection.

At the district level, systemic reform for 21st century learning has a higher mountain to climb. In Tucson, Arizona, and Warrenville, Illinois, school leaders, starting with the school board and central administration, have gone public with a vision for 21st century learning and districtwide strategic plans. These plans are driving step-by-step actions that include new building designs, curriculum changes, long-term professional development for leaders and teachers, and the integration of technology in each school.

At the state level, West Virginia, an early 21st century skills partner, leads an increasing number of state offices of education in promoting 21st century skills. West Virginia has created a user-friendly website, Teach 21 (http://wvde.state.wv.us/teach21/), that offers 21st century *power standards*—instructional guides, unit plans, and sample project-based learning ideas—across content and special needs areas. West Virginia has also prepared a cadre of teacher leaders to facilitate teachers' use of project-based learning throughout the school year. Individual teachers and schools, such as tiny Washington District Elementary School in Buckhannon, are encouraged to revise instruction and assessment to align practice with this rich collection of resources and put project-based learning into daily practice.

Illinois has taken a different tack. When the Illinois State Board of Education formally signed on as a member of the Partnership, a group of education and business leaders formed an independent consortium to engage school districts in planning for implementation of the Partnership's Framework. The Illinois Consortium's vision includes plans to link multidistrict collaboratives that will provide long-term professional development and systemic change for member schools.

The Consortium's leadership, working closely with Illinois State Board of Education officials, is connecting its "bubble up" innovation process with the State Board's direction-setting initiative. The bubble-up process, named at New Trier East High School (Winnetka, Illinois) by then associate superintendent Mary Ida Maguire, encourages diverse constituent groups—teachers, parents, and administrators—to generate ideas for improvements to be funded for the next school year. The best ideas determined within each group rise to the top. A committee with members selected at random from each of the basic groups set criteria, agree on the best ideas, and make recommendations to the school board's budget committee. The Consortium's thirty member board of directors uses the bubble-up process to identify innovative projects for which it will pursue implementation funds.

On the national stage, a handful of professional organizations, most notably the National Council of Teachers of English, National Science Teachers Association, the National Council for Social Studies, and the American Library Association, have collaborated with the Partnership to develop online resource guides for integrating 21st century skills into content areas. Other organizations, such as the National Education Association and Association for Supervision and Curriculum Development, have taken steps to raise member awareness.

With the chapters in this volume, we begin the process of filling in the vision established by the Partnership. We know this collection will not be the last word on the subject, but we believe it is a valuable next step.

Our first task in envisioning this volume was to identify key issues that would contribute to the dialogue. We then identified a group of authors, each with the experience and farsightedness required to address these issues. We asked them to help answer three basic questions that would illuminate the theme of 21st century skills: (1) Why are the skills listed in the framework needed for learning in the future? (2) Which skills are most important? and (3) What can be done to help schools include these skills in their repertoire so that 21st century learning results?

Chapter Overviews

In his foreword, Ken Kay, president of the Partnership for 21st Century Skills, presents the Framework for 21st Century Learning advocated by his group. He responds to our three key questions and argues for realigning the teaching-learning relationship so that it focuses on outcomes.

In chapter 1, Howard Gardner identifies five types of minds society should encourage in future generations, three primarily cognitive and two in the human sphere. He outlines the major features of each type, the ways they can be shaped, and ways they could be distorted. He concludes by offering suggestions for how the five types might be integrated in a single, thriving human being.

In an interview for chapter 2, Linda Darling-Hammond calls for major policy changes to guide development of 21st century schools. She advocates deep alignment of standards, curriculum, instruction, and assessment; strengthening professionalism among teachers and school leaders; redesign of school time to allow for increased participation in professional decisions by teachers; and equitable distribution of resources among all schools. She insists that the United States must take a more balanced approach to school reform and that these changes are essential if the United States is to restore its lost leadership for educational excellence.

In chapter 3, Chris Dede compares several prominent lists of 21st century skills. He asks, "How diverse are these definitions for 21st century skills?" and notes that a lack of clarity about the nature of 21st century skills could be problematic. His examination illuminates what the various frameworks have in common and what each uniquely adds to the overarching concept.

In chapter 4, Richard and Rebecca DuFour discuss school settings for teaching 21st century skills. They observe that the most appropriate environment for teaching the life and career skills espoused by the Partnership for 21st Century Skills is a professional learning community (PLC) that models these skills. On this basis, they argue that the PLC is an essential tool for bringing about the changes that 21st century skills advocates envision.

In chapter 5, Robin Fogarty and Brian Pete carry the discussion to Singapore, where they have worked as educational consultants with the nation's ambitious "Teach Less, Learn More" initiative. Fogarty and Pete share the thoughts and feelings of teachers torn between the old ways of authoritarian, competitive schools and the new ways of shared decision making and collaborative study that encourage students to construct meaning rather than memorize facts.

In chapter 6, Bob Pearlman takes a walk through innovative school buildings designed for collaborative learning. He reminds us that the familiar box-based design of most current schools was suited for an outdated factory-model agenda. He shows us that form follows function in these innovative buildings as well—but the functions are now engagement, problem solving, and communication.

In chapter 7, Jay McTighe and Elliott Seif address the question of how to infuse 21st century outcomes into the overcrowded curriculum left over from the previous century with a systematic approach that takes advantage of the principles and practices of Understanding by Design. Using familiar concepts adapted from Schooling by Design, the authors outline five interrelated components: (1) the mission of schooling, (2) the principles of learning, (3) a curriculum and assessment system, (4) instructional programs and practices, and (5) systemic support factors. They examine how each of these components can help schools transform themselves to implement a viable approach to teaching and learning that ends in the acquisition of 21st century skills for all students.

In chapter 8, John Barell shows that problem-based learning is an ideal way to develop 21st century skills. He describes how teachers shift their standards-based curriculum from direct instruction of passive students to active engagement of problem solvers and question askers. His concrete examples illustrate ways problem-based inquiry can be adapted for meaningful use with students of all ages, talents, and challenges.

In chapter 9, David Johnson and Roger Johnson point out four important challenges of the 21st century: (1) greater global interdependence, (2) the increasing number of democracies throughout the world, (3) the need for creative entrepreneurs, and (4) the importance of interpersonal relationships that affect the development of personal identity. They discuss how cooperative learning, constructive controversy, and problem-solving negotiations will play a central role in teaching students the competencies and values they need to cope with these challenges and lead productive and fulfilling lives.

In chapter 10, Douglas Fisher and Nancy Frey describe three ways for teachers to respond to the extreme shifts in technological advancement and student needs for the 21st century: (1) considering functions rather than tools, (2) revising technology policies, and (3) developing students' minds through intentional instruction.

In chapter 11, Cheryl Lemke introduces three important innovations of 21st century learning: (1) visualization, (2) democratization of knowledge, and (3) participatory cultures for learning. She provides an impressive demonstration of ways technology permits greater balance between a visual approach and traditional language-based communication.

In chapter 12, Alan November reinforces Pearlman's rationale for redesigned schools. He cautions against using expensive technology to continue the trend of schools as managers of student learning. It's time, he says, to redesign not only the physical structure but the culture of schools. Technology makes it possible for students to become less dependent on schools and take more responsibility for managing their own learning.

In chapter 13, Will Richardson calls attention to the explosion of social network technologies. This powerful new landscape is fraught with danger, he says, but it is also rich with potential for learning. Richardson describes the rise of the virtual, global classroom, the challenge of this unrestricted learning, its potentials and pitfalls, and how educators can make the shift to network literacy in order to improve the quality of students' learning experiences.

In chapter 14, Douglas Reeves tackles the challenging problem of assessment. He argues that the new outcomes envisioned by advocates of 21st century skills can properly be measured only by abandoning standardized tests. He offers three criteria for determining how educators can know students are learning 21st century content and skills and shows how these might apply in practice.

In the afterword, Andy Hargreaves concludes the collection by asking tough questions about the 21st century skills movement. He uses metaphor to illuminate the historic ways that change has occurred in education and will occur in the future. He categorizes the emphasis on 21st century skills as the Third Way. He lists positive and negative results from each of the prior ways and looks ahead to an even more desirable Fourth Way.

Howard Gardner

Howard Gardner, Ph.D., is the John H. and Elisabeth A. Hobbs Professor of Cognition and Education at the Harvard Graduate School of Education. Among numerous honors, Gardner received a MacArthur Prize Fellowship in 1981. He has received honorary degrees from twenty-six colleges and universities. In 2005 and 2008, he was selected by *Foreign Policy* and *Prospect* magazines as one of the one hundred most influential public intellectuals in the world.

The author of over twenty books translated into twenty-eight languages, and several hundred articles, Gardner is best known in educational circles for his theory of multiple intelligences, a critique of the notion that there exists but a single human intelligence that can be assessed by standard psychometric instruments. Building on his studies of intelligence, Gardner has also authored *Leading Minds*, *Changing Minds*, and *Extraordinary Minds*. In 1994, in collaboration with psychologists Mihaly Csikszentmihalyi and William Damon, Gardner launched the GoodWork Project to study work that is excellent in quality, socially responsible, and personally meaningful. More recently, Gardner and collaborators at Harvard Project Zero have embarked on applications of good work insights in secondary schools and colleges, investigations of conceptions of trust and trustworthiness in young people, and studies of ethical issues associated with the new digital media.

In this chapter, Gardner identifies five types of minds society should encourage in future generations—three primarily cognitive and two in the human sphere. He outlines the major features of each type, the ways they can be shaped, and the ways they could be distorted. He concludes by offering suggestions for how the five types might be integrated in a single, thriving human being.

Chapter 1

Five Minds for the Future

Howard Gardner

Educational institutions change very slowly. In some ways, this conservatism is positive; it discourages faddism and encourages educators to build upon tried-and-true methods. Of course, such conservatism can go too far. I remember a revealing experience I had in China more than twenty years ago. I was invited to observe a college course in psychology and was dismayed to find that the class consisted entirely of students simply reciting the textbook content verbatim. Afterward, with the interpreter by my side, I engaged in a ten-minute debate with the instructor. I emphasized that the students all knew the rote material and suggested that it would be far more productive to raise provocative questions or ask the students to draw on the memorized material in order to illuminate a new phenomenon. The instructor was not the least bit convinced. Indeed, after we went back and forth, she finally cut off the discussion with the statement, "We've been doing things this way for so long, we *know* it is right."

With the benefit of historical insight, we can identify eras when education had to undergo fundamental changes. Probably the most dramatic changes occurred during classical times, when writing became common, and during the Renaissance, when print emerged. Within the United States, pivotal times included the rise of the American common school in the middle of the 19th century, and the commitment, in the middle of the 20th century, to educate all Americans, regardless of race, gender, social class, or ethnicity. At such times, we can no longer just carry on as before: we must consider whether fundamental changes may be in order.

I believe that, at the beginning of the 21st century, we live in such a time. The forces of globalization entail major changes in all of our lives: I refer here to the increasing power of and reliance on science and technology; the incredible connectivity that results; the enormous amount of information, often of dubious quality, that is at our fingertips; the convergence of cultures in economic, cultural, and social terms; and the incessant circulation, intermingling, and periodic clashing of human beings of diverse backgrounds and aspirations. Intimately and inextricably connected to others, we need to be able to communicate with one another, live with one another, and, where possible, make common cause.

In this chapter, I portray the kinds of minds that we should cultivate in the future. Three of these minds are primarily cognitive: the disciplined mind, the synthesizing mind, and the creating mind. Two minds deal with the human sphere: the respectful mind and the ethical mind. I indicate the major features of these forms of mind, the ways in which they can be shaped, and the ways in which they can be distorted. I describe some of the tensions among minds and offer suggestions of how to possibly integrate these minds within a single thriving human being.

Here are a few clarifying comments: First, in conceptualizing the future, I refer to trends whose existence is widely acknowledged; to be sure, none of the five minds is exclusive to the future: one could have called for them fifty or perhaps even five hundred years ago. Yet their individual and joint cultivation assumes particular urgency at the present time.

> To be sure, none of these five minds is exclusive to the future: one could have called for them fifty or perhaps even five hundred years ago.

My second point is that I intend to be both descriptive and prescriptive. I am descriptive in the sense that I seek to explain what these minds are; I am prescriptive in the sense that I believe we need to cultivate these kinds of minds. Certainly, thriving as individuals and as societies without a generous dosage of these five mental predispositions is not possible. Indeed, it is possible that the cultivation of the respectful and ethical mind will determine whether human beings survive as a species.

A third point concerns the scope of the enterprise. Increasingly, education will take place in all kinds of venues and continue throughout one's productive life. So, the minds under discussion here are as much the concern of the fifty-year-old executive or manager as of the teacher or mentor of the young. Moreover, throughout their life cycle, individuals must tend to the development of their own mind, as well as the minds of other individuals—their offspring, students, or employees—over whom they have responsibility.

Finally, as the individual who developed the concept of multiple intelligences, I should forestall a possible confusion. When I write as a psychologist investigating individual differences, I describe human beings as exhibiting different intellectual strengths and different intellectual profiles; thus, William excels in linguistic intelligence, while Pablo is strong in spatial intelligence (Gardner, 2006). But when I wear the mantle of an educator, in the broad sense just described, I call for each person to develop all five kinds of minds. Considerations of differences among individuals fade into the background.

The Disciplined Mind

In English, the word *discipline* has two distinct connotations. We speak of the mind as having mastered one or more disciplines: arts, crafts, professions, or scholarly pursuits. By rough estimate, an individual takes approximately one decade to learn a discipline well enough to be considered an expert or master. In most cases, individuals acquire such mastery through some kind of tutelage: either formally, in a school, or less formally, through some combination of apprenticeship and self-instruction.

Perhaps at one time, an individual could rest on his or her laurels after initially achieving such disciplinary mastery. No longer! Disciplines evolve and ambient conditions change, as do the demands on individuals who have achieved initial mastery. Over succeeding decades, an individual must continue to educate both himself or herself, and others. Such hewing of expertise can continue only if an individual possesses discipline—in the second sense of the word. That is, an individual needs continually to practice in a disciplined way to remain at the top of his or her game.

> Once basic literacies have been mastered, the chief burden of educational systems is ensuring the acquisition of an ensemble of scholarly disciplines.

Once basic literacies have been mastered, the chief burden of educational systems is the acquisition of an ensemble of scholarly disciplines. In my own work on precollegiate education, I stress four disciplines: mathematics, science, history, and at least one art form. I make a sharp distinction between subject matter and discipline. The subject matter of history consists of learning detailed factual information about the past. Such television quiz-show knowledge is always welcome and sometimes lucrative. But this amassing of information differs qualitatively from disciplinary competence. For example, an individual who has acquired the discipline of history can think like a historian. That is, the student of history appreciates that he or she must work with textual, graphical, and other kinds of records; and those records must be reconstructed and sensitively interpreted. Unlike science, historical events occur only once and cannot be replicated exactly or interpreted unambiguously. Historians must impute motives to personages from the past; each generation will necessarily rewrite history. Yet historians are bound to respect the facts and to strive for as accurate and comprehensive a record as possible. Other major disciplines, ranging from genetics to economics, exhibit analogous regularities and constraints.

Individuals first acquire a disciplined mind in school. But relatively few go on to become academic disciplinarians. The rest master disciplines that are not, strictly speaking, scholarly. Yet the same need to master *a way of thinking* applies to the range of workers—whether one is dealing with professionals, such as lawyers or engineers, or with those in business, such as individuals in personnel, marketing, sales, or management. Such education may occur in formal classes or on the job, explicitly or implicitly. In the end, a form of mastery is achieved, one that must continue to be refined over the years.

Nowadays, the mastery of more than one discipline is at a premium. We value those individuals who are genuinely interdisciplinary, but the claim must be real. We would not

Nowadays, the mastery of more than one discipline is at a premium.

acknowledge someone as bilingual unless he or she could speak more than one language. The claim of interdisciplinarity makes sense only if a person has genuinely mastered and can integrate two or more disciplines. For most individuals, the attainment of multiple perspectives is a more reasonable goal.

Pathological forms exist with respect to any kind of mind. Those related to the disciplined mind are, first, the individual who is overly disciplined, who approaches every issue, whether professional or personal, through the same set of beliefs and practices. Next is the individual who, at one time, had mastered the discipline but who no longer keeps up—exhibiting the patina of the disciplinarian but no longer possessing the requisite contents, skills, and understandings. Finally, there is the avowed interdisciplinarian, who may, in fact, be a jack-of-all-trades but the master of none.

Scholars of cognition generally believe it takes ten years to master a discipline. This leaves little time for multiple forms of mastery.

Scholars of cognition generally believe it takes ten years to master a discipline.

But thanks to excellent computer pedagogy, forms of expertise are more rapidly attainable, perhaps in half the time. Also, because of shrewd scaffolding for those who have yet to attain mastery, hope remains that we will nonetheless be able to participate in a number of disciplines and to synthesize knowledge obtained therefrom.

The Synthesizing Mind

Murray Gell-Mann, Nobel laureate in physics and an avowed multidisciplinarian, made an intriguing claim about our time: in the 21st century, the most valued mind will be the synthesizing mind—the mind that can survey a wide range of sources; decide what is important and worth paying attention to; and then put this information together in ways that make sense to oneself and, ultimately, to other persons as well.

Gell-Mann is onto something important. Information has never been in short supply, but with the advent of new technologies and media, most notably the Internet, vast and often overwhelming amounts of information now deluge individuals around the clock. Shrewd triage becomes an imperative. Those who can synthesize well for themselves will rise to the top of the pack; those whose syntheses make sense to others will become invaluable teachers, communicators, and leaders.

Strangely, my own discipline of psychology seems to have fumbled with regard to explicating the skill of synthesizing. Compared to a half century ago, a great deal of knowledge exists about how individuals learn to read, calculate, and master basic concepts in history, science, economics, or philosophy; but I have been unable to locate comparable knowledge about how an individual synthesizes.

Nonetheless, identifying the basic constituents of the synthesizing process is possible. To begin, a person must decide on the area that he or she wishes to synthesize. Sometimes, the individual has time to reflect on this; sometimes the demand for synthesis is pressing.

Consider an example from business. Suppose that you are an executive, and your company is considering the acquisition of a new company in a sector that seems important but about which you and your immediate associates know little. Your goal is to acquire enough information so that you and your board can make a judicious decision within the next two months.

The place to begin is with the best existing synthesis: fetch it, devour it, and evaluate it. If none exists, you turn to the most knowledgeable individuals and ask them to provide the basic information requisite to synthesis. Given this initial input, you then decide what information seems adequate and which important additional data you need. At the same time, and of great moment, you need to decide on the form and format of the ultimate synthesis: a written narrative, an oral presentation, a set of scenarios, a set of charts and graphs, an equation, a mind map, or an ordered list of pros and cons leading to a final judgment.

Then the actual work of synthesis begins in earnest. New information must be acquired, probed, evaluated, followed up with, or sidelined. The new information needs to be fit, if possible, into the initial synthesis; and where fit is lacking, mutual adjustments must be made. There is constant reflection and regular tinkering.

At some point before the final synthesis is due, you need to develop a protosynthesis that should be tested with the most knowledgeable associates, preferably an audience that is critical and constructive. To the extent that time and resources are available, more than one trial run is desirable. But ultimately there arrives a moment of truth, at which point the best possible synthesis must suffice.

What kind of mind is needed to guide the synthesis? Clearly, although he or she should have a "home" area of expertise, the synthesizer cannot conceivably be up to speed on every relevant discipline. As compensation, the synthesizer must know enough about the requisite disciplines to be able to make judgments about whom and what to trust—or to identify individuals who can help make that determination. The synthesizer must also have a sense of the relevant forms and formats for the synthesis, being prepared to alter when possible but to make a final commitment as the deadline approaches. The synthesizer must always keep his or her eyes on the big picture, while making sure to secure adequate details and arrange them in useful ways. It is quite possible that certain individuals are blessed with a *searchlight intelligence*—the capacity to look widely and to monitor constantly, thus making sure that nothing vital is missing—and that such individuals also have the capacity to value the complementary *laser intelligence* that has fully mastered a specific discipline or problem area. Such broad-gauged thinkers should be identified and cherished. But it is crucial that we determine how to nurture synthesizing capacities more widely, because this facility is likely to remain at a premium in the coming era.

Anyone who has read a clutch of textbooks or attended a variety of weekend seminars knows that not all syntheses are equally effective. Some syntheses are too sprawling, attempting to cover too much material. Some syntheses are too focused, serving as briefings for specialists, not nutrients for generalists. Some are too technical; others are too popular. Different aesthetics can also be brought to bear. I favor literary syntheses that make judicious use of organizers, stories, metaphors, and analogies. Others may prefer syntheses that are devoid of linguistic artifice and that instead rely heavily on charts, graphs, and captionless cartoons. The good synthesizer must know what works both for him and for those who must make use of his synthesis.

The Creating Mind

Most artists, scientists, and scholars plow the same paths as their peers; most politicians and executives are substitutable for one another. In sharp contrast to those conventional experts, those who possess the creating mind forge new ground. In the current popular argot, creators think outside the box. In our society we have come to value those individuals who attempt new things, monitor whether they work, cast about continually for new ideas and practices, pick themselves up after an apparent failure, and so on. Society gives special honor to those rare individuals whose innovations actually change the ideas and practices of their peers—in my trade, we call these individuals *big C creators*.

> In our society we have come to value those individuals who attempt new things, monitor whether they work, cast about continually for new ideas and practices, pick themselves up after an apparent failure, and so on.

What is special about our time? Put succinctly, nearly every practice that is well understood will be automated. Mastery of existing disciplines will be necessary but not sufficient. Whether at the workplace or in the laboratory, on the political platform or the theatrical stage, individuals face pressure to go beyond the conventional wisdom or the habitual practice—to try to improve upon previous practices and current efforts by themselves or their competitors.

Of course, sheer innovation is much easier to accomplish than effective creation. I could write this essay in numerous original ways—for example, putting nonsensical phrases between every sentence. These insertions may well be an original act, but such a ploy serves no useful purpose and is unlikely ever to influence future essayists. Suppose, however, I devise a set of Web links to key points, and those links can be varied, based on questions raised by particular readers or on a shrewd assessment of the interests and sophistication of various audiences. Were such a practice desirable, and my pilot work proved successful, such an innovation might eventually be judged as creative.

Ascertaining the relationship among the three kinds of minds introduced thus far is important. Clearly, synthesizing is not possible without some mastery of constituent disciplines—and perhaps there is, or will be, a discipline of synthesizing, quite apart from such established disciplines as mathematics, music, or management. Creation is unlikely to emerge in the absence of some disciplinary mastery and, perhaps, some capacity to synthesize; it's not possible to think outside the box unless you have a box.

Nonetheless, we must bear in mind that the most imaginative instances of creating typically emerge with individuals who are young—perhaps twenty or thirty years old in science or mathematics, perhaps a decade or so later in other pursuits. Disciplinary acumen and synthesizing capacities continue to accrue throughout a lifetime. This fact suggests that too much discipline, or excessive synthesizing, may actually prove counterproductive for the aspiring creator. The challenge is to acquire enough discipline and sufficient synthesis early in life in order to take the confident leap—to go beyond what is known, and stretch in new and unexpected directions.

In comparing creating with synthesizing, we should not minimize the originality of synthesizing. A valued synthesis is not simply an algorithmic exercise; rather, it gains power when it provides that sense of meaning, significance, and connectedness that so many seek today.

Let me put it another way. If synthesis were simply the following of rules, a well-programmed machine could carry it out. But if synthesis is to respond to human concerns, to concerns not just of the moment but also concerns *sub specie aeternitatis*, then it becomes a distinctly human endeavor. And so, I offer the suggestion that powerful synthesizing builds on the candidate human intelligence that I have been studying most recently: *existential intelligence*, defined as the capacity to raise and address the largest questions. When these questions are new ones, synthesizing blends into creating.

As a student of creativity, I long assumed that creating was primarily a *cognitive feat*—having the requisite knowledge and the apposite cognitive processes—but I now believe that personality and temperament are equally important, and perhaps even more important, for the would-be creator. Many individuals know a great deal, and most can

As a student of creativity, I long assumed that creating was primarily a *cognitive feat*—having the requisite knowledge and the apposite cognitive processes—I now believe that personality and temperament are equally important, and perhaps even more important, for the would-be creator.

acquire knowledge and skills indefinitely. Those who would reach for the Promethean fire must possess a robust personality and temperament. More than willing, creators must be eager to take chances, to venture into the unknown, to fail, and then, perhaps smiling, to pick themselves up and once more throw themselves into the fray. Even when successful, creators do not rest on their laurels. They have motivation again to venture into the unknown and to risk failure, buoyed by the hope that another breakthrough may be in the offing, able to frame an apparent defect as a valuable learning opportunity.

In 1909, psychoanalyst Sigmund Freud and his close associate Carl Jung went to America. It was Freud's first and last trip—he did not like the New World. Jung remained longer; he was lionized by audiences. With great enthusiasm, Jung wired back to Freud: "Great news: psychoanalysis big success in the United States." According to legend, Freud immediately wired back: "What did you leave out?" Far from enjoying the acclaim, Freud was more intent on raising the tension, on venturing beyond anything suggestive of easy acceptance or conventional wisdom.

In the United States, people often ask me how to cultivate creativity. I give two responses, which are neither expected nor immediately popular. First, I talk about the need to pose challenges, obstacles, and boulders. An individual cannot achieve a robust temperament without taking chances, often failing, and learning that the world does not thereupon end. Of course, the frustrations must be manageable; they cannot be allowed to break a person's spirits. Second, and at the risk of being politically incorrect, I question whether it is important to cultivate creativity in American schools. That is because messages about the importance—the cash value—of creativity are ubiquitous in American society: on the streets, in the media, and in the marketplace. Probably more emphasis on disciplines and synthesis would yield greater dividends. But in other countries, where rote instruction is entrenched and innovations are greeted with suspicion, I would favor a curriculum and a pedagogy oriented toward the cultivation of the creative person and the discovery and exploration of the creative idea.

Until this point, I've reviewed the kinds of minds most familiar to me as a cognitive psychologist. If I had written this essay a decade ago, I would probably have stopped here. Indeed, I could summarize the three minds very crisply: the disciplined mind involves depth; the synthesizing mind entails breadth; and the creating mind features stretch.

More recent events, however, prompted me to postulate and ponder two additional kinds of minds: the respectful mind and the ethical mind. To begin, there is my fifteen-year collaborative study of good work—work that is excellent, engaging, and ethical. This line of research sensitized me to kinds of minds that I might otherwise have ignored. In addition, many social and political trends in the world disturbed me. Sheer cultivation of cognitive capacities, in the absence of the human dimension, seems a dubious undertaking. I agree with Ralph Waldo Emerson's assertion that "character is higher than intellect."

The Respectful Mind

Almost from the start, infants are alert to other human beings. Absent frank pathology, even neonates display keen interest in anything that resembles a human face or voice. The attachment between parent (typically the mother) and child is predisposed to develop throughout the early months of life; and the nature and strength of that bond determines the capacity of individuals to form relationships with others throughout life.

Of equal potency is the young human's capacity to distinguish among individuals and among groups of individuals. Within months, the infant can distinguish his mother from other young females; by the end of the first year of life, the infant recognizes, and can modulate his reaction to, a range of individuals in his environment. By the age of two approximately, the toddler is able to make all manner of group discriminations: male versus female, young versus old, familiar versus unfamiliar, and, most revealingly, classification of members of different racial and ethnic groups.

Human beings are wired to make such distinctions readily; indeed, survival depends upon the ability to distinguish among those who are likely to help and nourish, and those who might do harm. But the particular messages in an individual's own environment determine *how* that person labels specific individuals or groups. An individual's own experiences, and the attitudes of the peers and elders to whom he or she is closest, determine whether he or she likes, admires, or respects certain individuals and groups; or whether, on the contrary, that individual comes to shun, fear, or even hate these individuals.

In earlier eras, when human beings met only a few hundred people in the course of a lifetime, the nature of their interpersonal or intergroup attitudes was of less moment. Today, individuals live in an era when nearly every person is likely to encounter thousands of other individuals personally, and when billions of people have the option of traveling abroad or of encountering individuals from remote cultures through visual or digital media.

A person possessed of a respectful mind welcomes this exposure to diverse persons and groups. Such a person wants to meet, get to know, and come to like individuals from remote quarters. A truly cosmopolitan individual gives others the benefit of the doubt, displays initial trust, tries to form links, and avoids prejudicial judgments. To be sure, such a posture is not uncritical or automatic; it is possible for another individual to lose one's respect, even to merit one's distrust or hatred. The respectful mind, however, starts with an assumption that diversity is positive and that the world would be a better place if individuals sought to respect one another.

> The respectful mind starts with an assumption that diversity is positive and that the world would be a better place if individuals sought to respect one another.

The threats to respect are intolerance and prejudice. A prejudiced person has preconceived ideas about individuals and groups, and resists bracketing those preconceptions. For example, if I am a disrespectful straight, white American and you are German, African American, or homosexual, I will assume that you are no good, distance myself, and take every opportunity to put you down verbally or physically. An intolerant person has a very low threshold for unfamiliarity; the default assumption is that strange is bad. No matter what you look like or who you are, if I don't already have a reason to embrace you, I won't.

Sham forms of respect exist. For example, I might "kiss up and kick down." That is, as long as you have power over me, or can do me a favor, I will treat you well; but once I am in a more important position, I won't give you the time of day. Or I might respect you publicly, but once you have left the room, I will make fun of you or the group to which you belong.

To come to respect others once feared, distrusted, or disliked is not easy. Yet, in an interconnected world, such a potential for growth, for freshly forged or renewed respect, is crucial. In war-torn lands, commissions of truth and reconciliation have taken on deserved importance; and at least at times, they succeed in reconstituting badly frayed ties. When countries are at loggerheads, sporting events (such as ping-pong diplomacy between Chinese and Americans) or cultural events (such as orchestras made up of young Israelis and Palestinians) can sometimes pave the way for reconciliation with "the other." When it comes to the causes of terrorism, these are no quick fixes; only genuine respect, nurtured and earned over the decades, can reduce the appeal of terrorism.

The Ethical Mind

The road to respect is paved from the earliest age, one smile or frown at a time. An ethical stance is in no way antithetical to a respectful one, but it involves a much more sophisticated stance toward individuals and groups. A person possessed of an ethical mind is able to think of himself or herself abstractly, and is able to ask, "What kind of a worker do I want to be? What kind of a citizen do I want to be?" Going beyond the posing of such questions, the person is able to think about himself or herself in a universalistic manner: "What would the world be like if all workers in my profession took the stance that I have, if all citizens in my region or my world fulfilled their roles in the way that I do?" Such conceptualization involves a recognition of rights and responsibilities attendant to each role. Crucially, the ethical individual behaves in accordance with the answers that he or she has forged, even when such behaviors clash with self-interest.

My own insights into the ethical mind come largely from fifteen years of study of professionals who are seeking to do good work—work that is excellent, engaging, and ethical (Gardner, Csikszentmihalyi, & Damon, 2001). Most individuals admire good work and want to achieve it. That is, they would like to behave ethically, and they would like others to behave ethically. But this wish does not translate automatically or smoothly into reality. Determining what is ethical is not always easy, and such a determination can prove especially challenging during times like our own, when conditions change very quickly, and when market forces are powerful and often unmitigated. Even when an individual determines the proper course, behaving in an ethical manner is not always easy; that proves particularly so when one is highly ambitious, when others appear to be cutting corners, when different interest groups demand contradictory things from workers, when the ethical course is less clear than one might like, and when such a course runs against one's immediate self-interest.

> Most individuals admire good work and want to achieve it.

Although most children lack the capability to conceptualize the ethical course, the building blocks that form the basis of an ethical life are identifiable: the words and actions of respected elders at home, at school, and in the community. Developing an ethical mind is much easier, so much more natural, when an individual inhabits an ethical environment. When adults are reflective about their decisions, and explicitly cite moral concerns, young people get the message even when the details elude them. Such an environment is rarely sufficient, however. Crucial contributions are made by the atmosphere at a person's first places of work: how do the adults in positions of authority behave; what are the beliefs and behaviors of one's peers; and, above all, what happens when there are clear ethical deviations, and—more happily if less frequently—when an individual or a group behaves in an ethically exemplary fashion? Education in ethics may not begin as early as education for respect, but neither "curriculum" ever ends.

I've suggested that an ethical stance requires the abstract attitude that typically does not develop until adolescence. But even young children are parts of communities—home, school classroom, or church—and they can be acculturated into the ideals, attitudes, and behaviors appropriate to their roles within these communities. Indeed, sensitivity to *institutional culture*—the norms of a particular group as manifest in daily operation—is certainly within the ken of the child in the elementary school. (Alas, so is acculturation into unethical frames of mind.) Thus, society should infuse ethics into the sinews of all important institutions in which the child is involved. An important step will have been taken toward an ethical career and citizenship.

Given the high standards necessary for an ethical mind, examples of failures abound. It is not difficult to recognize behaviors that are strictly illegal, such as theft or fraud, or behaviors that are obviously unethical—for example, the journalist who publishes a story that he knows is untrue or the geneticist who overlooks data that run counter to her hypothesis. More subtle discrimination is needed to detect instances of compromised work—for example, the journalist who fails to confirm a tip before publishing or the geneticist who elects quick publication over running an indicated control group. Compromised work and bad work can undermine institutions and societies; the former may occur more slowly, but unless the trends are reversed, the undermining of the profession is equally decisive.

My examples of ethics are drawn from the professional world, the one that I've studied. But none of us are simply professionals; we are also family members, citizens of a community, and inhabitants of the world. In each case, the ethical mind must go through the exercise of identifying the kind of individual one wants to be. And when a person's own words and behaviors run counter to that idealization, that individual must take corrective action.

I would add that as one gets older, it does not suffice simply to keep one's own ethical house in order. One acquires a responsibility over broader realms of which one is a member. For example, an individual journalist or geneticist may behave ethically, but if his or her peers fail to do so, the senior worker should assume responsibility for the health of the domain. I deem such individuals *trustees*: veterans who are widely respected, deemed to be disinterested, and dedicated to the legitimacy of the domain. As the French playwright Jean-Baptiste Molière commented, "We are responsible not only for what we do but for what we do not do."

Tensions Between and Among the Minds

Of the five minds, the ones most likely to be confused with one another are the respectful mind and the ethical mind. In part, this is because of ordinary language: we consider respect and ethics to be virtues, and we assume that it is impossible to have one without the other. Moreover, very often they correlate; persons who are ethical are also respectful, and vice versa.

However, as indicated, I see these as developmentally discrete accomplishments. An individual can be respectful from early child-hood, even without having a deep understanding of the reasons for respect. In contrast, ethical conceptions and behaviors presuppose an abstract, self-conscious attitude: a capacity to step away from the details of daily life and to think of oneself as a worker or as a citizen.

For example, even as a youth, Abraham Lincoln never liked slavery; he wanted to treat slaves as human beings with their own aspirations, not as mere property. Yet it took him many years to become a politi-cal opponent of slavery because as a citizen and as a political figure, Lincoln felt that it was his ethical obligation to obey the law, which protected slavery in much of the United States. As he put it, his own personal views—his own respect for Negroes—was irrelevant to his official role. Only after much soul-searching and many tumultuous political events did Lincoln reconceptualize his role as a political leader and begin to favor emancipation. In this particular case, he brought into closer alignment his respectful and ethical minds.

Whistle-blowers are another example. Many individuals observe wrongdoing at high levels in their company and remain silent. They may want to keep their jobs, and also to respect their leaders. It takes both courage and a mental leap to think of oneself not as an acquaintance—or even a friend—of one's supervisor but rather as a member of an institution or profession, with certain obligations attendant thereto. The whistle-blower assumes an ethical stance at the cost of a respectful relationship with his supervisor.

Economist Albert O. Hirschman (1970) wrote insightfully about such a sequence. Initially, he contends, one owes allegiance, or loyalty, to one's organization; this is a matter of respect. If, however, the offending situation remains or magnifies, then one has an obligation so speak up. At this point, voice trumps respect. Ultimately, if such an effort to alert and to change the organization is judged to be futile, then the individual should exit the organization; that is the only ethical course. Such a sequence is difficult to realize in a totalitarian society, where other options are few and the penalties for voice can be severe. Nor is it easy to realize if an individual has no other employment options.

Sometimes, respect trumps ethics. Initially, for example, I believed that the French government was correct in banning Muslim women from wearing scarves at school. By the same token, I defended the right of Danish newspapers to publish cartoons that poked fun at Islamic fundamentalism. In both cases, I took the American Bill of Rights at face value—no state religion, guaranteed freedom of expression. But I eventually came to the conclusion that this ethical stance needed to be weighed against the costs of disrespecting the sincere and strongly held religious beliefs of others. The costs of honoring the Islamic faith emerged as less than the costs of honoring an abstract principle. Of course, I make no claim that I came to the right conclusion—only that the tension between respect and ethics can be resolved in contrasting ways.

Here is another example: the creative mind often finds itself in conflict with other minds. In East Asia, an individual is expected to respect his or her mentor throughout life. This stance is difficult to maintain when that person engages in creative iconoclasm—more bluntly, when one's own work overthrows that of the mentor or, equally devastating, renders it irrelevant. For this reason, many aspiring creators from East Asia moved to the West in past decades so that they could avoid the appearance of disrespecting their teacher or mentor. By the same token, too much of an emphasis on discipline, or too much of a dedication to synthesis, also clashes with pursuit of creative breakthroughs. Some discipline and some synthesizing are necessary—but not too much.

The Minds and Multiple Intelligences

As the originator of the theory of multiple intelligences (MI theory), I am often asked about the various intelligences in the development of the five minds. The disciplined and creating minds can and do draw on any and all intelligences, depending on the area of work. Thus, whether disciplined or creative, a poet depends on linguistic intelligence, an architect on spatial intelligence, a therapist on interpersonal intelligence, and so on. Respect and ethics clearly draw on the personal intelligences. Ethics, reflecting an abstract way of thinking, draws as well on logical intelligence.

The synthesizing mind poses a problem for MI theory because synthesis often involves the operation of one, two, or even several intelligences. I suspect that gifted synthesizers achieve their goals in different ways. For example, as a synthesizer, I rely heavily on linguistic, logical, and naturalistic intelligences, but others may draw on spatial, artistic, or personal intelligences to achieve and convey their synthesis. And so, I offer the suggestion that powerful synthesizing may build on the candidate intelligence that I have been contemplating most recently: existential intelligence.

Assessment and the Five Minds

Once individuals hear about the five minds, they ask how to best assess their occurrence and their enhancement. In the United States, the assessment question almost always comes up soon. Assessing the minds is hardly a straightforward matter; and indeed, I worry about too rapid a move to the "test" for synthesizing or ethics. Nonetheless, a few preliminary thoughts are in order.

> Assessing the minds is hardly a straightforward matter.

We know the most about assessing the disciplined mind. Experts in nearly every discipline have developed both quantitative and more qualitative (or more subjective) ways of assessing individual attainment in the discipline. Indeed, educators could not legitimately teach the disciplines in the school, and award licenses or diplomas, without some reasonably consensual evaluation metrics.

As I formulate it, creativity can be assessed only after the fact. An individual work or product is creative if, and only if, it changes the ways in which others in the relevant field think and act. Sometimes this judgment about creativity can be made quite rapidly (as in the case of a riveting movie format), but this assessment can take years or even decades. And so, we can assess an individual's potential for achieving middle C or big C creativity only by looking at what small C creativities have already been achieved.

Syntheses are best judged by laying out beforehand the criteria for a successful synthesis and determining, by consensus, whether those criteria have been achieved. Chapter 3 of my book *Five Minds for the Future* (2007) provides an example of how to do this.

This leaves respect and ethics. If I have the opportunity of observing a person, a group, or an institution, particularly when no one is aware of my presence, I can readily determine whether an aura of respect pervades. In contrast, ethics can be assessed only if a set of explicit principles characterizes a role (professional, citizen). Those responsible for upholding the principles may then render judgments about who abides by the principles and who crosses the line into compromised or bad work.

Of course, even if it could not please a psychometrician, sometimes a general guideline can take an individual quite far. Hearing about the five minds, my friend and distinguished educator Patricia Graham commented, "We respect those who behave in an ethical manner." Indeed, although ethics might be judged in many ways, consensus that a person or institution in question is worthy of respect is an extremely persuasive indication.

Are There Other Minds?

When I wrote *Five Minds for the Future*, I was unaware of Daniel Pink's book *A Whole New Mind: Why Right-Brainers Will Rule the Future* (2006); and Daniel Pink does not mention my writings in his book. Ignorance is never to be preferred over knowledgeability; nonetheless, this state of affairs means that two writers could each put forth their own views independently, and readers could judge the extent to which these views were congruent or in conflict.

Pink is impressively alert to the softer sides of cognition, which he calls design, story, symphony, and play. Although much of my own research has probed the arts, I do not specify areas of discipline, synthesizing, and creating; a person can choose to work in architecture, dance, or film, as well as in business, finance, or management consultancies. However, I agree with Pink that those capacities that can be carried out automatically by machines, or far more cheaply in other parts of the world, will cease to be at a premium in the developed nations. Therefore, the so-called right-brain capacities will come increasingly to the fore.

My work brings out points that Pink ignores or minimizes. Even though mastery of a discipline seems old-fashioned and left-brained, mastery is still vital. Those who do not have a discipline, as well as a sense of discipline, will either be without work or will work for someone who does. Also, Pink leaves out how individuals behave toward others (respect) and how they carry out their roles as workers and citizens (ethics). He might respond that the new mind features "empathy," and that is true enough. Nonetheless, an empathetic person does not necessarily behave desirably. Empathy can be used to produce hurt—indeed, that is what sadism is, taking pleasure in the pain that others feel.

I endorse Pink's discussion of meaning. The thirst for significance has always existed in human beings. The faster the changes, the weaker the ambient religious and ideological systems, the more isolated the individual and the greater the thirst for meaning. I had considered the importance of meaning in my study of existential intelligence. The newly suggested link between synthesizing, on the one hand, and existential intelligence, on the other, resonates with Pink's interest in meaning.

As Pink reminds us, in a world that so honors the STEM disciplines (science, technology, engineering, and mathematics), we require extra efforts not to ignore the other fields of human knowledge and practice. I worry particularly about the arts and humanities. There is less demand for these topics, which were once seen as central to a liberal education. Parents, policymakers, and pupils are all pulled toward the professions, and particularly those that have the potential for making one wealthy (preferably quickly). Yet I believe that an individual cannot be a full person, let alone have a deep understanding of the world, unless he or she is rooted as well in art, literature, and philosophy. Moreover, these realms of knowledge should not be rewards for the harried middle-aged executive, but rather the cornerstone of education for all young persons. In the absence of a strong demand for these topics on the part of consumers, it is incumbent on those with the responsibility of trustee to make sure that humanistically oriented fields are protected. By the same token, those who would hope to continue teaching literature, music, philosophy, and history need to present these topics in ways that speak to new generations, while avoiding "inside baseball" curricula that speak only to those with a professional stake in the field.

Integrating Five Minds Into One Person

Even if one believes that all five of these minds ought to be cultivated, many questions remain about how best to accomplish this goal. One could, for example, randomly assign young persons to one of five classrooms or schools; or, more deliberately, one could attempt to assess mental affinities, and then place each child in the most congenial track (Johnny seems like he has a lot of potential to synthesize; let's put him in track two). I do not favor this alternative. I feel individuals will be better served if they have the opportunity to cultivate all five minds even if, in the end, some will emerge as stronger in one variety, while others exhibit a contrasting profile.

Among the minds is no strict hierarchy, such that one mind should be cultivated before the others, and yet a certain rhythm does exist. An individual needs a certain amount of discipline—in both senses of the term—before undertaking a reasonable synthesis; and if the synthesis involves more than one discipline, then each of the constituent disciplines must be cultivated. By the same token, any genuinely creative activity presupposes a certain disciplined mastery. Although prowess at synthesizing may be unnecessary, nearly all creative breakthroughs—whether in the arts, politics, scholarship, or corporate life—are to some extent dependent on provisional syntheses. Still, as argued previously, too much discipline clashes with creativity; those who excel at syntheses are less likely to effect the most radical creative breakthroughs.

> I feel individuals will be better served if they have the opportunity to cultivate all five minds even if, in the end, some will emerge as stronger in one variety, while others exhibit a contrasting profile.

Without question, the respectful mind can be cultivated well before an ethical stance is conceivable. Indeed, respect ought to be part of the atmosphere from the earliest moments of life. When it comes to the cultivation of creativity, it is important to underscore personality and temperament factors. The building of a robust temperament, and a personality that is unafraid of assuming reasonable risks—cognitive and physical—can begin early in life; these dispositions mark the future creator.

Whatever details of ordering may obtain, in the end it is desirable for each person to have achieved aspects of all five mental capacities, all five minds for the future. Such a personal integration is most likely to occur when individuals are raised in environments that exhibit and value all five kinds of minds. So much the better if role models—parents, teacher, masters, or supervisors—regularly display aspects of discipline, synthesis, creation, respect, *and* ethics. In addition to embodying these kinds of minds, the best educators at school or work can provide support, advice, and coaching that help to inculcate discipline, encourage synthesis, prod creativity, foster respect, and encourage an ethical stance.

In the end, however, no one can compel the cultivation and integration of the five minds. The individual must come to believe that the minds are important, that they merit the investment of significant amounts of time and resources, and that they are worthy of continuing nurturance even after external supports fade. The individual must reflect on the role of each of these minds at work, in a favored avocation, at home, in the community, and in the wider world. The individual must be aware that sometimes these minds will find themselves in tension with one another, and that any resolution will come at some cost. In the future, the mind that is likely to be at greatest premium is the synthesizing mind. And so, it is perhaps fitting that the melding of the minds within an individual's skin is the ultimate challenge of personal synthesis.

References

Gardner, H. (2006). *Multiple intelligences: New horizons in theory and practice.* New York: Basic Books.

Gardner, H. (2007). *Five minds for the future.* Boston: Harvard Business School Press.

Gardner, H., Csikszentmihalyi, M., & Damon, W. (2001). *Good work: When excellence and ethics meet.* New York: Basic Books.

Hirschman, A. O. (1970). *Exit, voice and loyalty: Responses to decline in firms, organizations, and states.* Cambridge, MA: Harvard University Press.

Pink, D. H. (2006). *A whole new mind: Why right-brainers will rule the future.* New York: Riverhead.

Linda Darling-Hammond

Linda Darling-Hammond, Ph.D., is Charles E. Ducommun Professor of Education at Stanford University, where she launched the Stanford Educational Leadership Institute and the School Redesign Network. She has also served as faculty sponsor for the Stanford Teacher Education Program. She is a former president of the American Educational Research Association and member of the National Academy of Education. Her research, teaching, and policy work focus on issues of school restructuring, teacher quality, and educational equity. Among Darling-Hammond's more than three hundred publications are *Preparing Teachers for a Changing World: What Teachers Should Learn and Be Able to Do* (with John Bransford, for the National Academy of Education, winner of the Edward C. Pomeroy Award for Outstanding Contributions to Teacher Education from the American Association of College Teachers for Education); *Teaching as the Learning Profession: A Handbook of Policy and Practice* (coedited with Gary Sykes, recipient of the National Staff Development Council's Outstanding Book Award for 2000); and *The Right to Learn: A Blueprint for Schools That Work* (recipient of the American Educational Research Association's Outstanding Book Award for 1998).

In this interview, Darling-Hammond calls for major policy changes to guide development of 21st century schools. She advocates deep alignment of standards, curriculum, instruction, and assessment; strengthening professionalism among teachers and school leaders; redesign of school time to allow for increased participation in professional decisions by teachers; and equitable distribution of resources among all schools. She insists that the United States must take a more balanced approach to school reform and that these changes are essential if the United States is to restore its lost leadership for educational excellence.

Chapter 2

New Policies for 21st Century Demands

Linda Darling-Hammond, Interviewed by James Bellanca

> *We badly need a national policy that enables schools to meet the intellectual demands of the twenty-first century.*

> —Linda Darling-Hammond (2007)

James Bellanca: *In your article for* The Nation *magazine (Darling-Hammond, 2007), you call for a national policy so that students can meet the intellectual demands of the 21st century. What are these demands?*

Linda Darling-Hammond: Our economy and our lives today are much more complex than many people understand. That complexity is exacerbated by the extraordinarily fast rate of knowledge growth in this century. Some people say that the amount of technological knowledge in the world is almost doubling every two years. Thus, the notion that we could take all of the facts that a person needs to know, divide them into twelve years of schooling, and learn those facts and be done does not clearly equip young people for the future. Twenty-first-century students need a deeper understanding of the core concepts in the disciplines than they receive now. In addition, students need to be able to design, evaluate, and manage their own work. Students need to be able to frame, investigate, and solve problems using a wide range of information resources and digital tools.

James Bellanca: *Does this mean that students have to get smarter?*

Linda Darling-Hammond: All students need to develop more complex cognitive abilities so that they can find, analyze, and use information for a range of purposes, including the development of new products and ideas. Students need to collaborate and communicate so that they can take advantage of each other's knowledge and expertise. Their communication abilities must include writing and speaking in world languages, as well as using mathematical symbols. These changes in student abilities and knowledge do not happen by accident; changes start at the top with national policy.

James Bellanca: *In the 1980s and 1990s, educators paid attention to the skills and understandings students were said to need to confront the 21st century work world. How is this different than our current perspective?*

Linda Darling-Hammond: I think we were on the right track in the early 1990s, especially in the efforts to create new content standards that incorporated the cognitive skills. However, pendulum swings in the conceptualization of what students need to learn and how they need to learn it have been very destructive. Back-and-forth swings between teaching for understanding and assessing authentic performances versus basic skills measured by multiple-choice and short-answer test items have cost the United States a lot of time and progress. The emphasis today on more complex skills is entirely different from what people were trying to pursue in the early 1990s. What is different today is the effort to correct from the extreme back-to-basics approach represented by the No Child Left Behind Act of 2001 and instead put cognitive skills into the context of what learners need to know for the work world of the 21st century.

I also think the impetus for the changes is different. In the last century, a handful of educators pushed to add "higher-order thinking skills" to instruction. Today, the move to change policy comes from multiple groups, including some groups from the business community, state education departments, and the president of the United States himself. And there is a new recognition that these skills cannot be taught in isolation. The only way to return the United States to a position of leadership in the international education community is with a comprehensive, systemic approach that reaches all children.

I also think the impetus for the changes is different. In the last century, a handful of educators pushed to add "higher-order thinking skills" to instruction. Today, the move to change policy comes from multiple groups, including some groups from the business community, state education departments, and the president of the United States himself.

James Bellanca: *What is the evidence that the United States has fallen behind?*

Linda Darling-Hammond: Let me focus on the most startling indicator—the data from the 2006 Programme for International Student Assessment (PISA). On that assessment of forty countries, the United States ranked thirty-fifth in mathematics and thirty-first in science. (No U.S. reading scores were reported because of editing problems.) Each assessment showed a glaring United States decline from the 2003 results. Furthermore, as I reported in a recent *Phi Delta Kappan* article (Darling-Hammond & McCloskey, 2008), in each disciplinary area tested, U.S. students scored lowest on the problem-solving items. I also noted that the United States had a much wider achievement gap than the most highly ranked jurisdictions, such as Finland, Canada, Australia, New Zealand, Hong Kong, Korea, and Japan.

James Bellanca: *What is it that separates the performances of the top-scoring nations from the United States?*

Linda Darling-Hammond: The competing nations do not experience the pendulum swings I spoke of. They do not zigzag back and forth every decade. These nations stay focused on developing a strong curriculum and a set of thoughtful assessments. Their assessments, most of which are open-ended performance assessments, require students to demonstrate what they can do with what they are learning. To prepare their students, these nations are steadily improving the quality of their instruction. In the meantime, the United States moves back and forth between polar extremes.

The competing nations do not experience the pendulum swings. . . . These nations stay focused on developing a strong curriculum and a set of thoughtful assessments.

James Bellanca: *How are these pendulum swings hurtful?*

Linda Darling-Hammond: The problem is the harm done to practitioners, teachers, and students. If you listen to great teachers, their answer about basic skills and thinking skills is always *both/and*, not *either/or*. These effective teachers balance how and what they teach. They prepare children *both* for decoding *and* for comprehending text. They ask students to build basic vocabulary *and* to understand literature, draw inferences, and use information for novel purposes. In math, these teachers teach students *both* how to compute math facts *and* how to reason, think, and communicate mathematically. In science, they prepare students *both* to understand key concepts in science *and* to engage in scientific investigation. These are the teachers who stay above the wars and reconcile the pendulum swings in daily practice.

James Bellanca: *Shouldn't this balanced practice be expected of all teachers?*

Linda Darling-Hammond: Many teachers are less sure of their own knowledge and abilities. They have had neither the preparation nor the support that enables them to stay out of the either/or trap. These teachers dutifully do what they are told. In one decade, it is back to basics; in the next, it is higher-order thinking. Although both practices are necessary, the every-decade administrative mandates to switch gears midstream confuse these teachers. To cope, many teachers respond by saying, "This, too, will pass."

James Bellanca: *What happens if we continue to have these pendulum swings?*

Linda Darling-Hammond: The United States has little chance to move ahead. Teachers will be unable to develop the foundation skills for thinking that their students need for real learning. Without that foundation, students will not know how to make sense of new information, apply knowledge in novel situations, or learn on their own. And if that happens, the United States will continue to compete poorly on international assessments.

James Bellanca: *Why are these international assessments important?*

Linda Darling-Hammond: Washington economic policy discussions often refer to international assessments rankings when emphasizing the need for the United States to benchmark expectations with those of the highest-performing nations. The aim is to make the school system more "internationally competitive." But analyses of results reveal other ways to approach teaching and learning than what occurs commonly in too many classrooms in the United States. For example, the analyses show that higher-achieving countries teach fewer topics more deeply each year; focus more on reasoning skills and applications of knowledge, rather than on mere coverage; and have a more thoughtful sequence of expectations based on developmental learning progressions within and across domains. This focus aligns closely with the many different frameworks for 21st century skills, including those from the Partnership for 21st Century Skills (see figure F.1 in the foreword on page xv).

James Bellanca: *So the assessment results can actually help us understand the cause of the differences?*

Linda Darling-Hammond: Yes. To understand why students from other countries do so well, we must examine *how* those students are taught and assessed. European and Asian nations that have steeply improved student learning have focused explicitly on creating curriculum and assessments that emphasize the so-called 21st century skills.

> The analyses show that higher-achieving countries teach fewer topics more deeply each year; focus more on reasoning skills and applications of knowledge, rather than on mere coverage; and have a more thoughtful sequence of expectations based on developmental learning progressions within and across domains.

James Bellanca: *What kinds of testing programs do these nations use?*

Linda Darling-Hammond: I have done analyses of assessment systems in the highest-achieving nations—Finland, Korea, Hong Kong, Singapore, The Netherlands, Sweden, Canada, and Australia. Unlike the continuous testing system required by the No Child Left Behind Act, which is accomplished primarily with externally provided multiple-choice tests, these top-performing countries have little external testing. These countries instead emphasize extensive school-based assessments driven by curriculum standards and teacher-developed syllabi that detail what is to be learned. In countries such as Finland, Hong Kong, and Singapore, only two grade levels have sample tests from the outside. The United Kingdom has a modest amount of external testing. And the external tests that are used include mostly open-ended items that require students to solve problems, show their work, write answers to questions, and sometimes actually demonstrate what they can do. Most importantly, teachers score and evaluate curriculum-based performance tasks that *they* developed. This approach is part of the accountability system that aligns the internal and external tests across the grade levels with the standards and with instruction.

James Bellanca: *How does this approach influence achievement?*

Linda Darling-Hammond: Several things are critically important here. When you have this alignment of standards, instruction, and assessments, teachers continually learn about what their students know. The teachers understand the standards deeply because they themselves are part of the assessment process around the standards. They learn how to refine curriculum so that they become increasingly more effective in teaching the standards. As a consequence, the school-based assessments result in greater curriculum equity for students. This method is the learning engine that drives all students to higher achievement.

James Bellanca: *How is this approach different from the approach in the United States?*

Linda Darling-Hammond: When I was in Australia learning about their assessment system, I talked about the American system. One of the Australian teachers asked me, "Do you mean that American teachers don't know what will be on the test?" I said, "They do *not* know. In the United States, testing is conceptualized as the measurement of factual recall. The tests are secret; they arrive in brown-paper wrappers. The completed scoring sheets go out in the same wrappers." She said, "How can they teach productively if they don't know what will be on the assessment?" This question shows how assessment is considered differently in other countries. For the most part, teachers in the United States teach facts, often covering every page of a textbook or a workbook; they have little idea about what facts will be tested. In the high-achieving countries, teachers are involved in designing tests that assess understanding and cognitive skills. Because these teachers also design and teach the lessons that lead students to these more rigorous outcomes, they align standards, instruction, and assessment. These educators know full well what they must do to ensure that every student achieves the intended results.

James Bellanca: *What are the implications for the United States?*

Linda Darling-Hammond: Abandoning the conception of assessment as a checkup on teachers whom we cannot trust to be involved in the assessment process is extremely important. It is also important that the United States move toward assessments in which teachers and students are intimately engaged in work that is intellectually ambitious, challenging, and worthwhile. Testing is not just what can be done in a couple of hours in April on a machine-scored instrument; it is also finding what students understand and can do cognitively as called for by rigorous standards. With this information, teachers can make real adjustments to how they instruct and assess so that every child really succeeds.

James Bellanca: *What kind of assessments should teachers use with their own students?*

Linda Darling-Hammond: True assessment does not limit students to quizzes and fact tests for grades. Effective assessment means assigning a piece of student work—whether it is an essay, a research project, a scientific inquiry, or a sculpture—and allowing a student to work on that selected task with support while scaffolding instruction and giving feedback that expands the student's understanding and skill. Teachers may combine peer assessment, student self-assessment, or their own assessment so that the students learn how to look at their work, learn strategies for framing and solving problems, and then understand how to continually revise their work so that they are getting closer and closer approximations to expert practice. This process produces

> Effective assessment means assigning a piece of student work—whether it is an essay, a research project, a scientific inquiry, or a sculpture—and allowing a student to work on that selected task with support while scaffolding instruction and giving feedback that expands the student's understanding and skill.

a substantially more thoughtful and rigorous outcome. In this way, grades, tests, and quizzes give way to the students' products, which show clearly what the students have come to know and understand.

James Bellanca: *The change from grades and quizzes to more authentic assessment sounds like a difficult challenge.*

Linda Darling-Hammond: Yes, but it's necessary. To use authentic assessment, teachers must rethink their understanding of the curriculum and the teaching process. Rather than expecting to just cover some information, give a test, and then assign a grade on whether students remember the information given, teachers need to think about what kind of skills and applications their students should develop. This assessment style requires that teachers develop a process that results in the learning of those skills and applications. Teachers must provide time for students to refine their work, receive feedback, revise their work, and gradually become more expert.

James Bellanca: *Why do you call this kind of assessment "authentic"?*

Linda Darling-Hammond: Because this type of assessment is like the development of expertise in the real—or authentic—world by real workers. How often do sculptors just sit down and knock off a new piece? Which authors don't write multiple drafts? How many scientists make a big break with the first experiment? In order for their students to develop expertise, teachers need a lot of professional development that is embedded in the content they teach; around the kinds of tests they want students to engage in; with colleagues trying strategies and debriefing them together, fine-tuning their plans, developing what I think of as a two-way pedagogy in which teachers learn to listen to students and look at student work, so that they get information about the learning process, as well as directly instruct students and provide information. That reciprocal kind of pedagogy is part of what gets refined in professional development with colleagues when teachers continually bring student work to the table and problem solve the teaching and learning process with colleagues.

James Bellanca: *How can we stop the pendulum swings you refer to and make progress toward a more aligned and balanced approach?*

Linda Darling-Hammond: Progress starts with respectful discourse. All must agree that both content and skills are important for serious schooling in the 21st century. For example, the American Enterprise Institute and others recently launched a set of volleys against the 21st century skills concept. These organizations fear that the "skills people" will lose sight of valuable content. They envision that the skills people will put an undisciplined emphasis on collaboration, teamwork, and project-based learning. They see students working with clay and toothpicks without actually mastering challenging intellectual content. On the other side, skills people are worried that the "content people" will try to reduce what is to be known and demonstrated to a list of dry, disconnected facts tested by multiple-choice items without attention to meaning or application.

A more respectful discourse can result in agreement about the value of both positions. With such an agreement, all could engage in serious conversation about rigorous content standards being paired with well-disciplined ways to promote the important skills. With that agreement, everyone will have to acknowledge that we must develop and prepare teachers and school leaders much more deeply. All teachers need the ability to engage in high-quality instruction that adequately represents both the content and the cognitive skills that enhance all students' deep understanding of content. And all teachers need to be more disciplined in order to move toward an integrated vision that invests in what practitioners need to know and be able to do.

> A more respectful discourse can result in agreement about the value of both positions.

James Bellanca: *If leaders on both sides could reach that kind of agreement, what national policies would advance our schools in a way that is free of the extreme pendulum swings?*

Linda Darling-Hammond: There are four necessary policy changes, and they are interdependent. First, we need an aligned standards, instruction, and assessment system. This alignment will be most apt if it includes not only the thinking and learning skills I have described, but also is firmly rooted in a deep understanding of each content area. In this process, we cannot do what we have done in the past, which is jump from standards to tests while we ignore curriculum. The development of a lean, not overly prescribed, curriculum that outlines the expected learning progressions applicable to all students and is assessable by teachers in authentic ways is essential.

There are four necessary policy changes, and they are interdependent:

1. An aligned standards, instruction, and assessment system
2. An infrastructure that gives teachers and school leaders sufficient time to do the alignment work
3. Schools that are more supportive of in-depth teaching and learning
4. More equitable distribution of resources

James Bellanca: *And we don't have such an aligned system now?*

Linda Darling-Hammond: Not in a way or to the degree that provides the necessary help. Currently, we have a loose system in which teachers in each school must guess at what the mandated state tests will cover. Teachers may be left on their own to choose what to teach each day, or perhaps they are given scripts to read that ignore student differences. In the aligned vision I propose, teachers would participate in solid curriculum development. They would know how their curriculum aligns with the mandated standards.

We cannot expect individual teachers to develop all this curriculum on their own, but the opportunity to sequence, organize, and create strong learning units is essential. Each unit must be one that they can use productively with real children in very diverse classrooms to accomplish common standards. To be most effective, teachers need the opportunity to use their professional judgment to determine what is appropriate for their classrooms. Overly prescriptive scripts only continue to thwart increased learning.

James Bellanca: *If I were a teacher with my day-to-day workload, I might feel overloaded by your long list. I might be inclined to resist.*

Linda Darling-Hammond: I hear a lot about teacher resistance to change. I have been in the field for more than thirty years, working with people from all different parts of different school systems, and I have three observations about so-called teacher resistance.

First, to the extent that *sometimes* teachers are resistant to change, resistance is actually not an irrational response. We throw so many changes at teachers with such blistering speed that mandated changes come and go in the blink of an eye. And then the changes change—based on who the current superintendent is, which company came and sold the latest hot product, what the school board has decided to do now, what the state legislature has decided to do now, what money is coming into the system, and so on. So, for teachers who know that the latest change is only temporary, resistance is a rational response.

Second, I have seen many reform-minded school settings in which the school board, the parent leadership, or the administration is more resistant to a change than the teachers. Sometimes teachers are saying, "We really want to do this," or "We have a great idea for our students, and we are ready to get on it." Meanwhile, the principal or a central office administrator is not ready to move in that direction or does not want to rock the boat. I have found, more often than not, that teachers are more progressive in their interest to shape instruction in better ways than the policy and administrative forces that stand over them.

Third, the problem in making constructive change is not how to get around perceived teacher resistance. The problem is how to get everybody onto the same path—and sticking to that path—rather than indulging in these pendulum swings. In the long run, we must buffer education more effectively from the vicissitudes of politics. High-achieving nations typically have a highly professionalized ministry of education. They try to identify the core values of the system, the essential beliefs about teaching and learning, and then continually refine practice. There are changes always being made, but changes in this context are more in the direction of refining the system rather than throwing out the system every time a new fad pops up or the next administrator plays a personal card.

> The problem is how to get everybody onto the same path—and sticking to that path—rather than indulging in these pendulum swings.

James Bellanca: *How can American education be more like that?*

Linda Darling-Hammond: We need to strengthen professionalism in the American education enterprise. We need to be sure that capable teachers and administrators have access to a strong knowledge base and trust them to be responsible for teaching and learning.

James Bellanca: *In many schools, teachers have limited time to do the work you describe. What do you propose?*

Linda Darling-Hammond: That answer is not difficult. It leads to the second policy change I mentioned earlier: one that allows us to build an infrastructure so that teachers and school leaders have sufficient time to do the alignment work I described. Again, we can learn about this from high-performing nations.

> Build an infrastructure so that teachers and school leaders have sufficient time to do alignment work.

James Bellanca: *What sorts of things could we learn?*

Linda Darling-Hammond: To begin, you get what you pay for. These systems completely underwrite three to four years of high-quality teacher preparation during which teachers receive a full salary. Teachers do not have to teach full time at their regular job and pay out of their pockets for a step-and-scale salary increase for a degree that may have little to do with their classroom work. Instead, they engage in a strong clinical experience that readies them to work with the most struggling students who have a wide range of needs. They prepare to develop formative and summative performance assessments that align with the prescribed standards. They spend intense hours developing their content knowledge and pedagogy, learning to use research and how to conduct action research to improve their own practice. This preparation is done universally—for all teachers in all contexts.

James Bellanca: *You also mentioned significant changes in leadership preparation.*

Linda Darling-Hammond: Yes. I believe leadership preparation needs a similar—if not greater—emphasis. School leaders need an undistracted engagement in learning to lead a school. This must include an intense clinical experience that prepares potential leaders to work in the most diverse and difficult schools. Shadowing a few administrators for a few weeks will not suffice. Leader candidates must prove their success as effective teachers, including use of performance assessments aligned with standards, knowledge of high-quality instruction that is based firmly in research, and helping other teachers develop their expertise. Those selected should already display leadership potential. Once selected, they need to have multiple years of high-quality, purposeful preparation without worrying about where the money will come from.

James Bellanca: *What you want leaders to study doesn't seem to align with the standard certification requirements for school administrators.*

Linda Darling-Hammond: No, it doesn't. I believe that the school leader's major responsibility is to enable excellent teaching in every classroom. Although we have given lip service to instructional leadership, little has happened in the last decades to make it a common or significant reality. School leaders in the next decades need to engage in three practices that we haven't always seen as part of school administration. First is constructing time for teachers to work together on the development of curriculum and assessments. Second is designing and implementing comprehensive professional development programs. This includes formation of professional learning communities, providing coaching and mentoring for teachers who have been identified as needing additional assistance, and encouraging peer support teams that address the special needs of struggling students. Third is helping teachers to find another profession if they are unable to improve after having received purposeful support.

> The school leader's major responsibility is to enable excellent teaching in every classroom.

James Bellanca: *That is a strong statement.*

Linda Darling-Hammond: Yes, it is. We can no longer tolerate bad teaching in any school. If a leader recognizes that a teacher needs improvement and he or she provides the types of support that are part of a professional learning community but still sees no constructive change, then the leader must counsel that teacher into a more appropriate career.

James Bellanca: *Does a school leader need other skills in order to be an instructional leader?*

Linda Darling-Hammond: Yes, being an instructional leader in the type of school I have described requires organizational development knowledge and skill. When an individual takes charge of a school, it most likely will be organized in an assembly-line fashion, which is the factory model we inherited. Leaders will have to redesign their schools. This redesign often starts with the creation of more sustained, productive relationships between adults and children. At the high school level, for example, leaders can make sure that students have advisors who work with a small number of students and have time to reach out and work with the parents. They can form students into smaller houses with teacher teams and advisors to prevent students from getting left behind. Leaders can push for school rubrics and performance assessments that create shared norms about the intellectual work expected.

Finally, I would say good leaders must be able to manage constructive change. They must be able to engage all the stakeholders, manage distributed leadership so that teachers are part of the leadership cadre, and ensure that parents and students have a voice and are engaged. They must develop the faculty as a professional learning community ready and able to take on the many challenges for aligning curriculum, instruction, and assessment to match 21st century learning needs. The days in which principals are expected just to manage the school bells, make the buses run on time, order the textbooks, keep order in the cafeteria, quote the school manual, and ensure that everyone is in their place must soon end. Without the changes required to bring all schools to up 21st century standards, we cannot expect 21st century results.

James Bellanca: *As you said, the second policy change involves finding the time for the intense experiences you're describing.*

Linda Darling-Hammond: Again, we can look at the PISA high-performing nations. In most of those nations, teachers have fifteen to twenty-five hours each week in which they plan their lessons together. They may engage in lesson study and action research. They may observe each other in the classroom. They may meet with students or parents, evaluate student work together or alone, conference with their site leaders or mentors, build assessments aligned to the standards, investigate models of teaching, study best practice research, or develop deeper understanding of their course content. These professional, collegial learning experiences inform their practice in ways that allow for rich improvements in what and how they teach. It is a well-prepared leader who makes these events happen.

Jim Bellanca: *Are these changes possible without other more substantive changes?*

Linda Darling-Hammond: No. The recommendation for giving teachers time to work together on the improvement of practice gets us to the third policy I recommend: redesigning schools so that they become more supportive of in-depth teaching and learning. We continue to struggle with the factory model that we inherited one hundred years ago. That model neither values relationships between adults and children nor the time for in-depth study. To make the school factory model work, we adopted the age-grading system that sends elementary school students to a different teacher every year and middle and high school students to a different teacher every forty-five or fifty-five minutes. If students get to high school, their teachers may face 100–125 students a day; if they attend high school in an urban area, students may join 150–175 others in each teacher's stamp-and-pass-on day. The notion that anyone can get deep, rigorous, high-quality learning in a system that treats students as assembly-line widgets is implausible. If we are serious about the kind of learning needed in the 21st century, redesigning our schools is imperative.

> I recommend redesigning schools so that they become more supportive of in-depth teaching and learning.

James Bellanca: *What sorts of things need redesigning?*

Linda Darling-Hammond: Foremost among these changes is use of time. To accomplish the outcomes being discussed now, teachers need the opportunity to work with students over longer periods of time. It takes time to teach content deeply, to challenge students to apply what they know with projects, to investigate ideas in depth, to solve significant learning problems, and to assess what students can do.

James Bellanca: *I believe you said you are seeking four changes in policy.*

Linda Darling-Hammond: Yes. The fourth policy calls for more equitable distribution of resources. Currently, the United States has the most inequitable system of education of any leading industrialized country. Most countries fund schools centrally and equally; they may add additional funding for high-need students.

In the United States, huge funding differences exist between the highest- and lowest-spending schools. The ratio between the highest- and lowest-spending schools in the United States is 10:1. Within most states, the ratio is 3:1, exacerbated by differences among states. The education of some children is well supported, with every imaginable accoutrement. These students receive superior support in terms of teacher quality, curriculum offerings, specialists, technology, textbooks, athletic facilities, and so on. In contrast, other students attend schools in third-world conditions or worse.

James Bellanca: *How does the issue of resource inequity relate to your other policy points?*

Linda Darling-Hammond: The four policy changes I recommend are connected systemically. Each depends on the others. For any one policy to work effectively, all are needed. In our continued use of the factory model, we see the degree of inequity, the spread of outcomes that is related to the spread of input. We cannot expect to radically change the outcomes unless we also ensure adequate resources in every school, including time for teachers to work on the alignment issues, time for professional learning so that teachers can develop the knowledge and skills they need to do this development, and so on.

James Bellanca: *What would you like to see happen to put these policy changes in place?*

Linda Darling-Hammond: Policy implementation should be done in a systematic, sustained way, based on a set of reforms that allows

teachers and administrators in every school to develop more thoughtful instruction. We have great schools in some places and great classrooms in some schools, but we need to be able to spread that greatness more uniformly across the national system, following a straighter path without those destructive pendulum swings.

References

Darling-Hammond, L. (2007, May 2). Evaluating No Child Left Behind. *The Nation.* Accessed at www.thenation.com/doc/20070521/darling-hammond on November 2, 2009.

Darling-Hammond, L., & McCloskey, L. (2007, December). Assessment for learning around the world: What would it mean to be internationally competitive? *Phi Delta Kappan, 90*(4), 263–272.

Chris Dede

Chris Dede, Ed.D., is the Timothy E. Wirth Professor in Learning Technologies at Harvard's Graduate School of Education. His fields of scholarship include emerging technologies, policy, and leadership. His funded research includes three grants from the National Science Foundation (NSF) and the U.S. Department of Education Institute of Education Sciences to explore immersive and semi-immersive simulations as a means of student engagement, learning, and assessment. In 2007, he was honored by Harvard University as an outstanding teacher. Dede has served as a member of the National Academy of Sciences Committee on Foundations of Educational and Psychological Assessment and a member of the 2010 National Educational Technology Plan working group. He serves on advisory boards and commissions for PBS TeacherLine, the Partnership for 21st Century Skills, the Pittsburgh Science of Learning Center, and several federal research grants. He is coeditor of *Scaling Up Success: Lessons Learned From Technology-Based Educational Improvement* (2005) and editor of *Online Professional Development for Teachers: Emerging Models and Methods* (2006).

In this chapter, Dede compares several prominent lists of 21st century skills. He asks, "How diverse are these definitions for 21st century skills?" and notes that a lack of clarity about the nature of 21st century skills could be problematic. His examination illuminates what the various frameworks have in common and what each uniquely adds to the overarching concept.

Chapter 3

Comparing Frameworks for 21st Century Skills

Chris Dede

Many groups have called for all students to learn 21st century skills. In response, some organizations have developed, as part of their institutional brand, frameworks for the new millennium that delineate content and processes teachers should convey as part of students' schooling. How diverse are these definitions for 21st century skills, and is the term becoming an umbrella phrase under which advocates from various groups can argue for almost any type of knowledge? Lack of clarity about the nature of 21st century skills could be problematic; many educational reforms have failed because people use the same terminology, but mean quite different things. What do the various frameworks for 21st century skills have in common? What can they add to the overarching concept of knowledge necessary for new graduates to be effective workers and citizens?

The Rationale for Formulating 21st Century Skills

The 21st century is quite different from the 20th in regard to the skills people now need for work, citizenship, and self-actualization. Proficiency in the 21st century differs primarily due to the emergence of very sophisticated information and communication technologies (ICTs). For example, the types of work done by people—as opposed to machines—are continually shifting as computers and telecommunications expand their capabilities to accomplish human tasks. Economists Frank Levy and Richard Murnane (2004) highlight a crucial component of what constitutes 21st century knowledge and skills:

> Declining portions of the labor force are engaged in jobs that consist primarily of routine cognitive work and routine manual labor—the types of tasks that are easiest to program computers to do. Growing proportions of the nation's labor force are engaged in jobs that emphasize expert thinking or complex communication—tasks that computers cannot do. (pp. 53–54)

These economists go on to explain the "components of expert thinking: [1] effective pattern matching based on detailed knowledge; and [2] metacognition, the set of skills used by the stumped expert to decide when to give up on one strategy and what to try next" (Levy & Murnane, 2004, p. 75). Inventing new problem-solving heuristics when standard protocols have failed is an important skill; when all diagnostics are normal, but the patient is still feeling unwell, for instance, a skilled physician can think outside the box and become an expert decision maker. According to Levy and Murnane (2004), "complex communication requires the exchange of vast amounts of verbal and nonverbal information. The information flow is constantly adjusted as the communication evolves unpredictably" (p. 94). Therefore, a skilled teacher is an expert in complex communication, able to improvise answers and facilitate dialogue in the unpredictable, chaotic flow of classroom discussion.

Sophisticated ICTs are changing the nature of "perennial" skills valuable throughout history, as well as creating novel "contextual" skills unique to new millennium work and citizenship (Dede, in press). For example, collaboration is a perennial ability, valued as a trait in workplaces for centuries. Therefore, the fundamental worth of this suite of interpersonal skills is not unique to the 21st century economic context. However, the degree of importance for collaborative capacity is growing now that work in knowledge-based economies is increasingly accomplished by teams of people with complementary expertise and roles, as opposed to individuals doing isolated work in an industrial setting (Karoly & Panis, 2004).

Further, the nature of collaboration is shifting to a more sophisticated skillset. In addition to collaborating face-to-face with colleagues across a conference table, 21st century workers increasingly accomplish tasks through mediated interactions with peers halfway across the world whom they may never meet face-to-face. Thus, even though perennial in nature, collaboration is worthy of inclusion as a 21st century skill because the importance of cooperative interpersonal capabilities is higher and the skills involved are more sophisticated than in the prior industrial era.

In contrast, the ability to rapidly filter huge amounts of incoming data and extract information valuable for decision making is a contextual capability. Due to the prevalence of ICTs, people are—for the first time in human history—inundated by enormous amounts of data that they must access, manage, integrate, and evaluate. Rather than rummaging through library stacks to find a few pieces of knowledge, an activity characteristic of information access in the 20th century, users of modern search engines receive thousands or even millions of "hits." However, many of these resources are off-target, incomplete, inconsistent, and perhaps even biased. The ability to separate signal from noise in a potentially overwhelming flood of incoming data is a suite of 21st century skills not in *degree*, as with collaboration, but in *type*.

Weinberger (2007) describes the power of "digital disorder," which takes advantage of the fact that virtual information can transcend the limited properties of physical objects (like books or index cards). Rather than relying on a single method of organization with a fixed terminology (such as the Dewey Decimal System as a means of categorizing knowledge), modern information systems can respond to natural language queries and can instantly sort digital data into whatever category structure best suits a particular person's immediate needs. This approach creates a new set of contextual 21st century skills centered on "disorderly" knowledge co-creation and sharing.

Overall, the distinction between perennial and contextual skills is important because, unlike perennial capabilities, new, contextual types of human performances are typically not part of the legacy curriculum inherited from 20th century educational systems. Conventional, 20th century K–12 instruction emphasizes manipulating predigested information to build fluency in routine problem solving, rather than filtering data derived from experiences in complex settings to develop skills in sophisticated problem finding. Knowledge separated from skills and presented as revealed truth, rather than as an understanding that is discovered and constructed, results in students simply learning data about a topic instead of learning how to extend their understanding beyond information available for assimilation. In 20th century instruction, problem-solving skills are presented in an abstract form removed from their application to knowledge; this makes transfer to real-world situations difficult. The ultimate objective of that type of education is presented as learning a specific problem-solving routine to match every situation, rather than developing expert decision-making and metacognitive strategies that indicate how to proceed when no standard approach seems applicable.

> In 20th century instruction, problem-solving skills are presented in an abstract form removed from their application to knowledge; this makes transfer to real-world situations difficult.

In 20th century instruction, little time is spent on building capabilities in group interpretation, negotiation of shared meaning, or co-construction of problem resolutions. The communication skills it stresses are those of simple presentation, rather than the capacity to engage in richly structured interactions that articulate perspectives unfamiliar to the audience. Face-to-face communication is seen as the gold standard, so students develop few capabilities in mediated dialogue and in shared design within a common virtual workspace.

Given that the curriculum is already crowded, a major political challenge is articulating what to deemphasize in the curriculum—and why—in order to make room for students to deeply master core 21st century skills. This is not a situation in which an equivalent amount of current curriculum must be eliminated for each 21st century skill added, because better pedagogical methods can lead to faster mastery and improved retention, enabling less reteaching and more coverage within the same time frame (VanLehn, 2006). However, what education should emphasize as core is politically controversial even if substantial sections of the 20th century curriculum are not eliminated.

Beyond curricular issues, classrooms today typically lack 21st century learning and teaching, in part because high-stakes tests do not assess these competencies. Assessments and tests focus on measuring students' fluency in various abstract routine skills, but typically do not assess their strategies for expert decision making when no standard approach seems applicable. Essays emphasize simple

> Given that the curriculum is already crowded, a major political challenge is articulating what to deemphasize in the curriculum—and why—in order to make room for students to deeply master core 21st century skills.

presentation rather than sophisticated forms of rhetorical interaction. Students' abilities to transfer their understandings to real-world situations are not assessed, nor are capabilities related to various aspects of teamwork. The use of technological applications and representations is generally banned from testing, rather than providing an opportunity to measure students' capacities to use tools, applications, and media effectively. Abilities to successfully utilize various forms of mediated interaction are typically not assessed either. As discussed later, valid, reliable, practical assessments of 21st century skills are needed to improve this situation.

Lack of professional development is another reason 21st century skills are underemphasized in today's schooling. Providing educators with opportunities to learn about the ideas and strategies discussed in this volume is only part of the issue. A major, often unrecognized challenge in professional development is helping teachers, policymakers, and local communities unlearn the beliefs, values, assumptions, and cultures underlying schools' industrial-era operating practices, such as forty-five-minute class periods that allow insufficient time for all but superficial forms of active learning by students. Altering deeply ingrained and strongly reinforced rituals of schooling takes more than the superficial interchanges typical in "make and take" professional development or school board meetings. Intellectual, emotional, and social support is essential for "unlearning" and for transformational relearning that can lead to deeper behavioral changes that create next-generation educational practices. Educators, business executives, politicians, and the general public have much to unlearn if 21st century skills are to assume a central place in schooling.

Current approaches to using technology in schooling largely reflect the 20th century pedagogy of applying information and communication technologies as a means of increasing the effectiveness of traditional instructional approaches: enhancing productivity through tools such as word processors, aiding communication by channels such as email and threaded asynchronous discussions, and expanding access to information via Web browsers and streaming video (Dede, 2009a). All these have proven worthy in conventional schooling, as they have in workplace settings; however, none draw on the full power of ICTs for individual and collective expression, experience, and interpretation—human capabilities emerging as key work and life skills for the first part of the 21st century. So how are various organizations that advocate for 21st century skills formulating these capabilities?

Current Major Frameworks for 21st Century Skills

Current conceptual frameworks for 21st century skills include the Partnership for 21st Century Skills (2006), the North Central Regional Education Laboratory (NCREL) and the Metiri Group (2003), the Organisation for Economic Co-operation and Development (OECD, 2005), and the National Leadership Council for Liberal Education and America's Promise (LEAP, 2007). In the particular area of information and communications technology—which, as mentioned previously, is richly interwoven with 21st century skills—these frameworks include the revised International Society for Technology in Education (ISTE) student standards for technology in the curriculum (2007), as well as digital literacy standards from the Educational Testing Service (ETS, 2007). Individual scholars such as Dede (2005) and Jenkins (2009) have also formulated lists of "digital literacies" that complement reading, writing, and mathematics as core capabilities for the 21st century. The figures that follow highlight each framework and are followed by an analysis of what each formulation adds to the Partnership for 21st Century Skills Framework for 21st Century Learning (2006).

The Partnership's Framework (2006) and the many ancillary publications produced since then serve as a baseline for this analysis because the Partnership's conceptualization of 21st century skills is more detailed and more widely adopted than any of the alternatives discussed later. For reasons of space, this chapter presents only a bare-bones outline of the Partnership's Framework (figure 3.1). The complete framework is available at www.21stcenturyskills.org, and an additional abridged version appears in the foreword on page xv of this volume.

Core subjects. The No Child Left Behind Act of 2001, which reauthorizes the Elementary and Secondary Education Act of 1965, identifies the core subjects as English, reading, or language arts; mathematics; science; foreign languages; civics; government; economics; arts; history; and geography.

21st century content. Several significant, emerging content areas are critical to success in communities and workplaces. These content areas typically are not emphasized in schools today: global awareness; financial, economic, business, and entrepreneurial literacy; civic literacy; and health and wellness awareness.

Learning and thinking skills. As much as students need to learn academic content, they also need to know how to keep learning—and make effective and innovative use of what they know—throughout their lives. Learning and thinking skills are comprised of critical-thinking and problem-solving skills, communication skills, creativity and innovation skills, collaboration skills, contextual learning skills, and information and media literacy skills.

ICT literacy. Information and communications technology literacy is the ability to use technology to develop 21st century content knowledge and skills, in the context of learning core subjects. Students must be able to use technology to learn content and skills—so that they know *how* to learn, think critically, solve problems, use information, communicate, innovate, and collaborate.

Life skills. Good teachers have always incorporated life skills into their pedagogy. The challenge today is to incorporate these essential skills into schools deliberately, strategically, and broadly. Life skills include leadership, ethics, accountability, adaptability, personal productivity, personal responsibility, people skills, self-direction, and social responsibility.

Figure 3.1: The Partnership for 21st Century Skills Framework for 21st Century Learning.

continued on next page →

21st century assessments. Authentic 21st century assessments are the essential foundation of a 21st century education. Assessments must measure all five results that matter: core subjects, 21st century content, learning and thinking skills, ICT literacy, and life skills. Assessment of 21st century skills should be integrated with assessments of core subjects. Separate assessments would defeat the purpose of infusing 21st century skills into core subjects. To be effective, sustainable, and affordable, assessments must use modern technologies to increase efficiency and timeliness. Standardized tests alone can measure only a few of the important skills and knowledge students should learn. A balance of assessments, including high-quality standardized testing along with effective classroom assessments, offers students and teachers a powerful tool to master the content and skills central to success.

Source: Partnership for 21st Century Skills, 2006. Reprinted with permission.

Figure 3.1: The Partnership for 21st Century Skills Framework for 21st Century Learning.

In contrast to the Partnership's Framework used as baseline in this analysis, NCREL and the Metiri Group produced a 21st century skills framework three years earlier, in 2003 (figure 3.2).

Digital-age literacy. Basic, scientific, economic, and technological literacies; visual and information literacies; multicultural literacy and global awareness

Inventive thinking. Adaptability, managing complexity, and self-direction; curiosity, creativity, and risk taking; higher-order thinking and sound reasoning

Effective communication. Teaming, collaboration, and interpersonal skills; personal, social, and civic responsibility; interactive communication

High productivity. Prioritizing, planning, and managing for results; effective use of real-world tools; ability to produce relevant, high-quality products

Source: North Central Regional Educational Laboratory & the Metiri Group, 2003.

Figure 3.2: enGauge Framework from the North Central Regional Education Laboratory and the Metiri Group.

The enGauge Framework adds "visual literacy" as related to information literacy. It includes "curiosity" and "risk taking" as core skills, as well as "managing complexity." It stresses "prioritizing, planning, and managing for results." "Multicultural literacy" is an explicit component. With the exception of the "effective communication" category, this shorter list focuses less on the overlap with 20th century curriculum than does the Partnership's Framework. More emphasis is placed on new contextual skills and knowledge.

In 2005, the OECD provided its conception of 21st century skills as shown in figure 3.3.

Competency category 1: Using tools interactively. Use language, symbols, and texts interactively; use knowledge and information interactively; use technology interactively.

Competency category 2: Interacting in heterogeneous groups. Relate well to others; cooperate and work in teams; manage and resolve conflicts.

Competency category 3: Acting autonomously. Act within the big picture; form and conduct life plans and personal projects; defend and assert rights, interests, limits, and needs.

Source: Organisation for Economic Co-operation and Development, 2005.

Figure 3.3: Organisation for Economic Co-operation and Development Competencies.

The OECD competencies highlight "using language, symbols, and texts," as well as "managing and resolving conflicts." "Acting autonomously" is a major category in this framework that includes "life plans" and "defending and asserting rights, interests, limits, and needs." Compared to the Partnership's Framework, this framework focuses less on overlaps with the 20th century curriculum and, like the NCREL/Metiri skillset, more on new contextual skills. Affective and psychosocial skills receive greater emphasis than in frameworks generated by U.S. organizations.

In 2007, LEAP developed a framework delineating the 21st century skills that graduates of higher education should attain (figure 3.4, page 60).

Beginning in school, and continuing at successively higher levels across their college studies, students should prepare for 21st century challenges by gaining:

Knowledge of human cultures and the physical and natural world, including study in
- Sciences and mathematics, social sciences, humanities, histories, languages, and the arts

Focused by engagement with big questions, both contemporary and enduring

Intellectual and practical skills, including
- Inquiry and analysis
- Critical and creative thinking
- Written and oral communication
- Quantitative literacy
- Information literacy
- Teamwork and problem solving

Practiced extensively across the curriculum in the context of progressively more challenging problems, projects, and standards for performance

Personal and social responsibility, including
- Civic knowledge and engagement—local and global
- Intercultural knowledge and competence
- Ethical reasoning and action
- Foundations and skills for lifelong learning

Anchored through active involvement with diverse communities and real-world challenges

Integrative learning, including
- Synthesis and advanced accomplishment across general and specialized studies

Demonstrated through the application of knowledge, skills, and responsibilities to new settings and complex problems

Source: National Leadership Council for Liberal Education and America's Promise, 2007.

Figure 3.4: National Leadership Council for Liberal Education and America's Promise Essential Learning Outcomes.

The LEAP college-level essential learning outcomes (presumably developed as a foundation in K–12 schooling) add "knowledge of human cultures" to the Partnership's Framework. This skillset stresses "engagement with big questions, both contemporary and enduring," an intellectual capability that higher education has long sought to inculcate. "Inquiry" and "quantitative analysis" are specifically cited as important analytic skills. Learning by doing, rather than by assimilation of information, is tacitly stressed in the language LEAP uses.

Current Conceptual Frameworks for Digital Literacies

In part to emphasize the ways in which ICT skills are central to the 21st century, in 2007 the ISTE revised its student standards for technology in the curriculum as shown in figure 3.5.

Creativity and innovation. Students demonstrate creative thinking, construct knowledge, and develop innovative products and processes using technology by:

- Applying existing knowledge to generate new ideas, products, or processes
- Creating original works as a means of personal or group expression
- Using models and simulations to explore complex systems and issues
- Identifying trends and forecasting possibilities

Communication and collaboration. Students use digital media and environments to communicate and work collaboratively—including at a distance, to support individual learning, and to contribute to the learning of others by:

- Interacting, collaborating, and publishing with peers, experts, or others employing a variety of digital environments and media
- Communicating information and ideas effectively to multiple audiences using a variety of media and formats
- Developing cultural understanding and global awareness by engaging with learners of other cultures
- Contributing to project teams to produce original works or solve problems

Figure 3.5: International Society for Technology in Education National Education Technology Standards for Students.

continued on next page →

Research and information fluency. Students employ digital tools to gather, evaluate, and use information by:

- Planning strategies to guide inquiry
- Locating, organizing, analyzing, evaluating, synthesizing, and ethically using information from a variety of sources and media
- Evaluating and selecting information sources and digital tools based on the appropriateness to specific tasks
- Processing data and reporting results

Critical thinking, problem solving, and decision making. Students draw on critical thinking skills to plan and conduct research, manage projects, solve problems, and make informed decisions using appropriate digital tools and resources by:

- Identifying and defining authentic problems and significant questions for investigation
- Planning and managing activities to develop a solution or complete a project
- Collecting and analyzing data to identify solutions and/or make informed decisions
- Using multiple processes and diverse perspectives to explore alternative solutions

Digital citizenship. Students show understanding of human, cultural, and societal issues related to technology and practice legal and ethical behavior by:

- Advocating and practicing safe, legal, and responsible use of information and technology
- Exhibiting a positive attitude toward using technology that supports collaboration, learning, and productivity
- Demonstrating personal responsibility for lifelong learning
- Exhibiting leadership for digital citizenship

Technology operations and concepts. Students demonstrate a sound understanding of technology concepts, systems, and operations by:

- Understanding and using technology systems
- Selecting and using applications effectively and productively
- Troubleshooting systems and applications
- Transferring current knowledge to learning of new technologies

Source: National Educational Technology Standards for Students, Second Edition, © 2007, ISTE® (International Society for Technology in Education), www.iste.org. All rights reserved.

Figure 3.5: International Society for Technology in Education National Education Technology Standards for Students.

Beyond the Partnership's Framework, the ISTE ICT skills stress "creating original works as a means of personal or group expression," "using models and simulations to explore complex systems and issues," and "identifying trends and forecasting possibilities." Other capabilities include "identifying and defining authentic problems and significant questions for investigation" and "using multiple processes and diverse perspectives to explore alternative solutions." It highlights "safe, legal" use of information and technology, as well as "digital citizenship." "Troubleshooting systems and applications" and "transferring current knowledge to learning of new technologies" are seen as key skills. As might be expected, the digital literacies this educational technology organization articulates are more detailed than those in the Partnership's overall framework.

In a similar vein, in 2007, the ETS released its ICT Digital Literacy Framework as shown in figure 3.6 (page 64). The framework delineates five levels of progressive mastery for each literacy.

The ETS Digital Literacy Framework adds "technical proficiency: a foundational knowledge of hardware, software applications, networks, and elements of digital technology." The example digital literacy activities provided in this framework seem less sophisticated than those implied by the other frameworks analyzed here; the illustration is closer in spirit to the ISTE framework for digital literacies developed in the late 1990s.

As the ISTE and ETS ICT frameworks suggest, much of what distinguishes 21st century skills from 20th century competencies is that a person and a tool, application, medium, or environment work in concert to accomplish an objective that is otherwise unobtainable (such as the remote collaboration of a team scattered across the globe via groupware). However, ICTs are not mere mechanisms for attaining the desired behavior; through distributed cognition, the understandings they enable are intrinsic to the fluent performance (such as a group co-constructing a sophisticated conceptual framework using the representational tools available in a wiki).

Frameworks that discuss new literacies based on the evolution of ICTs help to illuminate this aspect of 21st century learning. With funding from the Macarthur Foundation, Henry Jenkins and his colleagues (2009) produced a list of digital literacies as shown in figure 3.7 (page 65).

Cognitive proficiency. The desired foundational skills of everyday life at school, at home, and at work. Literacy, numeracy, problem solving, and spatial/visual literacy demonstrate these proficiencies.

Technical proficiency. The basic components of digital literacy. Includes a foundational knowledge of hardware, software applications, networks, and elements of digital technology.

ICT proficiency. The integration and application of cognitive and technical skills. ICT proficiencies are seen as enablers; that is, they allow individuals to maximize the capabilities of technology. At the highest level, ICT proficiencies result in innovation, individual transformation, and societal change.

An illustration of a five-level literacy in ICT proficiency follows:

Access—Select and open appropriate emails from the inbox list.

Manage—Identify and organize the relevant information in each email.

Integrate—Summarize the interest in the courses provided by the company.

Evaluate—Decide which courses should be continued next year, based on last year's attendance.

Create—Write up your recommendation in the form of an email to the vice president of human resources.

Source: Educational Testing Service, 2007, pp. 18, 20.

Figure 3.6: Educational Testing Service ICT Digital Literacy Framework.

These digital literacies have a different tone than the ISTE and ETS frameworks presented earlier. The emphasis is not on proficiency with the tool, but on types of intellectual activity performed by a person working with sophisticated ICTs. While some perennial capabilities—like judgment—are listed, other skills—such as performance—are contextual in their emphasis on new types of 21st century capacities.

These digital literacies not only represent skills students should master for effective 21st century work and citizenship, but also describe the learning strengths and preferences people who use technology now bring to educational settings. Dede (2005) presents a framework of neomillennial learning styles that are based on new digital literacies as shown in figure 3.8 (page 66).

Play. The capacity to experiment with one's surroundings as a form of problem solving

Performance. The ability to adopt alternative identities for the purpose of improvisation and discovery

Simulation. The ability to interpret and construct dynamic models of real-world processes

Appropriation. The ability to meaningfully sample and remix media content

Multitasking. The ability to scan one's environment and shift focus as needed to salient details

Distributed cognition. The ability to interact meaningfully with tools that expand mental capacities

Collective intelligence. The ability to pool knowledge and compare notes with others toward a common goal

Judgment. The ability to evaluate the reliability and credibility of different information sources

Transmedia navigation. The ability to follow the flow of stories and information across multiple modalities

Networking. The ability to search for, synthesize, and disseminate information

Negotiation. The ability to travel across diverse communities, discerning and respecting multiple perspectives, and grasping and following alternative norms

Source: Jenkins, 2009.

Figure 3.7: Jenkins' digital literacies based on new media.

Since the articulation of this framework, the emergence of Web 2.0 media has fueled a shift in online leading-edge applications that reinforces these learning strengths and preferences. The predominant learning activities on the Internet have changed from the presentation of material by website providers to the active co-construction of resources by communities of contributors. Whereas the 20th century Web centered on developer-created material (such as informational websites) generated primarily by a small fraction of the Internet's users, Web 2.0 tools (such as Wikipedia) help large numbers of people build online communities for creativity, collaboration, and sharing.

Fluency in multiple media. Valuing each medium for the types of communication, activities, experiences, and expressions it empowers

Active learning. Collectively seeking, sieving, and synthesizing experiences rather than individually locating and absorbing information from some single best source

Expression through nonlinear, associational webs of representations. Authoring a simulation and a webpage to express understanding, in contrast to writing a paper

Codesign by teachers and students. Personalizing learning experiences to individual needs and preferences

Source: Dede, 2005.

Figure 3.8: Dede's neomillennial learning styles.

Dede (2009b) delineates a category system for current Web 2.0 tools:

1. *Sharing*

   - Communal bookmarking
   - Photo/video sharing
   - Social networking
   - Writers' workshops/fan fiction

2. *Thinking*

   - Blogs
   - Podcasts
   - Online discussion forums

3. *Co-creating*

   - Wikis/collaborative file creation
   - Mashups/collective media creation
   - Collaborative social change communities

This framework shows a loose progression from top to bottom, with sharing leadership to thinking together to collective action in which sophisticated groups seeking change use subsets of the nine media listed before the last entry—collaborative social change communities—to accomplish their shared objectives. Overall, growing use of these Web 2.0 tools has led to an intensification of the learning styles and digital literacies described earlier.

Leu and his colleagues (2007) described four characteristics of the "new literacies" generated by ICTs. First, emerging ICT tools, applications, media, and environments require novel skills, strategies, and dispositions for their effective use. Second, new literacies are central to full economic, civic, and personal participation in a globalized society. Third, new literacies constantly evolve as their defining ICTs are continuously renewed through innovation. Fourth, new literacies are multiple, multimodel, and multifaceted. These characteristics are in accord with the media-based styles of learning presented in this section and with the 21st century capabilities this chapter discusses.

Comparing Alternative Frameworks for 21st Century Skills

In summary, these 21st century skills frameworks are generally consistent with each other. The additions to the Partnership's skillset that the alternative frameworks offer are of two types. First, other groups identify some subskills within Partnership categories as particularly important. As an illustration, the ISTE subskill "troubleshooting systems and applications" easily falls within the Partnership's overall category of ICT literacy; it also requires "technical proficiency: a foundational knowledge of hardware, software applications, networks, and elements of digital technology," which is a foundational subskill advocated by ETS. Highlighting this subskill may reflect an assessment of which 21st century skills teachers are likely to overlook given the current culture of schooling; for example, students seldom have opportunities to learn "troubleshooting" because teachers instinctively don't want problems to emerge in an instructional situation.

Second, groups other than the Partnership stress some areas they feel are underemphasized in its categories. As an illustration, "students acting autonomously" is a major category for OECD that, again, is contrary to the current culture of U.S. schooling. Similarly, the NCREL/Metiri framework stresses student "risk taking," but this is unlikely to be encouraged by many U.S.

> These 21st century skills frameworks are generally consistent with each other.

teachers unless special emphasis is put on this skill as crucial to 21st century work and citizenship.

The stress on skills that may be underemphasized because they are inconsistent with current classroom culture highlights a substantial challenge to infusing these 21st century skills frameworks into educational practice and policy. At this point in history, the primary barriers to altering curricular, pedagogical, and assessment practices are not conceptual, technical, or economic, but instead psychological, political, and cultural. We now have all the means necessary to move beyond teaching 20th century knowledge in order to prepare all students for a future quite different from the immediate past. Whether society has the professional commitment and public will to actualize such a vision remains to be seen.

Advances in the Assessment of 21st Century Skills

The Education Sector's report, *Measuring Skills for the 21st Century* (Silva, 2008), discusses several metrics for assessing 21st century skills. Which parts of the synthesized 21st century skills framework do these assessments cover?

The College and Work Readiness Assessment

The College and Work Readiness Assessment (CWRA) measures how students perform on constructed-response tasks that require an integrated set of critical thinking, analytic reasoning, problem solving, and written communication skills. The CWRA is delivered entirely over the Internet in a proctored setting. Critical thinking, analytical reasoning, problem solving, and writing are "collective outcomes" that cannot fully be taught in any one class or year; so all teachers and faculty have a responsibility to teach for such skills within each subject area and discipline.

Performance tasks. Students must complete a real-life activity (such as preparing a memo or policy recommendation) that involves reviewing and evaluating a series of documents. Completion of these instruments does not require the recall of particular facts or formulas; instead, the measures assess the demonstrated ability to interpret, analyze, and synthesize information.

Analytic writing tasks. These tasks evaluate students' ability to articulate complex ideas, examine claims and evidence, support ideas with relevant reasons and examples, sustain a coherent discussion, and use standard written English.

The Programme for International Student Assessment

Several metrics for assessing 21st century skills are discussed in the Education Board's report *Measuring Skills for the 21st Century* (Silva, 2008).

The Programme for International Student Assessment (PISA) is based on the OECD Definition and Selection of Competencies project (DeSeCo). PISA seeks to measure how well fifteen-year-olds, approaching the end of compulsory schooling, are prepared to meet the challenges of today's knowledge societies—what PISA refers to as "literacy." The assessment is forward looking, focusing on young people's ability to use their knowledge and skills to meet real-life challenges, rather than merely on the extent to which they have mastered a specific school curriculum. This orientation reflects a change in the goals and objectives of curricula themselves, which increasingly address what students can do with what they learn at school and not merely whether they can reproduce what they have learned.

The assessment covers the domains of reading, mathematical, and scientific literacy not merely in terms of mastery of the school curriculum, but in terms of important knowledge and skills needed in adult life. Tests are pencil-and-paper, with the assessment lasting a total of two hours for each student. Test items are a mixture of multiple-choice items and questions requiring students to construct their own responses. The items are organized in groups based on a passage setting out a real-life situation. Assessment covers a total of about seven hours of test items, with different students taking different combinations of test items. Students also answer a background questionnaire, which takes twenty to thirty minutes to complete, providing information about themselves and their homes. School principals are given a twenty-minute questionnaire about their schools as well.

Key Stage 3 ICT Literacy Assessment

Also discussed in Silva (2008) is the Key Stage 3 ICT Literacy Assessment. This gauges students' ICT capabilities at the end of "Key Stage 3" (ages twelve to thirteen) in Great Britain's national curriculum. The test not only assesses students' ICT skills, but also their ability to use those skills to solve a set of complex problems involving research, communication, information management, and presentation. Test results provide both summative information—in the form of a national score for each student—and detailed formative feedback about student performance that could be used to inform future teaching and learning.

The ICT test is set in a complex virtual world, within which students carry out tasks using a "walled garden" of assets (such as text, pictures, data, and "canned" websites) without access to the Internet. Students are also provided with a toolkit of applications to enable them to complete the tasks; all of these assets are generic software programs developed by the Qualifications and Curriculum Authority to provide the same capabilities as familiar productivity software on the level playing field of a nonbrand-specific platform. As students work through the test session, their actions are tracked by the computer and mapped against expected capabilities for each level of the national curriculum; this includes both technical skills and learning skills, such as "finding things out," "developing ideas," and "exchanging and sharing information." The information collected about a student's performance allows a score to be awarded along with a profile of individual strengths and weaknesses.

All three assessments potentially could cover substantial amounts of the 21st century skills delineated in the frameworks presented in this chapter. However, CWRA and PISA are limited in their effectiveness by their formats: paper based and, at times, test-item focused. The Key Stage 3 has more potential to measure the full range of 21st century capabilities, including digital literacies, because it is conducted in a virtual world and based on activities more sophisticated than making forced-choice decisions among a limited number of alternatives.

Beyond these current assessments, many researchers are working on virtual performance assessments for specific higher-order intellectual performances, such as scientific inquiry, that soon may provide reliable, usable, and valid measures for many 21st century skills (Ketelhut, Dede, Clarke, Nelson, & Bowman, 2008). Research has documented that higher-order thinking skills related to sophisticated cognition (such as inquiry processes, formulating scientific explanations, communicating scientific understanding, and approaches to novel situations) are difficult to measure with multiple choice or even with constructed-response pencil-and-paper tests (Quellmalz & Haertel, 2004; Resnick & Resnick, 1992; Wilson & Bertenthal, 2006). In the late 1980s and 1990s, educators attempted to use performance assessments in accountability programs. However, the developers of both hands-on and virtual performance assessments encountered a number of technical, resource, and reliability problems in large-scale administration (Cronbach, Linn, Brennan, & Haertel, 1997; Shavelson, Ruiz-Primo, & Wiley, 1999). At that time, these problems were substantial enough to undercut the potentially greater construct validity for science inquiry that performance assessments can provide over pencil-and-paper tests. Now, however, teams of scholars are using modern technologies to develop virtual performance assessments of various types (such as http://virtualassessment.org) that may solve this problem of providing reliable, valid measurements for sophisticated intellectual and psychosocial skills (Quellmalz & Pellegrino, 2009).

Overall, the increasing availability of valid assessments for 21st century skills is leading to calls for all states to participate in "international benchmarking," or comparing their educational processes and outcomes to the best models around the world (National Governors Association, 2008). Widely used international assessments centered on curricular areas include the Trends in International Mathematics and Science Study for grades 4, 8, and 12, as well as

The increasing availability of valid assessments for 21st century skills is leading to calls for all states to participate in "international benchmarking," or comparing their educational processes and outcomes to the best models around the world.

the Progress in International Reading Literacy Study of fourth-grade reading levels (Silva, 2008). *Benchmarking for Success: Ensuring U.S. Students Receive a World-Class Education* calls on states to implement five types of benchmarking:

- **Action 1**—Upgrade state standards by adopting a common core of internationally benchmarked standards in math and language arts for grades K–12 to ensure that students are equipped with the necessary knowledge and skills to be globally competitive.

- **Action 2**—Leverage states' collective influence to ensure that textbooks, digital media, curricula, and assessments are aligned to internationally benchmarked standards and draw on lessons from high-performing nations and states.

- **Action 3**—Revise state policies for recruiting, preparing, developing, and supporting teachers and school leaders to reflect the human capital practices of top-performing nations and states around the world.

- **Action 4**—Hold schools and systems accountable through monitoring, interventions, and support to ensure consistently high performance, drawing upon international best practices.

- **Action 5**—Measure state-level education performance globally by examining student achievement and attainment in an international context to ensure that, over time, students are receiving the education they need to compete in the 21st century economy. (Adapted from National Governors Association, 2008, p. 6)

Recent U.S. federal activities to promote coordination among states in developing comparable, high-quality curriculum standards are building momentum to generate and use assessments that can measure sophisticated intellectual and psychosocial skills needed for the 21st century.

Reconceptualizing for the 21st Century

Fortunately, groups developing conceptualizations of 21st century skills have built sufficiently on each other's ideas to avoid speaking a different language about the same topic. As this analysis shows, organizations that argue for 21st century skills have frameworks largely consistent in terms of what should be added to the curriculum. However, each group has different areas of emphasis within the overarching skillset. For instance, taking the Partnership's Framework as a baseline, groups focused on technical skills—such as ISTE, ETS, and those who advocate for digital literacies—emphasize that aspect of the Partnership's Framework and articulate in greater detail which fluencies in information and communications technologies are most important.

Each organization also introduces complementary ideas to the concept of 21st century skills. For example, as discussed earlier, additions to the Partnership's Framework from OECD and NCREL/ Metiri incorporate autonomous actions by students that typically are not a part of conventional classroom culture. This highlights a metacognitive challenge for the 21st century skills movement: to systematically examine all the tacit beliefs and assumptions and values about schooling that are legacies from the 20th century and the industrial age. Compilations such as this volume are making important contributions in aiding this reconceptualization of education for the 21st century.

References

Cronbach, L. J., Linn, R. L., Brennan, R. L, & Haertel, E. H. (1997). Generalizability analysis for performance assessments of student achievement or school effectiveness. *Educational and Psychological Measurement, 57*, 373–399.

Dede, C. (2005). Planning for neomillennial learning styles: Implications for investments in technology and faculty. In D. G. Oblinger & J. L. Oblinger (Eds.), *Educating the net generation* (pp. 226–247). Boulder, CO: EDUCAUSE.

Dede, C. (2009a). Determining, developing and assessing the capabilities of North Carolina's future-ready students. *Friday Institute White Paper Series.* Raleigh: North Carolina State University.

Dede, C. (2009b, May). Comments on Greenhow, Robelia, and Hughes: Technologies that facilitate generating knowledge and possibly wisdom. *Educational Researcher, 38*, 260–263.

Dede, C. (in press). Technological supports for acquiring 21st century skills. In P. Peterson, E. Baker, & B. McGaw (Eds.), *International Encyclopedia of Education* (3rd ed.). Oxford, England: Elsevier.

Educational Testing Service. (2007). *Digital transformation: A framework for ICT literacy.* Princeton, NJ: Author. Accessed at www.etsliteracy.org/Media/

Tests/Information_and_Communication_Technology_Literacy/ictreport .pdf on December 13, 2009.

International Society for Technology in Education. (2007). *National educational technology standards for students* (2nd ed.). Eugene, OR: Author.

Jenkins, H. (with Purushotma, R., Weigel, M., Clinton, K., & Robison, A. J.). (2009). *Confronting the challenges of participatory culture: Media education for the 21st century*. Cambridge, MA: MIT Press.

Karoly, L. A., & Panis, C. W. A. (2004). *The 21st century at work: Forces shaping the future workforce and workplace in the United States*. Santa Monica, CA: RAND Corporation.

Ketelhut, D., Dede, C., Clarke, J., Nelson, B., & Bowman, C. (2008). Studying situated learning in a multi-user virtual environment. In E. Baker, J. Dickieson, W. Wulfeck, & H. F. O'Neil (Eds.), *Assessment of problem solving using simulations* (pp. 37–58). New York: Lawrence Erlbaum.

Leu, D. J., Zawilinski, L., Castek, J., Banerjee, M., Housand, B. C., Liu, Y., et al. (2007). What is new about the new literacies of online reading comprehension? In L. S. Rush, A. J. Eakle, & A. Berger (Eds.), *Secondary school literacy: What research reveals for classroom practice* (pp. 37–68). Urbana, IL: National Council of Teachers of English.

Levy, F., & Murnane, R. J. (2004). *The new division of labor: How computers are creating the next job market*. Princeton, NJ: Princeton University Press.

National Governors Association. (2008). *Benchmarking for success: Ensuring U.S. students receive a world-class education*. Washington, DC: Author.

National Leadership Council for Liberal Education and America's Promise. (2007). *College learning for the new global century*. Washington, DC: Association of American Colleges and Universities.

North Central Regional Educational Laboratory & the Metiri Group. (2003). *enGauge 21st century skills: Literacy in the digital age*. Chicago: North Central Regional Educational Laboratory.

Organisation for Economic Co-operation and Development. (2005). *The definition and selection of key competencies: Executive summary*. Paris: Author.

Partnership for 21st Century Skills. (2006, July). *A state leaders action guide to 21st century skills: A new vision for education*. Tucson, AZ: Author.

Quellmalz, E. S., & Haertel, G. (2004). *Technology supports for state science assessment systems*. Washington, DC: National Research Council.

Quellmalz, E. S., & Pellegrino, J. W. (2009, January). Technology and testing. *Science, 323*, 75–79.

Resnick, L. B., & Resnick, D. P. (1992). Assessing the thinking curriculum: New tools for educational reform. In B. R. Gifford & M. C. O'Connor (Eds.), *Changing assessments: Alternative views of aptitude, achievement, and instruction* (pp. 37–75). Boston: Kluwer Academic.

Shavelson, R. J., Ruiz-Primo, M. A., & Wiley, E. W. (1999). Note on sources of sampling variability in science performance assessments. *Journal of Educational Measurement, 36*, 61–71.

Silva, E. (2008, November). *Measuring skills for the 21st century.* Washington, DC: Education Sector.

VanLehn, K. (Ed.). (2006). *The Pittsburgh Science of Learning Center theoretical framework.* Pittsburgh, PA: Pittsburgh Science of Learning Center. Accessed at www.learnlab.org/clusters/PSLC_Theory_Frame_June_15_2006.pdf on December 13, 2009.

Weinberger, D. (2007). *Everything is miscellaneous: The power of the new digital disorder.* New York: Times Books.

Wilson, M. R., & Bertenthal, M. W. (Eds). (2006). *Systems for state science assessment: Committee on test design for K–12 science achievement.* Washington, DC: The National Academies Press.

Richard DuFour

Richard DuFour, Ed.D., was a public school educator for thirty-four years, serving as a teacher, principal, and superintendent at Adlai Stevenson High School in Lincolnshire, Illinois. During his tenure, Stevenson became what the United States Department of Education (USDE) described as "the most recognized and celebrated school in America." Stevenson is one of three schools in the United States to win the USDE Blue Ribbon award on four occasions and one of the first comprehensive schools designated a New America High School by the USDE as a model of successful school reform. DuFour has written multiple books on the theory and practice of professional learning communities (PLCs) emphasizing the model used at Stevenson.

Rebecca DuFour

Rebecca DuFour, M.Ed., has served as a teacher, school administrator, and central office coordinator. As a former elementary principal, DuFour helped her school earn state and national recognition as a model professional learning community. DuFour is coauthor of many books and video series on the topic of PLCs.

In this chapter, DuFour and DuFour discuss school settings for teaching 21st century skills. They observe that the most appropriate environment for teaching the life and career skills espoused by the Partnership for 21st Century Skills is a professional learning community that models these skills. On this basis, they argue that the PLC is an essential tool for bringing about the changes that 21st century skills advocates envision.

Chapter 4

The Role of Professional Learning Communities in Advancing 21st Century Skills

Richard DuFour and Rebecca DuFour

When the Partnership for 21st Century Skills articulated the knowledge and skills essential to the future success of students in the United States, it stressed that the traditional school culture was not designed to deliver those outcomes. To its credit, the Partnership recognized that if its initiative were to have a positive impact on student achievement, educators would need to transform their schools and districts into professional learning communities (PLCs).

The Partnership (2009) was emphatic on this point and stipulated that the environments best suited to teach 21st century skills "support professional learning communities that enable educators to collaborate, share best practices and integrate 21st century skills into classroom practice." The Partnership called for schools to be organized into "professional learning communities for teachers that model the kinds of classroom learning that best promote 21st century skills for students" and urged educators to encourage "knowledge sharing among communities of practitioners, using face-to-face, virtual and blended communications."

The Three Big Ideas of the PLC concept mirror this emphasis from the Partnership. These three ideas are as follows:

1. A commitment to high levels of learning for *all* students

2. The imperative of a collaborative and a collective effort to fulfill that commitment

3. The intense focus on results that enables a school to respond to the needs of each student, inform teacher practice, and fuel continuous improvement

We agree that the best environment for teaching the 21st century life and career skills espoused by the Partnership—setting goals, managing time, prioritizing work, engaging in ongoing learning, contributing to a team, being responsible to others, and focusing on and producing results—is one in which adults model those behaviors and skills. The PLC concept is designed to help educators develop their individual and collective capacity to utilize these precise skills. Thus, we fully concur with the conclusion by the Partnership that students are unlikely to acquire the skills and knowledge essential for the 21st century unless schools function as PLCs.

We hope that this national initiative to impact what and how students learn will be far more successful than its predecessors. We advocate this view precisely because this reform effort is grounded in the recognition that substantive and sustainable school improvement will require new school cultures. Successful implementation of 21st century skills will require more than the creation and adoption of new curriculum; it will require educators to embrace different assumptions, develop interdependent relationships, and, most importantly, act in new ways.

As John Kotter and Daniel Cohen (2002) conclude in their seminal study of the change process, the central challenge and core problem of all improvement initiatives is *changing people's behavior* . . . [addressing] what people do, and the need for significant shifts in what people do" (p. 2).

In our past work (DuFour, DuFour, Eaker, & Many, 2006), we attempted to identify the nature of the cultural shifts necessary for schools and districts to function as PLCs. Those shifts are highlighted in table 4.1.

Table 4.1: The Cultural Shifts From Traditional Schools to Professional Learning Communities

From	To
The job of teachers is to teach; the job of students is to learn.	Teaching without learning isn't teaching at all; it's just presenting. The purpose of school is to ensure all students *learn*.
Professionals are free to use their own judgment and discretion regarding how they go about their work.	Professionals have an obligation to seek out best practices for those they serve.
Protecting individual teacher autonomy is more important than ensuring students have access to a guaranteed curriculum, are assessed according to the same criteria, or receive similar support and assistance when they struggle.	Professionals must address the crucial issues impacting student learning collectively rather than in isolation. Teachers must build a collaborative culture and systems that promote effectiveness and equity.
Teachers work best when they work alone.	Teachers who work in isolation will never help all students learn at high levels. Teachers must take collective responsibility for their students.
Schools work best when districts provide them with site-based autonomy.	Schools work best when they operate within clearly defined and clearly communicated parameters regarding their purpose and priorities, receive assistance in aligning their practices with the specified purpose and priorities, are held accountable for doing so, and have latitude regarding how to best achieve goals.
Teachers have no control over the factors that cause students to learn.	The individual and collective efforts of educators can have an enormous positive impact. The key factors that impact student learning are within their sphere of influence.

An abundance of research establishes that changes in behavior *precede* the changes in the assumptions, beliefs, expectations, and habits that constitute the culture of an organization.

Educators must begin to act in new ways in order for these cultural shifts to occur. An abundance of research establishes that changes in behavior *precede* the changes in the assumptions, beliefs, expectations, and habits that constitute the culture of an organization (Elmore, 2004; Fullan, 2007; Kotter & Cohen, 2002; Pfeffer & Sutton, 2006; Reeves, 2006). As Kotter and Cohen point out, "In a change effort, culture comes last, not first" (p. 175). Culture changes only when new behaviors become the norm—"the way we do things around here." Thus, educators must engage in behaviors that reflect the PLC culture, but recognize those behaviors "will not take hold until the very end of the process" (p. 176).

Changing Behavior

A study of the men and women who are extraordinarily effective in bringing about change reveals that they all focus on behavior (Patterson, Grenny, Maxfield, McMillan, & Switzler, 2008). These "influence geniuses" start the change process by asking, "In order to improve our existing situation, what must people actually *do*?" (p. 26). They identify and focus on a few high-leverage vital behaviors, create new structures and revise existing structures to align with the behaviors, coach the behaviors, provide resources and rewards to reinforce the behaviors, and confront those people who fail to act appropriately.

So what are the vital behaviors of a school seeking to become a PLC? People must work collaboratively rather than in isolation. They must engage in collective inquiry to address the issues most essential to student learning. They must resolve issues and answer questions by building shared knowledge about both their current reality and the most promising practices occurring both within and outside of the school and district. They must continuously monitor student learning and gather evidence of that learning in order to inform and improve their professional practice, respond to students who need additional support, and drive their continuous improvement process. When these behaviors become the norm in a school or district, educators are in a position to meet the challenge of providing students with the knowledge and skills essential to their future success.

To illustrate, imagine a staff is committed to implementing 21st century skills in their school. An abundance of evidence indicates that an essential step in helping students learn at high levels is to ensure that each teacher is clear on exactly what students are to learn and committed to providing the curriculum and instruction that ensures each student acquires the intended outcomes. Whether these outcomes are referred to as "essential curricular goals" (Lezotte, 1991), "power standards" (Reeves, 2002), a "guaranteed and viable curriculum" (Marzano, 2003), "a crystal clear curriculum that includes a compact list of learning intentions and success criteria" (Saphier, 2005), or "clear learning intentions" (Hattie, 2008), research and common sense indicate that educators improve their effectiveness when they are clear on and committed to the knowledge, skills, and dispositions each student is to acquire. This clarity and commitment require teachers to participate in collective inquiry and build shared knowledge on vital issues of curriculum, pacing, instruction, and assessment. In short, if schools are to teach students 21st century skills, educators must collaboratively engage in the process to clarify what those skills are, the indicators they will monitor to ensure each student has acquired the skills, and the best strategies they can employ in helping students develop the skills.

In districts still using traditional quick-fix inservice, educators receive a copy of the 21st century skills and perhaps attend a workshop or two to get an overview of the initiative. In contrast, educators in PLCs jointly study the resources with the members of their collaborative teams. They honor the 21st century skills framework that calls for schools to eschew shallow coverage of many topics and focus instead on helping students to acquire a deep understanding of the knowledge and skills necessary for success in work and in life. These educators engage in vertical dialogue with those who teach the course or grade level above theirs to enhance their understanding of the learning that is most essential to the success of their students. They seek clarification where there is confusion or disagreement. They

> In short, if schools are to teach students 21st century skills, educators must collaboratively engage in the process to clarify what those skills are, the indicators they will monitor to ensure each student has acquired the skills, and the best strategies they can employ in helping students develop the skills.

establish time frames for when to teach key concepts. Most importantly, at the end of the process, they commit to their colleagues that all students will have access to the same knowledge and skills regardless of the teacher to whom they are assigned.

One of the most critical elements of successful implementation of 21st century skills involves assessing whether or not students are acquiring those skills.

One of the most critical elements of successful implementation of 21st century skills involves assessing whether or not students are acquiring those skills. Once again, a growing body of research supports the power of assessment to improve, rather than merely report, student achievement (Black & Wiliam, 1998; Hattie, 2008; Little, 2006; Marzano, 2006; National Commission on Teaching and America's Future, 2003; Popham, 2008; Stiggins, 2004; Wiliam & Thompson, 2008). In PLCs, collaborative teams of teachers work together to develop their assessment literacy. They explore the nature of effective assessments and apply their learning to establish effective formative assessments in their classrooms each day. They work together to create a balanced and varied *common* assessment process. They agree on the criteria they use in assessing the quality of student work and practice applying those criteria to authentic performance-based and project-based assessments until they can do so with great consistency. They help their students become active participants in monitoring the progress of their own learning. They make frequent and varied common formative assessments one of the most potent weapons of their assessment arsenal.

In PLCs, conversations regarding student achievement focus on evidence from ongoing assessments, the particular skill that a specific student has yet to master, and the precise prerequisite learning that the student needs in order to become proficient. It will not be enough to say, "Johnny failed the last test," or even "Johnny needs help in math." The team will be able to say, "Johnny struggles with this particular skill, and here are the specific steps we can take to bring him to mastery," because members are clear on the sequence of skills needed to close the gap between Johnny's current level of learning and the intended outcomes he must achieve. Generalities about groups give way to specificity about individuals, and precision in intervention replaces generic oversimplification about remedies.

Of course, in order for all students to acquire 21st century skills, some students need additional time and support. In a PLC, every educator, parent, and student knows that the school has a plan to *ensure* each student who struggles to acquire an essential skill will receive additional time and support for learning in a timely, directive, and systematic way that never removes the student from new direct instruction. Administrators develop schedules to reflect this priority, and educators have increased access to the students who need them most during the school day. Furthermore, the plan has multiple levels of intervention so that if the existing amount of time and support does not produce the desired results, additional steps built into the process provide even more time and more support. The *school* responds when a student struggles rather than leaving the issue to the individual classroom teacher.

This collaborative and collective effort requires educators to function not merely as groups, but as teams—people working *interdependently* to achieve a *common* goal for which members are *mutually accountable*. Therefore, teams must establish specific, measurable, attainable, results-oriented, timebound (SMART) goals directly tied to student learning and then work interdependently to achieve them. Students who are not learning are the concern of the entire team rather than their individually assigned teacher. The dialogue focuses on evidence of student learning and is specifically intended to impact instructional practice in ways that have a positive effect on student achievement.

> This collaborative and collective effort requires educators to function not merely as groups, but as teams—people working *interdependently* to achieve a *common* goal for which members are *mutually accountable*.

Because student learning is the priority, evidence of student learning is easily accessible and openly shared among members of collaborative teams. Educators transform data into information by using common assessments that provide them with a basis of comparison. They seek out indicators of the strengths and weaknesses of their individual and collective efforts and put processes in place to ensure that they are able to learn from one another. Teachers who are struggling to help their students acquire a skill have timely and direct access to colleagues who are highly effective in teaching that skill. Schools and districts identify and study *positive deviants*—teachers and schools that are achieving exceptional results—so that others can benefit from their expertise. Teams are hungry for evidence of the most effective instructional practices, and members support one another as they implement those practices and assess their impact. This constant collective inquiry into effective practice fuels the continuous improvement process for the individual, the team, the school, and the district.

The Work of Professional Learning Communities in the Future

We believe that the future work of PLCs in implementing 21st century skills will continue to revolve around the same critical issues that drive the collaborative work of effective PLCs today: what do we want each student to learn, how will we know when each student is learning, how will we respond when a student is not learning, and how will we enrich and extend the learning for those who are proficient? We suggest, however, that the manner in which the work is conducted will differ in the following ways.

PLCs Will Have a Clearer Understanding of 21st Century Essential Skills

In the United States, the question of what is essential for students to learn is left to each of the fifty states. The commonality among all fifty states is that their attempt to answer the question has resulted in far too many standards. We anticipate that the future will bring greater consensus and clarity regarding the knowledge, skills, and dispositions all students should acquire as a result of their education, and greater recognition of the fact that all students—whether they live in Kansas or California—need these outcomes. The 21st century skills initiative is an important step in this direction. The Common Core State Standards project is another. This project—launched by the Council of Chief State School Officers; the National Governors Association Center for Best Practices; Achieve, Inc.; ACT, Inc.; and the College Board—intends to establish standards for grades K–12 that will be "fewer, clearer, and higher" and "internationally benchmarked and evidence- and research-based" (Council of Chief State School Officers, 2009, p. 2). Upon completion, individual states will be invited to adopt the standards. As of September 2009, forty-eight states had agreed to participate in the project, moving the United States closer to establishing a shared understanding regarding what students must learn.

As the specific elements of the essential learning come more sharply into focus, the conversations of teachers in collaborative teams will change. Teams not only will grapple with the challenge of how to develop curriculum, instruction, and assessments that lead students to deeper understanding of important concepts, but also will consider ways to engage students in work that fosters the collaboration, creativity, critical thinking, problem solving, and self-directed learning called for in the Partnership for 21st Century Skills Framework for 21st Century Learning. These skills, in turn, will call for much more varied and sophisticated methods of assessment. Once again, an abundant amount of research demonstrates that the best structure and strategy for providing educators with the skills needed to become more proficient in assessment is the collaborative team engaged in job-embedded professional development (Hattie, 2008; Little, 2006; Popham, 2008; Stiggins, 1999; Wiliam & Thompson, 2008). High-quality assessment has always been the linchpin of the PLC process, and it will be vital to the effort to provide students with 21st century skills.

PLCs Will Use Technology to Support and Accelerate the PLC Process and Expand the Concept of Community

Although technological innovation does not have the power to transform traditional school cultures into PLCs, technology can support educators who are determined to make that transformation. For example, imagine a team of algebra teachers that has identified a particular set of skills students must acquire to advance their ability in mathematical reasoning. The team accesses a national network of demonstration lessons to observe some of the most effective math educators in the country teaching the skills. The website provides lessons for every course, discipline, and grade level, and for all of the essential skills and concepts students are expected to acquire. The team not only observes and discusses how the lesson is taught, but also has free access to the lesson plans, handouts, informal and formal assessments, teaching tips, and frequently asked questions about the skills they will teach.

> Although technological innovation does not have the power to transform traditional school cultures into PLCs, technology can support educators who are determined to make that transformation.

As team members introduce the unit in their respective classrooms, they use the available technology to gather instant feedback on each student's level of understanding of each new skill or concept. Because the classroom has been structured into collaborative learning teams, the instant a student experiences difficulty, that student receives immediate clarification and support from members of his or her team, as well as from the teacher.

When the team utilizes more formal assessments, such as quizzes and tests, members have access to national assessment banks that provide hundreds of sample items for each skill and indicators of how students across the United States performed on those items. Teams integrate some of those items into their assessments and create their own items as well. On the day of these more formal assessments, a student is able to pass a wand over his or her answer sheet and get immediate feedback regarding performance. Furthermore, the feedback points out the nature of any mistakes and provides clarification to address those mistakes. Meanwhile, the results for the entire class are available both to the individual teacher and the team the moment students complete the assessment. The team reviews the results and can pinpoint with precision the exact skill or concept a particular student has yet to acquire, and then returns to the national network of effective teaching to examine the scaffolding of learning that will be most powerful in helping bring that student to proficiency.

When the team uses projects or various forms of performance-based assessments, members have access to the clear and challenging recommended criteria they should use in assessing the quality of student work. Members practice applying the criteria to actual examples of student work until they establish consistency and inter-rater reliability, and then teach those criteria to their students.

This scenario is not a pipedream. The technology exists, and small steps have been taken to give educators greater and more instantaneous access to the quality materials, pedagogy, and feedback that can assist them in their important work. We remain hopeful that, at some point, educators will have free and open access to a powerful knowledge base that supports their profession.

Technology can also help educators redefine their concept of collaboration. We frequently hear the lament that "I am the only person who teaches my course or grade level in my school and, thus, I cannot collaborate." The assumption behind such a statement is that it is impossible to collaborate with anyone outside of the walls of one's own school. This notion is patently untrue. As Ken Blanchard (2007) writes, "There is no reason that time and distance should keep people from interacting as a team. With proper management and the help of technology, virtual teams can be every bit as productive and rewarding as face-to-face teams" (p. 173). The combination of agreed-upon standards and increased access to technology means teachers who are not in the same building or even the same state could, nevertheless, work interdependently to achieve common goals for their students. Teachers interested in working in collaborative teams can look to many websites and professional organizations that facilitate collaboration. We recommend Parry Graham and Bill Ferriter's (2010) persuasive and pragmatic insights regarding the use of technology to support powerful collaboration that contributes to the effectiveness of teams and the ongoing professional development of each member.

The PLC Concept and the Teaching Profession Will Align

We are hopeful that the profession will take meaningful steps to align all its practices with the PLC concept. Those who enter the teaching profession through university training will go through programs specifically designed to prepare them to work in a PLC. When student teaching, they will be placed in schools that have brought the concept to life and assigned to a team of teachers rather than an individual. Accreditation agencies will require universities to demonstrate that their graduates in education have training in such areas as effective instructional practice, group processes, assessment literacy, data analysis, working interdependently with team members to achieve common goals, implementing action research, and accessing the knowledge base on best practice.

As a teacher enters the profession, his or her collaborative team will play a role in the hiring process and will assume responsibility for providing a smooth transition. Instead of the traditional sink-or-swim introduction to teaching, neophytes will have the advantage of a guaranteed curriculum, agreed-upon pacing guidelines, common team assessments, and criteria for assessing the quality of student work—all of which contribute to the clarity essential to effective teaching. More importantly, each member of the team will have the benefit of ongoing evidence of the learning of his or her students compared to the learning of students taught by their colleagues. When members of the team discover problem areas, they will have multiple sources of support to help improve their instructional practices. Colleagues whose students demonstrated high achievement on a particular skill or concept will provide the initial support, and support will then expand beyond the team to others in the school. Support continues to expand beyond the school to educators in the district who have demonstrated particular expertise in that area. Finally, the team will have access to the national video bank of effective practice referenced previously. As John Hattie (2008) concludes in his exhaustive study of the factors that impact student learning, individual teachers who reflect on their practice in isolation are unlikely to improve their effectiveness. Reflection leads to improved practice only when it is based on actual evidence of student learning and when it is done collectively. When reflection includes not only the individual teacher, but also an entire team, and when the team has access both to expertise within the district and vivid national examples of proven effective practice, educators will be in a much better position to meet the challenges they face.

Teachers will abandon traditional practices and structures that reinforce working in isolation. Principals will spend less time trying to supervise individual teachers into better performance through formal evaluation and will spend more time working on building the capacity of collaborative teams. The practice of rewarding individual teachers for pursuing isolated courses and workshops through varied colleges and programs will give way to professional development that is ongoing rather than episodic, collective rather than individual, job-embedded rather than external, and systematically aligned with school and district priorities rather than random.

For example, at Adlai Stevenson High School in Lincolnshire, Illinois, a teacher's contribution to his or her team is a significant factor in his or her evaluation because the collaborative team is regarded as vital to the effectiveness of the school. The time for collaboration that is built into the school calendar each week provides teachers with the continuing professional development credits required for their ongoing certification. The school offers its own graduate courses, taught by its own staff, on topics that represent priorities for the district, and those who complete the courses receive credit on the salary schedule. The success stories of collaborative teams are told at every faculty meeting, and a team reports on its work at every meeting of the board of education. Everything the school does—hiring, evaluation, professional development, scheduling, rewards, and recognition—is designed to support the message that helping all students learn at high levels requires a collaborative and collective effort.

Can Professional Learning Communities Become the Norm in Education?

If, as the Partnership for 21st Century Skills has concluded, schools must function as PLCs in order for students to acquire the knowledge and skills essential to their future, then the ability of educators to develop PLCs is crucial. But in order for the concept to become the norm in schools and districts throughout North America, educators must assume a more realistic position regarding the complexity of substantive change. Although many school reform initiatives of the past engaged educators in superficial change at the margin of professional practice, the PLC concept calls upon them to engage in deep, substantive, real change. And real change is *really hard*! False starts, mistakes, and setbacks are inevitable, and how educators respond to those mistakes determines their success or failure in implementing the concept.

Although many school reform initiatives of the past engaged educators in superficial change at the margin of professional practice, the PLC concept calls upon them to engage in deep, substantive, real change. And real change is *really hard!*

To assume that educators can flawlessly execute the complex transformation that the PLC concept requires is naïve, unrealistic, and counterproductive. Niels Bohr, the Nobel Prize–winning physicist, once observed, "An expert is a person who has made all the mistakes that can be made in a very narrow field." The only way to develop expertise in the concept is to learn by doing, which, to a large extent, is learning through mistakes.

It is equally unrealistic to assume that the profound cultural changes required to move a traditional school to a PLC can occur without tension and conflict. In fact, the absence of tension and conflict suggests the changes being made are probably too superficial. Educators must learn to surface the conflict, acknowledge and honor the varying perspectives, build shared knowledge, identify the criteria to be used in making decisions, and search for common ground. Developing these skills in managing conflict will not occur until educators recognize and embrace the inevitability of conflict and see it as a problem to be solved rather than an issue to be glossed over or an indication of failure. The crucial differences between those who succeed and those who fail in implementing the PLC concept often come down to resilience, tenacity, and persistence in overcoming mistakes and resolving conflict.

Despite the magnitude of the challenge, there is reason for optimism. As Michael Fullan (2007), one of the leading authorities on the change process in schools concludes, "I believe we are closer than ever in knowing what must be done to engage all classrooms and schools in continuous reform" (p. 19). The reason for his optimism, he explains, is that "developing [PLCs] has turned out to be one of the leading strategies of reform," and "PLCs are becoming . . . more sharply defined" (p. 98). Moreover, "the press for PLCs and the resources to aid and abet them are becoming increasingly explicit" (p. 151).

Fullan is not alone. In *The Tipping Point*, Malcolm Gladwell describes that "magic moment when an idea, trend, or social behavior crosses a threshold, tips, and spreads like wildfire" (2002, back cover).

The tipping point is reached when a few key people in the organization who are highly regarded by and connected to others (the Law of the Few) present a compelling argument in a memorable way (the Stickiness Factor) that leads to subtle changes in the conditions of the organization (the Power of Context).

The Law of the Few seems to be at work as key influencers in the profession have lined up to support the PLC concept. Virtually every leading educational researcher and almost all professional organizations for educators have endorsed it.

The increasing number of schools and districts that have become high-performing PLCs contributes to the "stickiness" of the argument to support the concept. Today, model sites throughout North America help to persuade educators that the concept is not only desirable but also feasible. The fact that entire districts have implemented the concept in ways that have raised student achievement in all of their schools demonstrates that the PLC concept is not limited to isolated success stories of individual schools, but can instead represent the norm for larger organizations.

Finally, unlike most educational reforms, which have focused on structure, the specific intent of the PLC concept is to change the context and culture of the school and district. Furthermore, the contextual changes it creates align with the most powerful levers for changing people's behavior. Kerry Patterson (2008) and his colleagues found that the peer pressure of social networks was one of the most powerful and accessible tools for influencing the behavior of others. This tool is unavailable in organizations in which people work in isolation. So the PLC concept changes the context by breaking down the walls of isolation to ensure people are on meaningful teams that work interdependently to achieve common goals for which members are mutually accountable.

A second powerful lever for change, particularly for educators, is concrete evidence of irrefutably better results (Elmore, 2004; Fullan, 2008; Patterson et al., 2008). This tool is unavailable in schools and districts where teachers are buffered from sharing results and the analysis of assessment data is left to each individual teacher. So the PLC concept changes the context by using frequent *common* assessments and making results transparent so that educators can identify their individual and collective strengths and weaknesses and take action accordingly.

Finally, Patterson (2008) argues the "greatest persuader" and the "mother of all cognitive map changes" is "personal experience" (p. 51). Schools and districts that implement the concept successfully are very purposeful in their efforts to create new experiences for people throughout the organization. This concept is a new experience for educators who have worked in traditional schools—to work collaboratively rather than in isolation, to use common formative assessments to inform their professional practice rather than merely to assign grades, and to contribute to a system of intervention and enrichment rather than leaving these issues to the discretion of each individual. Thus, PLCs change the context of schooling, and as Fullan (2007) concludes, "improvement occurs only when you change context" (p. 302).

Perhaps we are approaching that moment in history described by the National Commission on Teaching and America's Future (2003) when PLCs will no longer "be considered utopian" but will in fact "become the building blocks that establish a new foundation for America's schools" (p. 17). Perhaps we are nearing "a tipping point—from reform to true collaboration—[that] could represent the most dramatic shift in the history of educational practice. . . . We will know we have succeeded when the absence of a 'strong professional learning community' in a school is an embarrassment" (Schmoker, 2004, p. 431).

Learning by Doing

Educators committed to helping students acquire the knowledge, skills, and dispositions essential to their future must operate from the assumption that improvement in student outcomes will require changes in adult behavior. Teachers, principals, and central office administrators must develop their own individual and collective capacity to function as members of a PLC, and the best strategy for developing that capacity is to learn by doing—that is, to engage in the behaviors that are vital to a PLC.

Assuming that the skills vital to student success will remain static for the foreseeable future is unrealistic. Students and those who teach them will confront formidable challenges that we cannot anticipate today. But the chances of overcoming those challenges dramatically increase in schools and districts where educators have learned to work collaboratively rather than in isolation; engage in collective inquiry to address the issues most essential to student learning; resolve issues and answer questions by building shared knowledge regarding the most promising practices; and continuously gather evidence of student learning to inform and improve professional practice, respond to the learning needs of students, and drive continuous improvement. Those skilled in the PLC process are best positioned to prepare not only their students but also themselves for the challenges and opportunities of an uncertain future.

> Educators committed to helping students acquire the knowledge, skills, and dispositions essential to their future must operate from the assumption that improvement in student outcomes will require changes in adult behavior.

References

Black, P., & Wiliam, D. (1998). The formative purpose: Assessment must first promote learning. In M. Wilson (Ed.), *Towards coherence between classroom assessment and accountability* (pp. 20–50). Chicago: University of Chicago Press.

Blanchard, K. (2007). *Leading at a higher level: Blanchard on leadership and creating high performing organizations.* New York: Prentice Hall.

Council of Chief State School Officers. (2009). *Common core state standards initiative.* Accessed at www.CoreStandards.org/Files/CCSSIOne-Page.pdf on August 8, 2009.

DuFour, R., DuFour, R., Eaker, R., & Many, T. (2006). *Learning by doing: A handbook for professional learning communities at work.* Bloomington, IN: Solution Tree Press.

Elmore, R. F. (2004). *School reform from the inside out: Policy, practice, and performance.* Cambridge, MA: Harvard Educational Press.

Fullan, M. (2007). *The new meaning of educational change* (4th ed.). New York: Teachers College Press.

Fullan, M. (2008). *The six secrets of change: What the best leaders do to help their organizations survive and thrive.* San Francisco: Jossey-Bass.

Gladwell, M. (2002). *The tipping point: How little things can make a big difference.* Boston: Back Bay Books.

Graham, P., & Ferriter, W. M. (2010). *Building a professional learning community at work™: A guide to the first year.* Bloomington, IN: Solution Tree Press.

Hattie, J. A. C. (2008). *Visible learning: A synthesis of meta-analyses relating to achievement.* New York: Routledge.

Kotter, J. P., & Cohen, D. S. (2002). *The heart of change: Real-life stories of how people change their organizations.* Boston: Harvard Business School Press.

Lezotte, L. W. (1991). *Correlates of effective schools: The first and second generation.* Okemos, MI: Effective Schools Products.

Little, J. W. (2006, December). *Professional community and professional development in the learning-centered school.* Washington, DC: National Education Association. Accessed at www.nea.org/assets/docs/mf_pdreport.pdf on November 25, 2009.

Marzano, R. J. (2003). *What works in schools: Translating research into action.* Alexandria, VA: Association for Supervision and Curriculum Development.

Marzano, R. J. (2006). *Classroom assessment and grading that work.* Alexandria, VA: Association for Supervision and Curriculum Development.

The National Commission on Teaching and America's Future. (2003, January). *No dream denied: A pledge to America's children.* Washington, DC: Author.

Partnership for 21st Century Skills. (2009). *21st century support systems.* Accessed at www.21stcenturyskills.org/route21/index.php?option=com_content&view=article&id=58&Itemid=17 on July 1, 2009.

Patterson, K., Grenny, J., Maxfield, D., McMillan, R., & Switzler, A. (2008). *Influencer: The power to change anything.* New York: McGraw-Hill.

Pfeffer, J., & Sutton, R. I. (2006). *Hard facts, dangerous half-truths, and total nonsense: Profiting from evidence-based management.* Boston: Harvard Business School Press.

Popham, W. J. (2008). *Transformative assessment.* Alexandria, VA: Association for Supervision and Curriculum Development.

Reeves, D. B. (2002). *The leader's guide to standards: A blueprint for educational equity and excellence.* San Francisco: Jossey-Bass.

Reeves, D. B. (2006). *The learning leader: How to focus school improvement for better results.* Alexandria, VA: Association for Supervision and Curriculum Development.

Saphier, J. (2005). *John Adams' promise: How to have good schools for all our children, not just for some.* Acton, MA: Research for Better Teaching.

Schmoker, M. (2004, September). Learning communities at the crossroads: Toward the best schools we've ever had. *Phi Delta Kappan, 86*(1), 84–88.

Stiggins, R. (1999, November). Assessment, student confidence, and school success. *Phi Delta Kappan, 81*(3), 191–198.

Stiggins, R. (2004, September). New assessment beliefs for a new school mission. *Phi Delta Kappan, 86*(1), 22–27.

Wiliam, D., & Thompson, M. (2008). Integrating assessment and learning: What will it take to make it work? In C. A. Dwyer (Ed.), *The future of assessment: Shaping teaching and learning.* New York: Lawrence Erlbaum.

Robin Fogarty

Robin Fogarty, Ph.D., is president of Robin Fogarty and Associates, Ltd., a Chicago-based educational consulting and publishing company. A leading proponent of the thoughtful classroom, Fogarty has trained educators throughout the world in curriculum, instruction, and assessment strategies. She has taught at all levels, from kindergarten to college, served as an administrator, and consulted with state departments and ministries of education across the globe. She is the author of numerous articles and books.

Brian M. Pete

Brian M. Pete is cofounder of Robin Fogarty & Associates. He comes from a family of educators—college professors, school superintendents, teachers, and teachers of teachers—and has a rich background in professional development. Pete has observed and recorded classroom teachers and professional experts in schools throughout the world. Pete is the author of numerous educational videos.

In this chapter, Fogarty and Pete carry the discussion to Singapore where they have worked as educational consultants with the nation's ambitious "Teach Less, Learn More" initiative. Fogarty and Pete share the thoughts and feelings of teachers torn between the old ways of authoritarian, competitive schools and the new ways of shared decision making and collaborative study that encourage students to construct meaning rather than memorize facts.

Chapter 5

The Singapore Vision:
Teach Less, Learn More

Robin Fogarty and Brian M. Pete

Singapore's visionary education framework—*Teach Less, Learn More*—was created for the nation's entry into the 21st century (Singapore Ministry of Education, 2004). It is part of a larger framework consisting of four separate but interrelated components: (1) a vision for the whole nation, (2) a vision for Singaporean education, (3) a vision for implementing school change, and (4) a vision for the collaborative constructs—the professional learning communities—that are necessary to anchor the change in each school.

The synergy created by these four distinct, yet interdependent, visions provides the catalyst for significant change efforts in Singapore's schools. In fact, it is the blending of these components that makes the country's journey of change an educational exemplar. Together, these four visions propel substantive change to previously accepted practices, and they support the transformation of Singapore's education system to meet the challenges of the 21st century. The visions create a landscape for others to contemplate as they begin their own journeys of 21st century change. The framework is shown in table 5.1 (see page 98).

Table 5.1: Singapore's Framework

Vision One	The Vision for a Nation: *Thinking Schools, Learning Nation*
Vision Two	The Vision for Education: *Teach Less, Learn More*
Vision Three	The Vision for Implementation: *Tight, Loose, Tight*
Vision Four	The Vision for Collaboration: *Professional Learning Communities*

Vision One: The Vision for a Nation

Thinking Schools, Learning Nation is the first vision in the framework. This, the nation's overarching vision, is deeply embedded in the education philosophy for all of Singapore's schools. It defines the proud plan of an entire country committed to an educational system of prestige and excellence. Thinking Schools, Learning Nation is about building a core set of life skills (thinking, creating, problem solving), attitudes (collaboration, wonderment), and dispositions (tolerance for ambiguity, persistence) in students that will create a mindset of innovation and enterprise, which is integral to the prosperity and well-being of the individual and the country. The vision is a national signature that inspires and brings hope.

Singapore possesses a unique synchronicity of city, state, and country that allows the government to plan, implement, and support expansive change. With this synchronicity, they are able to coordinate planning, implementation, and institutionalization at all levels of the change process. They are able to develop support within the community, the schools, and the state. In essence, they are able to create the critical mass necessary for meaningful and lasting change.

Vision Two: The Vision for Education

Teach Less, Learn More is the second vision in the framework. It is integral to the first vision and speaks to the goal of "teaching in ways that help students learn without being taught" (Loong, 2004). The Teach Less, Learn More vision for education provides a strong and steady anchor for transformational bridging from 20th century education to 21st century skills.

The 21st century skills as defined by the Partnership for 21st Century Skills (2007) are the skills inherent in the Teach Less, Learn More vision. They include the global skills of learning and innovation; career skills; information, media, and technology skills; and practical life skills (family, school, community, state, and nation). These are juxtaposed with core subjects from the various and traditional disciplines, and laced with timely 21st century themes of global awareness, and financial, economic, business, entrepreneurial, civic, and health and wellness literacies. Teach Less, Learn More is manifested in the work of pilot schools, called Teach Less, Learn More (TLLM) Ignite Schools. The TLLM Ignite Schools are focused on promoting intrinsic interest in learning. They are primary and secondary schools of various sizes guided by carefully crafted missions. They seek admission to the pilot program through a competitive application process.

Vision Three: The Vision for Implementation

Tight, Loose, Tight is the third component in Singapore's framework for the 21st century. A school reform with a goal of Teach Less, Learn More has little sustainability if it is not flexible enough to address a variety of local school needs or able to accommodate immovable constraints. The Tight, Loose, Tight formula combines an adherence to central design principles (tight) with expected accommodations to the needs, resources, constraints, and particularities that occur in any school or district (loose), when these don't conflict with the theoretical framework (tight) and, ultimately, with the stated goals and desired results (tight). Singapore's leaders wisely encourage implementation that adheres to a tight, loose, tight philosophy (Wylie, 2008). While leadership does not provide specific models, they encourage inventiveness and far-reaching thinking through the theoretical underpinnings of the Tight, Loose, Tight model, and they advocate a framework for change shaped by the innovative thinking of the particular school staffs.

Vision Four: The Vision for Collaboration

Professional Learning Communities is the fourth component. Grounded in the seminal work on professional learning communities (PLCs) by Richard DuFour and Robert Eaker (DuFour & Eaker, 1998;

see also DuFour and DuFour on page 77 of this volume), it completes Singapore's framework for change. As part of the national reform initiative, schools receive professional development to function as PLCs with resources available through the Ministry of Education, the TLLM network of schools, and through their own professional-development planning teams. While every PLC is not yet expert at this process, PLCs are in place in every TLLM Ignite School, in varying stages of effectiveness.

The TLLM Ignite Schools are committed to the Professional Learning Communities vision. These schools are held accountable by the Ministry of Education to demonstrate results. They are expected to perform and to show evidence of their progress each year. Schools are made up of learning teams with members who work interdependently through structured collaboration to propel the implementation process. The collaborative work—the back-and-forth and imperfect process of articulation orchestrated within and across PLCs—distills the essence of each group's thinking. Believing that social discourse bears the fruit of creative thought (Vygotsky, 1978), educators embrace this as their instrument of change, and they welcome the collaborative spirit and the camaraderie that accompanies the teamwork. Team members are committed to implementing their PLC efforts with fidelity. And in the end, the proven PLC process yields insightful and inspired teaching and learning connections. This, in fact, is the hallmark of PLCs. They tend to emerge as the "think tanks" for differentiation, emergent creativity, and real innovation.

Teach Less, Learn More

Couched within the national mantra of Thinking Schools, Learning Nation, the concept of Teach Less, Learn More speaks to lifelong, life-fulfilling, and life-sustaining learning. For the Ministry of Education, this paradoxical statement—Teach Less, Learn More—calls for a subtle look at "remembering why we teach, reflecting on what we teach, and reconsidering how we teach" (Ministry of Education, Singapore, 2004). It is a story told quietly, through the collective voices of the PLCs, as they come to know and understand the meaning of teaching less and learning more.

At first glance, Teach Less, Learn More sounds contradictory. Why do teachers need to teach less? If they do, how do students learn more? When moved beyond the literal interpretation, Teach Less, Learn More naturally becomes a central topic of discussion in the PLCs. These professional discussions reveal answers, but subsequently move the teams along the endless stream of additional questions they generate in their journey. For example, as a team of teachers discusses the perceived need to develop more creative thinking and genuine risk taking from students, teachers question how they might foster that kind of thinking. That question leads to others about the impact of the traditional behaviors of competition and compliance on creative thinking and risk taking. The theory is clear, but the practical path to implementation is complex.

The PLCs undertake and embrace the dedicated process as they learn together and teach together. The change process is about evolutionary thinking, not revolutionary thinking, and it all begins with these critical collaborative conversations.

Teach Less

Teach Less is the first of the complex concepts teachers struggle to embrace within the structure of PLCs. The idea of teaching less is hard to comprehend in a country such as Singapore with an undeniable and well-known focus on traditional subject-matter content and ever-looming high-stakes examinations, with class sizes of forty or more, with traditional didactic teaching models firmly and at times fiercely in place, all in a world ripe with data, facts, figures, images, and in an endless flow of information.

> The change process is about evolutionary thinking, not revolutionary thinking, and it all begins with these critical collaborative conversations.

The world of knowledge expands every day at a rate that is almost incomprehensible. Teachers are expected to absorb a growing body of work in their fields of study. The curricula balloons with information. Teachers are expected to be current and conversant in a wide array of subjects—from politics, economics, and ever-changing geographical data, to medicine, technology, and space exploration; from business, industry, and educational innovation, to literature, art, music, and the dramatic media.

In addition, the world of instant communication complicates the work of teachers. In the early lifetime of many of Singapore's teachers, the fax machine was an unknown tool. Now, it is already almost obsolete. School leaders, busy appropriating funds to create and wire computer labs, incredulously, had no real knowledge of or access to the Internet. Now, the simple cell phone debuts as the new laptop for ten to fifteen million schoolchildren. It presents just one of the impending technology challenges teachers struggle to keep pace with in this information-rich society. Within a brief span of time, entire newspapers, complete literary works, and classic dictionaries have become electronic, and interactive encyclopedias and global positioning devices have become everyday phenomena. The world is the world of high-speed connections, online communications, blogs, wikis, podcasts, and RSS feeds with Time Machine and Mozy backup systems. Search engines such as Google, Yahoo, and Bing locate targets in milliseconds. Visual media, film libraries, video inventories, YouTube, TeacherTube, Hulu, comedy hours, sportscasts, and online gaming are readily available all day, every day.

Today, the digital world of schooling is immersed in an era of anytime, anywhere learning with Blackboard and Moodle platforms and interactive whiteboards. There are web-based graduate courses, online master's and doctoral programs, webinars and video confer-encing, Kindle and Wikipedia. In turn, social-networking tools, such as MySpace, Facebook, Linkedin, Twitter, and Skype, provide platforms for instant and immediate personal connections both near and far-reaching.

Hand-held PDAs, with hundreds of applications for the savvy user, permeate the environment both in and out of school. Phoning, texting, emailing, indexing, organizing, and crunching data merely scratch the surface of the sophisticated surfing functions savvy users can perform. The iPhone has over 135,000 applications on its open-source platform. Why, indeed, would a transformational education policy advocate teaching students *less* when there is so much *more* to know, as all of these new tools put even more information at our fingertips on a daily basis?

Professional learning communities must address the Teach Less question, even as they recognize that they could so easily teach more. Through conversations, Singapore's teachers come to understand that Teach Less does not mean that they should actually teach less—not less in terms of hours of teaching time, not less in terms of fundamental discipline-based knowledge, and not less in terms of a watered-down or minimalist curriculum. They know that Teach Less does not mean reduce the core curriculum and teach less essential material. Nor does it mean eliminate, omit, or slight parts of the basic curriculum. Over time, and with many meetings and conversations, they come to accept that Teach Less has a strikingly different connotation that is far removed from the literal translation.

The PLCs' deeper understanding of Teach Less often happens as the teams address two essential concerns: what to teach and how to teach it. *What to teach* involves the quantity/quality conundrum of a standards-based curriculum. *How to teach* refers directly to the delivery methods teachers employ. Members of the PLCs address the quantity and quality question. They know that there is a core curriculum for the various disciplines that has always reigned supreme in their schools. Yet while they are still tied to Singapore's traditional discipline-based curriculum, they are committed to its Teach Less, Learn More vision. They know they must find a way to manage the enormous quantity of content in the curriculum, and, at the same time, look at the issue of the quality of that content as it relates to 21st century skills.

One example of teaching less is the emergent focus on cooperative learning in the TLLM Ignite Schools. TLLM schools frequently incorporate student teamwork for uncovering what they know and think about the learning at hand—a major shift from the traditional Singaporean methods of covering the content in a didactic manner; however, these emergent methodologies can cause concern for teachers as they try to balance the new instructional strategies with the old. The feature box on page 104 shows an example of the kind of conversations that often take place.

Teacher 1: Let's use cooperative teams for our investigations of environmental issues. We can jigsaw the various aspects, and let student teams research and unpack the essential information.

Teacher 2: How will we guarantee students are addressing the key issues required for the examination? Students could get pretty freewheeling when the teams strike out on their own.

Teacher 3: I know exactly what you mean. I have the same concern, yet I know from past projects that even though the use of student teams does present content-management challenges, the student results are always worth it.

Teacher 1: What do you mean?

Teacher 3: I mean that the students often take the research in a direction of genuine interest that motivates them to go deeper and to really own the learning. It's in their hands, but we are always there to guide the process and to point them in the direction of the essential learnings.

Teacher 2: You're right. I have had that same feeling with authentic project learning. It's just tough to let go of the control. But I'm in agreement. Let's use the collaborative team approach.

Learn More

Through the articulation process inherent in the PLCs, teachers in the TLLM Ignite Schools begin to look at the quantity/quality issue through a different lens. While their system has traditionally compartmentalized the curriculum by disciplines that honor *quantity* of subject matter, they find that this structure can be deliberately shifted to focus on essential 21st century questions, conceptual themes, and life skills that honor the *quality* of student outcomes.

> In addition to raising essential questions, PLCs in Singapore begin to examine conceptual themes—the 21st century themes of change, design, conflict, structure, and justice—that broaden the scope of learning beyond the traditional subject-matter content.

When PLCs explore the idea of essential questions—characterized by authentic inquiry learning models that require active, engaged learning—they discover these are universal questions that have many possible answers. For example, how is justice served? How literate must one be? What is the nature of conflict? How is balance achieved?

The "what" questions. In addition to raising essential questions, PLCs in Singapore begin to examine conceptual themes—the 21st century themes of change, design, conflict, structure, and justice—that broaden the scope of learning beyond the traditional subject-matter content. While the study of economics as a subject is a robust part of the core curriculum, teachers soon see how the concept has more lasting impact when it becomes a 21st century theme. For example, when the theme *entrepreneurship* is the pivot point for integrating core economics subject matter, students sense the excitement of a dynamic, modern-day theme. This theme adds a needed relevancy for students and produces opportunities ripe for rich projects in which students take on the simulated roles of entrepreneurs in authentic classroom projects.

Finally, discussions in the PLCs turn to the idea of life skills. Team members see how the skills of learning to learn, problem-based learning, decision making, and technology should be woven into the subject-matter content, not merely as implicit tools used to navigate a unit of study, but rather as a set of invaluable lifelong learning tools, explicitly taught and purposefully imbedded into meaningful core curriculum.

The "how" questions. Over the course of many PLC sessions, the teachers' focus moves to the second type of critical question: how? The team reflects on *how* they teach, *how* they deliver the information, and their options as they embrace 21st century skills as the basis for designing dynamic curriculum.

How can we teach less? In deep discussions peppered with personal stories of classroom experiences, teachers gradually come to understand that Teach Less does mean teaching less in the traditional didactic delivery of information—less teacher talk, less "pour and store," and less-frequent one-way broadcasts.

They discover that Teach Less means using a wider and deeper instructional repertoire: interactive methodologies, hands-on learning, collaborative interactions, and multimodal

> They discover that Teach Less means using a wider and deeper instructional repertoire: interactive methodologies, hands-on learning, collaborative interactions, and multimodal learning in the classroom.

learning in the classroom. As the PLCs examine models of authentic, engaged learning and learning-to-learn skills, members discover, uncover, view, and review the wide range of complex and powerful curricular models available. These include cooperative learning, brain-compatible learning, Habits of Mind, problem-based learning, multiple intelligences, integrated thematic instruction, integrated curriculum, Understanding by Design, mediated learning, case studies, creativity and innovation, differentiated instruction, assessment as learning, drama as pedagogy, use of the arts as a teaching and learning tool in mathematics and English, and art and teaching for understanding. The PLCs explore and investigate what makes these models worthy of their scrutiny. This is where the conversation of the vision for implementation—Tight, Loose, Tight—begins to surface. This is when teams begin to feel empowered in the freedom to choose widely and wisely within the established structure of the Teach Less, Learn More vision *how* they will teach *what* so that their 21st century students learn more, faster and deeper.

While the PLCs actively seek appropriate theoretical models for their students, the discussion often leads to other insights. They talk about how they *already know* about these authentic, hands-on, student-centered learning models and how they have never felt able to stray from the traditionally accepted, more didactic Singaporean classroom template. And they marvel at the fact that they are now being asked to radically reconceptualize the teaching and learning process. They realize that they are, in fact, being urged to honor the Teach Less initiative, with all of its potential power, and they begin to feel a sense of urgency about renewing their approach to the curriculum. Figure 5.1 tracks this shift in thinking as it often occurs in the journey of the PLCs.

As these critical conversations about what teachers teach and how they teach begin to surface, parallel conversations weave their way into the PLC sessions. The teachers subsequently attend to the idea of more student-centered models of learning and how those theoretical structures fuel the second part of the first vision—Learn More.

How can students learn more? From a student perspective, Learn More addresses two crucial foundational questions about the

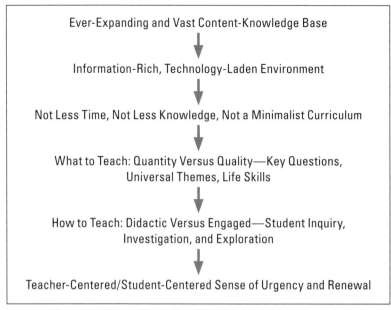

Ever-Expanding and Vast Content-Knowledge Base

↓

Information-Rich, Technology-Laden Environment

↓

Not Less Time, Not Less Knowledge, Not a Minimalist Curriculum

↓

What to Teach: Quantity Versus Quality—Key Questions, Universal Themes, Life Skills

↓

How to Teach: Didactic Versus Engaged—Student Inquiry, Investigation, and Exploration

↓

Teacher-Centered/Student-Centered Sense of Urgency and Renewal

Figure 5.1: Flow chart showing PLCs' thinking about the Teach Less concept.

teaching and learning process. Just as with the earlier questions: What do students learn? And how do they learn it?

As the PLCs explore what students learn, again, the core curriculum is front and center. Even when bridging learning to 21st century skills, these teachers understand that there is no argument about the basics. It is a given that students need core content knowledge. What is not a given—yet—is the urgent need to equip students with skills of life, skills of learning, and skills of an already-present future.

> Even when bridging learning to 21st century skills, these teachers understand that there is no argument about the basics.

Teachers are aware that the students they are teaching are already immersed in a plethora of future skills. Teachers talk about how effortlessly students adapt to technology tools. They gobble up shiny new hardware, and they show no hesitation with the ever-expanding repertoire of software applications available. Teachers lament that students are omnivores when it comes to "playing around" with the technological tools that debut almost daily. Professional learning communities provide the perfect platform to discuss this well-known and often dismissed dilemma: students are ahead of the curve with technology in every way, shape, and manner. Students in today's schools have known no other way in their short lifetimes. Yet it is sometimes acknowledged, but rarely addressed with interest and integrity, how the school curriculum often lags far behind the students in the integration and blending of available technologies.

With this context in mind, conversations in the PLCs invariably lead to the idea that students do need more than a knowledge-based curriculum. Teachers realize that students need a curriculum that goes above and beyond the present state of affairs; that they need a dynamic, more relevant curriculum that is laced with cutting-edge technologies—one that truly does bridge to the 21st century of fast-paced, ever-changing, technology-rich living and learning.

Conversations in the PLCs invariably lead to the idea that students do need more than a knowledge-based curriculum.

As the discussion unwinds, teachers begin listing the litany of life and learning skills: skills of reasoning, research, and resilience; skills of technology, team building, and teamwork; skills of communication, collaboration, and collegiality; and skills of innovation, invention, and industry. The PLCs talk about how students need to learn skills that develop attitudes, dispositions, and habits of mind; that students need rich, rigorous, and relevant learning experiences that bridge a core content-knowledge base with the unknown and unforeseen challenges of the 21st century and beyond. When discussing what students need to learn, the PLCs see that the list is long and full of new items. They realize that learning cannot be just about discipline-specific knowledge. What students learn must go much further than the status quo. This is an exciting breakthrough for PLCs, and the conversations continue.

In the natural course of events, these collegial conversations find their way into talks of how students learn the curriculum best. The team discusses teaching methods, what works for them as teachers, and what does not, what other teachers do, and what they have not yet tried. Within these coveted collegial conversations, a whole repertoire of teaching strategies is revealed. This beginning of authentic professional dialogue and articulation sparks changes in practice.

While most teachers agree that their primary mode of delivery is in a straightforward blast of facts, data, and reasons, they also know that in those all-too-rare moments when they diverge from the didactic—in those moments when they orchestrate a unit-driven project or a meaningful excursion—their students are engaged quite differently. They recall the intensity and the involvement of a classroom of eager learners. As the teachers exchange scenarios of these experiences that transform passive learners into lively, active, and engaged participants, they know they have struck a chord.

The teams have more breakthroughs. Realizing that Teach Less, Learn More calls for this kind of learner engagement, teacher teams are motivated to try new methods apart from the traditional class instruction. Of course, all this robust conversation occurs over time, over several or many meeting sessions, as the PLCs struggle to come to agreement on their theoretical model. They discuss the various models of student inquiry, investigations, discovery learning, hands-on experimentation, exploration, and problem solving. They consider team collaborations; a deeper, not wider curriculum focus; and a definite and aggressive technology thread. They weigh the pros and cons of each of the many models, narrowing the choices down as they unearth concerns and priorities.

And the PLCs address, again and again, the ever-present concern about the core curriculum, as they are always cognizant of Singapore's high-stakes examinations. Yet they now know that core curriculum can be presented not as inert knowledge to be "covered," but as a dynamic flow of information that incorporates life's challenges in ways that are structured yet experiential, and in ways that are authentic, relevant, and meaningful.

Some Teach Less, Learn More school applications are simple, yet they are eloquent in their mindfulness of what and how to teach differently. Other school implementations of Teach Less, Learn More are intricate and exquisite in their applied methodologies as they follow the Tight, Loose, Tight implementation vision. Note in figure 5.2 (page 110) the flow of thinking that occurs when school teams move toward their ultimate goal of implementing an innovative model of curriculum that bridges learning to the demands of the 21st century.

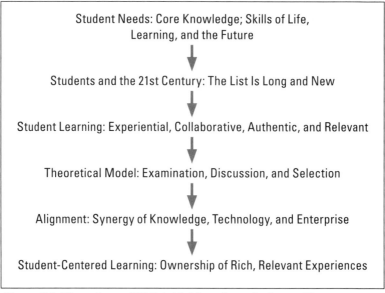

Figure 5.2: Flow chart of PLCs' thinking about the Learn More concept.

What do the implementation results from a collegial conversation look like? The examples presented in the following sections show the results in two schools. One profile is a primary school implementation plan that marries traditional content with 21st century skillsets. The second depicts a secondary school curriculum plan that reaches rigorously into the rich technologies of the 21st century.

An Elementary School Example

Changkat Primary School's PLC chose to adopt a simple but eloquent model of instruction (Ministry of Education, Singapore, 2004). They use Costa and Kallick's (2000) *Integrating and Sustaining Habits of Mind* as a theoretical model for understanding narrative text. Teachers at Changkat know the weight comprehension skills carry in terms of continued student success, so they teach about metacognition and the learning-to-learn skills of awareness and control over one's learning. They emphasize student understanding of (1) knowing what they know, (2) knowing what they don't know, and (3) knowing what to do when they don't know. As students learn to take responsibility for reading with understanding, they focus on such habits of mind as managing impulsivity, persistence, continuous learning, and monitoring, and modifying and managing their own learning. These same students are taught how to systematically code narrative text for more explicit comprehension, using a set of specific symbols: (+) New; (rr) Reread; (?) Question; (_____) Connection; (!) WOW; (^) Empathy; (V) Visualize; (*) Research; (I) Infer; and (=) Clue.

This explicit coding provides concrete evidence of the students' understanding and use of specific strategies that deepen their comprehension. The coding engages complex thinking skills used in qualitative data analysis and interpretation of ethnographic studies. The coding process raises the bar significantly for student understanding of informational text.

This elementary school PLC decided that these are habits of mind and learning-to-learn skills that will serve their students for years to come. While this may appear at first glance to be a more traditionally focused application of Teach Less, Learn More, in truth, it establishes noble goals for these primary students.

The difference between a common and an uncommon application of Teach Less, Learn More lies in the subtle shift in teachers' understanding and execution of core content. The explicitness with which comprehension of a narrative is approached takes comprehension from a "phantom skill" that is often alluded to, but not often actually taught, to explicit skillsets for reading with comprehension (inference, visualization, empathy, and so on), enhanced by lifelong skills of learning to learn.

A Secondary School Example

The team at Jurong Secondary School collaborates with industry partners and uses a problem-based learning approach (Barrows & Tamblyn, 1980) with differentiated learning (Tomlinson, 1999), and a unique set of e-PBL tools (problem-based learning tools) tools that immerse students in information-communication technology (Ministry of Education, Singapore, 2004). As part of this unique experience, an engine with artificial intelligence capacity processes student data about learning dispositions. This media-literacy project in which students are evaluating sources of information, communicating ideas through various media tools, and making use of technology with responsibility and ethics is truly an intricate and eloquent adaptation of the 21st century vision.

The Challenge of Change

While significant change is happening in these pilot schools, teachers come to realize that what they are doing is not a perfect science. It is an imperfect, messy, human process. Ultimately, however, the PLCs understand the overriding benefits to students. Teachers come to realize that by moving toward student-centered curriculum models, students willingly and assertively take over the ownership of the learning experiences inherent in the innovative curriculum projects being planned and implemented.

These are the trials and tribulations, the tools and techniques of reflective practice that come to the surface as the PLCs mature—as team members adjust to other members, build a sense of community, and begin to feel empowered to move forward with their mission.

A sense of instructional renewal slowly emerges from the dual focus on the core curriculum and student-centered 21st century skills. With the Teach Less, Learn More dichotomy of ideas tediously, intensely, and thoroughly sorted and exposed through the collaborative conversations of PLCs, these school teams continue to dig into their theoretical models of choice and advance the process of alignment to their core curricular content.

As curriculum designs develop, the Learn More aspect of the vision takes shape. The teacher teams begin to grasp why Teach Less, Learn More is neither more nor less of the same. They begin to realize that the Teach Less, Learn More vision is about teaching with passion and foresight about what to teach along with relevancy and richness in how to teach. Teachers begin to look past the isolated subject area boundaries toward a richer, fuller, and more meaningful curriculum intertwined with 21st century skills.

> Teachers begin to look past the isolated subject area boundaries toward a richer, fuller, and more meaningful curriculum intertwined with 21st century skills.

This examination of what students learn and how students learn lies at the center of the Learn More element of Singapore's educational vision. As these PLCs proceed with their dynamic discussions, they think more about student learning—learning that is relevant to the world students live in and the world they will live in. Teachers talk about students learning more when they are given responsibility for that learning and when they are given the tools needed to meet the challenges they encounter. Teachers discuss how students learn more when they "own" their learning, when they have choices and options, when they must struggle a little to complete the task, and when they feel the joy of accomplishment and achievement. There is no way to measure the power of these collegial conversations as the teachers shift from notions of traditional schooling to teaching for the 21st century. It shows, over and over again, that teachers, working as professional communities of learners, come to embrace the emerging philosophy of Teach Less, Learn More, and, in turn, evolve as more reflective practitioners who focus on the outcomes they have created.

A Bridge to the 21st Century

All is not perfect in this imperfect process of change, engineered by imperfect humans, functioning as imperfect PLCs. Yet as the process unfolds, as the school teams fight to keep their nation's global stature by producing the highest standardized test scores, they are striving at the same time to shift toward more engaged learning that may not herald the examination at the same priority level as in times past. Nevertheless, these schools continue to demonstrate success for students and are still among the most acclaimed and esteemed in the world's educational community for their willingness to accept the challenges involved in this dual task.

This is the story of how TLLM Ignite Schools conceptualize the 21st century core curriculum above and beyond the basic, foundational learning of traditional schooling. These schools are attempting to unlock the creative minds of teachers and students, set in motion the talents and abilities of the students in their care, and honor Singapore's mission of Thinking Schools, Learning Nation. This is the story of how Singapore's educators are preparing for the 21st century.

This story is not yet complete, and many questions about the future course of the journey still remain: What does Singapore's journey have to do with schools in other nations? What are the lessons

As the process unfolds, as the school teams fight to keep their nation's global stature by producing the highest standardized test scores, they are striving at the same time to shift toward more engaged learning that may not herald the examination at the same priority level as in times past.

learned that apply to different systems? What can our school leaders take away in their quest to bridge learning to 21st century skills? How does Singapore's journey relate to others leading the way to 21st century skills?"

What any educational community can take away from this visionary framework begins with the four visions within Singapore's framework. Singapore's visions can inspire, guide, and bridge; they can crystallize, teach, and empower. They can embrace, embody, transfer, and transform. They can begin conversations, spur debate, and provide a source for reflection.

Teach Less, Learn More! The mantra is simple. This vision is the frame and the fuel for the conversation within the school system's PLCs. What begin as ordinary conversations among colleagues evolve into practical missions for school teams. There are no miracles here. The lessons learned by these PLCs are the lessons of collaboration, communication, and celebration. These lessons translate to other schools and other teachers and other places around the world—the lessons of visionary journeys, creative thinking, authentic learning, and spirited collaborations, the universal lessons of challenge and change.

References

Barrows, H. S., & Tamblyn, R. M. (1980). *Problem-based learning: An approach to medical education.* New York: Springer.

Costa, A. L., & Kallick, B. (Eds.). (2000). *Integrating and sustaining habits of mind.* Alexandria, VA: Association for Supervision and Curriculum Development.

DuFour, R., & Eaker, R. (1998). *Professional learning communities at work: Best practices for enhancing student achievement.* Bloomington, IN: Solution Tree Press.

Loong, L. H. (2004, August 12). *Our future of opportunity and promise.* Speech presented at the Singapore National Day Rally, Singapore. Accessed at www.pmo.gov.sg/NR/rdonlyres/63C7AA0A-FC1B-45C8-9FC3-3310E29E5057/0/2004NDR_English.doc on April 30, 2009.

Ministry of Education, Singapore. (2004). *Teach less, learn more: Reigniting passion and mission.* Singapore: Ministry of Education. Accessed at www.MOE.edu.sg/bluesky/tllm on May 30, 2009.

Partnership for 21st Century Skills. (2007). Framework for 21st century learning. Accessed at www.21stcenturyskills.org/index.php?Itemid=120&id=254&option=com_content&task=view on May 30, 2009.

Tomlinson, C. A. (1999). *The differentiated classroom: Responding to the needs of all learners.* Alexandria, VA: Association for Supervision and Curriculum Development.

Vygotsky, L. S. (1978). *Mind in society: The development of higher psychological processes.* Cambridge, MA: Harvard University Press.

Wylie, E. C. (Ed.). (2008). *Tight but loose: Scaling up teacher professional development in diverse contexts.* Accessed at www.ets.org/Media/Research/pdf/RR-08-29.pdf on April 30, 2009.

Bob Pearlman

Bob Pearlman has been a key leader of national educational reform efforts in his unique thirty-year career as a teacher, codirector of computer education, teacher union leader and negotiator, foundation president, and director of education and workforce development. Pearlman's experience and expertise includes whole-district reform, new school development, business-education partnerships and coalitions, school-to-career and workforce development, union–school district negotiations, school restructuring and technology, project-based learning, professional development, educational finance, and school-site assessment and accountability. Pearlman is currently a strategy consultant for 21st century school and district development. He served as the director of strategic planning for the New Technology Foundation from 2002 to 2009. Pearlman consults in the United States and in the United Kingdom on 21st century learning, focusing on new school development and districtwide implementation of 21st century skills.

In this chapter, Pearlman takes a walk through innovative school buildings designed for collaborative learning. He reminds us that the familiar box-based design of most current schools was suited for an outdated factory-model agenda. He shows us that form follows function in these innovative buildings as well, but the functions are now engagement, problem solving, and communication.

Visit **go.solution-tree.com/21stcenturyskills** to view the graphics in this chapter in full color and to access live links to tools and materials.

Chapter 6

Designing New Learning Environments to Support 21st Century Skills

Bob Pearlman

Visit any number of new school buildings across the United States, and behind the beautiful, new (and sometimes green) facilities, you will still see the same old 700- to 900-square-foot classrooms, superbly designed for a teacher to stand in front of a class of thirty students set in neat rows, listening, taking notes, and doing worksheets. Yes, you might see wiring for computers and interactive whiteboards at the head of the classroom, but other than that, little has changed.

Go across the pond to England, where they are six years into the eighty-billion-dollar Building Schools of the Future (BSF) program to replace or renovate every secondary school in that country, and you will see some significant innovations beginning to emerge. The aspirations of many local education authorities are high: "BSF is being seen as the catalyst for transformation of education in [England]. BSF is not simply a buildings programme, and must not result in 'old wine in new bottles'" (Hertfordshire Grid for Learning, 2009). What you see, however, in the first wave of new builds and renovations, is still mostly the same "old wine"—traditional education. But because the United Kingdom's process is so much deeper, involving so many more institutions, companies, local education authorities, and student voices, some significant innovations are emerging.

The United States has always had pockets of innovation in schooling, and the first decade of the 21st century is no exception. But it is happening mostly through the work of not-for-profit school development groups. Little innovation has issued from the federal or state governments. Elliot Washor (2003), cofounder of Big Picture Learning, studied these trends and found little innovation in school facilities:

> Three themes emerge from a review of research and literature on school facilities design. First, facilities designs have been shown to have an impact on learning. Second, these designs have been shown to have an impact on students and others who work in the schools. Third, there have been few innovations in school facilities design. (p. 10)

Hasn't anything changed? Are students today different from their parents? Do they come to school with different capabilities and interests for learning than previous generations? Have new technology tools enabled more learner-centered approaches to education (Watson & Riegeluth, 2008)? Has the new flat world significantly expanded the knowledge and skills that students need to be successful workers and citizens?

If these changes are real, then schools are now enabled to move away from teacher-directed whole-group instruction to create learner-centered workplaces for a collaborative culture of students at work. Many new school designs in the United States and the United Kingdom have done this. A review of best practice illuminates these new 21st century learning environments and school facilities to help school designers and developers and education, civic, and business leaders launch the next generation of innovative schools.

The Digital Natives Are Restless

A torrent of publications are illuminating the new behaviors and capabilities of today's students, from Don Tapscott's *Growing Up Digital: The Rise of the Net Generation* (2001), to Marc Prensky's *Digital Natives, Digital Immigrants* (2001), to the more recent work of Frank S. Kelly, Ted McCain, and Ian Jukes, *Teaching the Digital Generation: No More Cookie-Cutter High Schools* (2008).

A key thesis in all of these publications is that students learn best when they are engaged and that students can now do most of the work. Prensky urges moving from "telling/lecturing" to the "'new' pedagogy of kids teaching themselves with the teacher's guidance" (Prensky, 2008).

Is this any surprise? These students are millenials—digital natives, social networkers, keen to work on their own or in collaboration with others. At home they are likely to be equipped with computers, Internet access, iPods, and smartphones. At school, they typically sit at small desks, push a pencil or pen, and do worksheets.

New Skills and Pedagogy for the 21st Century

There is a growing recognition in the United States and other countries that 21st century knowledge and skills not only build upon core content knowledge, but also include information and communication skills, thinking and problem-solving skills, interpersonal and self-directional skills, and the skills to utilize 21st century tools, such as information and communication technologies. The Partnership for 21st Century Skills (2003) has defined and articulated these 21st century skills. (See Ken Kay's foreword on page xiii of this volume.)

New standards in the United States, United Kingdom, and other countries often stress creativity, critical thinking, problem solving, communication, and so on; however, few curricula bring these standards to life as learning outcomes, and few countries assess them either in national or state tests or in classroom practice. Practitioners have made headway at the classroom level, however, by emphasizing projects, authentic assessment with rubrics that are transparent to students, products, presentations, and exhibitions.

We are now more than a decade into the standards and accountability movement in the United States and the United Kingdom, and already the limitations of a standards-based school accountability system that focuses on basic skills in a fast-changing, globalizing world have been revealed. Calls for change are coming from many places.

In the United Kingdom, the Innovation Unit, supported by the Paul Hamlyn Foundation, published *Learning Futures: Next Practice in Learning and Teaching* (2008), which "sets out the reasons why innovation in pedagogy is needed in order to inspire young people":

There is a new argument taking centre stage. It is no longer the usual debate over standards and structures but instead a discussion about how young people best learn in the 21st century, and how we can make schools (and those who work in them) catalysts for vibrant engagement, not simply achievement. By looking at how young people choose to learn, what motivation and love of learning mean in the context of school, and how we can give more emphasis to student engagement and voice, there is an almost inevitable sharpening of focus upon what goes on in and out of the classroom. This is a focus on new pedagogy, a domain which has not been prominent in recent secondary school initiatives, but forms the locus of a new programme of work. (Paul Hamlyn Foundation and the Innovation Unit, p. 3)

Innovators in the United States and abroad have adopted a new pedagogy—project-based learning (PBL), coupled with performance assessment—as the best way to engage and challenge students and provide them with the learning experiences that lead to 21st century knowledge and skills.

Project- and Problem-Based Learning—Keys to 21st Century Learning

How do schools move, as Marc Prensky urges, from "telling/lecturing" to the "'new' pedagogy of kids teaching themselves with the teacher's guidance" (Prensky, 2008)? According to Paul Curtis, chief academic officer for the New Technology Foundation, what is needed is "a new type of instruction that better reflects the goals we want each student to achieve, demonstrate, and document" (Pearlman, 2006).

Since 2001, the New Technology Foundation (NTF), based in Napa, California, has helped fifty-one communities in ten states launch and implement 21st century high schools based on the model and practices of New Technology High School in Napa, California. The New Tech network's experience is that students best work, produce, and construct knowledge through project-based learning (PBL).

The Buck Institute of Education, which shares the same rigorous PBL methodology as NTF, defines standards-focused PBL as "a systematic teaching method that engages students in learning knowledge and skills through an extended inquiry process structured around complex, authentic questions and carefully designed products and tasks" (Buck Institute of Education, 2003).

Projects at New Tech schools are typically one to three weeks long. New Tech teachers start each unit by introducing students to a realistic, real-world project that both engages their interest and generates a list of information students need to know. Projects are designed to tackle complex problems, requiring critical thinking. Some examples of projects include presenting a plan to Congress on solving the oil crisis, or inventing, under contract from NASA, new sports that astronauts can play on the moon so they can get exercise.

Innovators in the United States and abroad have adopted a new pedagogy— project-based learning (PBL), coupled with performance assessment— as the best way to engage and challenge students and provide them with the learning experiences that lead to 21st century knowledge and skills.

Through projects, New Tech teachers are able to embed all the learner outcomes (content and 21st century skills) and assess against them. Learner outcomes are the same across all subjects and inter-disciplinary courses. Projects have associated rubrics for content, collaboration, written communication, oral communication, critical thinking, and so on, and are all posted online for students so they can decide on their own whether to achieve basic, proficient, or advanced work.

Assessment for Learning

Effective assessment for learning provides students with just-in-time information about their own learning and links it to information on the criteria needed to do better. At New Tech schools, students access an online grade portal. Grades on projects and all learner outcomes are updated whenever new assessment information is available. The usual composite course grades are also available per subject, and across courses for the skills of the learner outcomes. Students and their parents can look at their grades anytime, from anywhere.

Self-assessment is a critical element of assessment for learning. Students look at their grades on a daily basis and check the online rubrics for a project's criteria for basic, proficient, and advanced work. By making the assessment criteria transparent and understandable, students are then able to make their own decisions about what performance target or level they wish to accomplish. Such just-in-time feedback, coupled with the assessment criteria, provides students with the information needed to foster self-directed behaviors.

Self-assessment is a critical element of assessment for learning.

At the end of a project, student teams present to an external audience of community experts and parents. They are assessed on their product and on their communication skills (oral and written). New Tech students also assess their team members on their collaboration skills and get to see how their peers assessed them on their collaboration skills. They also write reflections on what they learned and how the project can be improved.

From Innovative Pedagogy to Innovative School Facilities

Schools must embrace a new pedagogy today that will engage 21st century students and enable them to acquire and master 21st century skills. Once they embrace the necessary changes in pedagogy, they realize the need for change in the physical learning environment. "Instead of starting from the physical, you need to start with the program you know you need to have," says Betty Despenza-Green, former principal of the Chicago Vocational Career Academy. "Then you can see how your existing structure won't let you do that. And then you do the work of making physical changes" (Davidson, 2001).

Elliot Washor (2003) urges school developers to "translate pedagogical designs into facilities" (p. 22). Kenn Fisher, director of learning environments at Rubida Research, links pedagogy and space for the design of new learning environments (Fisher, 2005). Fisher further divides pedagogy into five distinct aspects: delivering, applying, creating, communicating, and decision making, all of which inform the new environments.

Designing 21st century schools and new learning environments starts with defining the outcomes. We must ask, "What knowledge and skills do students need for the 21st century?" But real design needs to go much further and address the following questions as well:

- What pedagogy, curricula, activities, and experiences foster 21st century learning?

- What assessments for learning, both school-based and national, foster student learning of the outcomes, student engagement, and self-direction?

- How can technology support the pedagogy, curricula, and assessments of a 21st century collaborative learning environment?

- What physical learning environments (classroom, school, and real world) foster 21st century student learning?

After defining these outcomes, the key design issues might be illustrated as depicted in Figure 6.1.

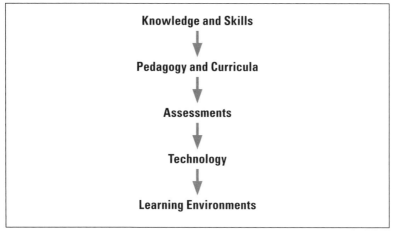

Figure 6.1: Design criteria for 21st century collaborative learning environments.

What Does 21st Century Learning Look Like?

Walk into a classroom in any school in any country today and what you will mainly see is teacher-directed whole-group instruction. Walk into a classroom at a New Technology High School and you will see *students at work* on their own learning—students writing journals online, doing research on the Internet, meeting in groups to plan and make their websites and their digital media presentations, and evaluating their peers for collaboration and presentation skills.

Walk into a classroom in any school in any country today and what you will mainly see is teacher-directed whole-group instruction.

Another teacher's students are also there, in a team-taught interdisciplinary course.

This classroom learning environment looks a lot different. It's double the size with a double group of students, two teachers, and a double-block period for an interdisciplinary course. The classroom is populated by worktables and rolling chairs, not individual student desks. Every student has access to a desktop or a laptop. The tables can be put together as needed for collaborative student project groups, or for teachers-led workshops or seminars constructed around student "need to knows." The classroom, or student workroom, can also serve as a design workshop or even as a space for end-of-project student presentations. The classroom can be set up to accommodate project teams, seminars, or workshops for some of the students while others continue working.

There is also a lot of glass. Glass walls or large glass windows make visible to the students and to visiting adults that this is a school where all students are at work.

Gareth Long (n.d.), a U.K.-based senior consultant on new secondary schools and school learning environments, writes on his work developing new secondary campuses in the Cayman Islands:

> The new learning environments being built are designed to promote total agilty *[sic]* and be capable of continuously reconfiguring themselves. They will allow project based learning rather than discipline based learning and will able teachers to respond to the "blurring" between phases and specific subjects. The ongoing trend towards longer lessons and interdisciplinary coursework reduces the need for student movement and increased effective use of spaces to allow for a variety of teaching and learning styles. They are also being designed for 24/7/360 use.

What Do Students Say?

In the United Kingdom, much work has been done to solicit student input into the design process for new or renovated secondary schools.[1] This student input has been inspired by "The school I'd like" (Birket,

---

[1] U.K. secondary schools go from year 7 to year 11 and sometimes include years 12 and 13.

2001), a national essay competition by *The Guardian*, for students across the United Kingdom (done in 1967 and 2001), followed by the books of the same name (Blishen, 1969; Burke & Grosvenor, 2003).

In the Knowsley Metropolitan Borough Council near Liverpool in North West England, during April to June 2005, School Works managed a participatory project involving local school communities in the design of eight new learning centers. Student participants identified key ways in which they learn:

- Looking
- Concentrating
- Thinking ahead
- Matching/comparing
- Creativity

- Listening
- Searching
- Negotiating
- Teamwork
- Learning

Knowsley's conclusion from student input and also from teacher and parent input was that pedagogy had to change to enable these learning modes, and that new learning environments and facilities should support these new modes (School Works, 2005).

Kids who have experienced the new pedagogy are even more emphatic in understanding their learning functions and the form that their learning environments need to take. Students from New Technology High School in Napa, California, commented on the design of a classroom of the future as participants with SHW Group architects in the 2009 Open Architecture Challenge (Open Architecture Network, 2008):

> *Colin:* To really be engaged, I need to have an interactive environment where I feel connected to others but can find a place to get away and think, too. I need easy access to all of the tools I might want to use for learning. I need to be able to adjust the space to be more comfortable and to fit the activities we are doing.

> *Zaira:* During project-based learning, we move through a variety of activities. We start with forming our teams and analyzing the problem. Then, we determine what we need to know and how to get the information. We have the research

phases, problem-solving phases, and presentation phases. For all of these activities, we need specific tools and need to be able to arrange the space accordingly. In addition, different teams are in different phases at different times, so we need the flexibility to have a variety of options in the same classroom.

"No More Classrooms!": The Language of School Design

"Classrooms are out! No more classrooms! Don't build them," says Roger Schank, founder of the Institute for Learning Sciences at Northwestern University (Fielding, 1999). Schank sees three key student work modes: computer work, talk with others, and making something. These modes, he argues, require three distinct environments for learning: focused work environments, collaborative work environments, and hands-on project work environment.

Innovators no longer speak of classrooms. Instead they have changed the language in order to change the mental model, as urged by Elliot Washor and also Randall Fielding and Prakash Nair of DesignShare and Fielding Nair International. Fielding and Nair are coauthors with Jeffrey Lackney of *The Language of School Design: Design Patterns for 21st Century Schools* (2005), a book that has strongly influenced new design in many countries. Students now work in learning studios, learning plazas, and home bases. They shift as needed into many varied extended learning areas and collaboration zones. These include project-planning rooms, workrooms, and other breakout areas.

Kenn Fisher (2005) translates pedagogy into many learning spaces: the student home base, the collaboration incubator, storage space, specialized and focused labs, project space and wet areas, outdoor learning space, display space, breakout space, the individual pod, group learning space, presentation space, and teacher meeting space. Most innovative schools still feature specialized classrooms for making things, including art, engineering, media, and design labs.

Classrooms, libraries, and labs used to be the only spaces where students spent their school hours. Wireless, laptops, and project learning have changed that. Until a few years ago, laptops were not powerful enough to handle high-level applications. Likewise, wireless was not powerful enough to handle continuous Internet access by even a small school of four hundred students in a one-to-one environment. Now it is. This has transformed all school spaces into potential extended learning areas, even the corridors and alcoves.

Technology in 21st Century Schools

The signature characteristic of 21st century schools is *students at work*. Pedagogy—a project-based curriculum and companion performance assessment—enables this new shape of schooling. But it is technology and new learning environments that support this new collaborative culture.

Students utilize new technology tools as investigators and producers of knowledge. The best 21st century schools provide every student with a computer, which increasingly means a laptop in a wireless environment. But personal computing by itself without the new pedagogy and learning environments, even when it is one computer for each student, is no solution at all. It doesn't work. Instead it often reinforces the old teacher-directed whole-group instruction.

> The signature characteristic of 21st century schools is *students at work.*

Students in 21st century schools first use computers and Internet access to research their projects. They find the information they need through Internet research, but also through email communication and Skype video interviews of experts. Then, working individually or in a collaborative team, they construct products—models, booklets, videos, podcasts, websites, PowerPoints, digital portfolios, and so on. Finally, they utilize technology to present their findings, often to an authentic audience of community experts.

Computers, cameras, and interactive whiteboards all come to life as student tools in a 21st century PBL classroom. Newer Web 2.0 tools—including blogs, wikis, and social networking sites—add greatly to the student toolset for individual and collaborative work. Students utilize all these tools to be investigators and producers of knowledge.

However, equipping students with appropriate technology and tools is the beginning, not the end. They also need 24/7 access to their project information, project calendar, assessment rubrics, and their just-in-time assessments. If

> Equipping students with appropriate technology and tools is the beginning, not the end.

they work in collaborative teams, they also need discussion boards, journals, email, and special evaluation tools.

The original New Tech High School in Napa, begun in 1996, built all these special technology tools and implemented them on a Lotus Notes platform. The New Technology Foundation took these tools and professionalized them into the New Tech High Learning System, a learning management system or learning platform specially designed for PBL schools. Since 2008, New Tech has developed that platform into a Web portal called PeBL. PeBL includes the online grade portal. The PeBL learning platform also provides teachers with the tools to design projects, assessments, and calendars and post them online for student access.

The New Learning Environments

New learning environments are needed to support technology-equipped students at work both individually and in collaborative teams, and to provide environments for what Roger Schank calls "focused work, collaborative work, hands-on project work," and for presentation and exhibition (Fielding, 1999).

There has been significant work on these issues by DesignShare and architects Randall Fielding, Prakash Nair, and Bruce Jilk in the United States, and by many parties in the United Kingdom, including the Partnership for Schools (PfS), the British Council on the School Environment (BCSE), the Specialist Trust, the Innovation Unit, and many individual architects and educators.

Five schools in the United States and the United Kingdom exemplify the best of the new learning environments. Each is original in its design and features:

- Columbus Signature Academy, Columbus, Indiana
- New Tech High @ Coppell, Coppell, Texas
- The Metropolitan Regional Career and Technical Center, Providence, Rhode Island
- High Tech High, San Diego, California
- New Line Learning Academy, South Maidstone Federation, Maidstone, Kent, England

Columbus Signature Academy

Columbus, Indiana, a small city forty-six miles south of Indianapolis, boasts the third-greatest assemblage of public and private architecture in the United States, behind New York City and Chicago. Years ago the CEO of Cummins Engine established a fund to support the architecture fees for all buildings built in the city, as long as the commissions went to a list of the ten top architects in the country.

The Bartholomew Consolidated School Corporation (BCSC) has benefited from this funding and the concomitant community spirit. BCSC hired CSO Architects, based in Indianapolis, to work with local educators to develop the new Columbus Signature Academy, launched in 2008 and built in two phases. The academy's program was to be modeled on that of New Tech High School, featuring project-based learning, collaborative teams, authentic assessment, and one-to-one computing. The story of the design process is captured by CSO in three videos available at www.csoinc.net/?q=node/172 (CSO Architects, 2008; for live links and to view graphics from this chapter in full color, visit go.solution-tree.com/21stcenturyskills).

Representatives from CSO visited four sites in California to see the actual implementation of the New Tech curriculum. The original New Tech High School in Napa has two distinct design characteristics that have been emulated in some form by all New Tech schools across the country. The first is the classroom footprint: it is typically double-sized, housing a double group of students in a two-teacher, team-taught interdisciplinary class in a double-block period (see the feature box on page 130 for examples of these interdisciplinary courses). Figure 6.2 (page 130) shows students in a learning studio at Columbus Signature Academy.

The second signature design characteristic is either no walls or glass walls separating classrooms from corridors and breakout spaces. This means that students and adult visitors walking the corridors can see what is going on everywhere. What they see are students at work on their projects. Recent projects have included projects on volcanoes, mitosis videos, electronic games, and motorized toys. This helps establish the collaborative culture of the school. (See figure 6.3, page 131, a 3-D floor plan of Columbus Signature Academy.)

**Examples of Team-Taught Interdisiplinary
Classes at New Tech High Schools**

Global Issues: English and Geography

World Studies: English and World History

American Studies: English and U.S. History

Political Studies: English, U.S. Government, Economics

Scientific Studies: Physics and Algebra 2

BioLit: Biology and Literature

Environmental Studies: Environmental Science and Environmental Issues

Biotechnology Ethics: Biology and Psychology

The CSO team, which included John Rigsbee and Rosemary Rehak, was especially inspired by a dinner meeting with Ted Fujimoto, who as a young business leader in Napa was one of the founders of New Tech High. "We asked Ted what should be done differently," recounted Rigsbee. "His response: 'Fewer barriers. Like a corporate office. Collaborative office space. Teachers as project managers'" (personal communication, June 8, 2009).

Rigsbee continued, "We saw students work as a project team, then break loose and work as individuals. This describes our architect's office, our design studios. That's why we decided not to use the word *classroom* anymore. Instead we now call all these spaces *studios.*"

Figure 6.2: A learning studio for an integrated interdisciplinary class at Columbus Signature Academy. Reprinted with permission.

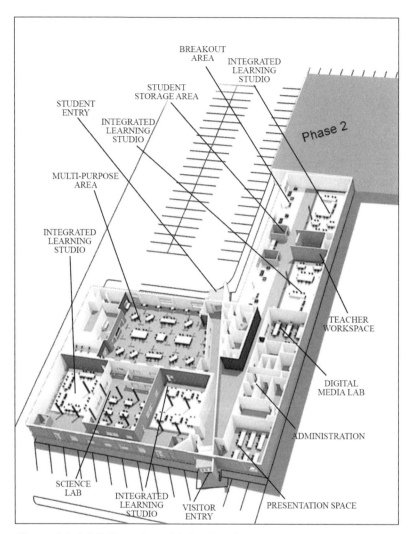

Figure 6.3: A 3-D floor plan of Columbus Signature Academy showing a double-sized integrated learning studio, presentation room, and multipurpose commons area. Drawing by CSO Architects. Reprinted with permission.

On their return, they brainstormed with BCSC personnel to plan the transformation of an auto parts warehouse into a model New Tech High campus. At 44,812 square feet, the academy is designed for four hundred students.

CSO designed these unique learning environments with integrated learning studios, breakout areas, distance learning and presentation rooms, and project conference rooms for preparing presentations. There are specialty labs for science and graphic media. They also designed a large multipurpose room to serve as a cafeteria and commons area, and to house large-group meetings and presentations, science fairs, and student exhibitions.

CSO wanted as few walls as possible in the new building, so learning studios do not have a fourth wall and instead are open on one end with breakout spaces, which are used for informal individual and small-group work.

Phase two will add more integrated learning studios and more specialty labs, including for engineering. "We know so much more now," says Rigsbee. "Our original plan was that students would go back to regular high schools for art, music, and physical education/fitness. Now students want their own specialty rooms, which we hope to provide in the phase two development."

Furniture is also unique to allow studios to be arranged flexibly for large-group, small-group, or individual work as needed. Studios feature rolling tables and chairs. Tables flip up for post-its and other displays.

New Tech High @ Coppell

At New Tech High @ Coppell, Coppell, Texas, a new small high school launched in 2008, there are no students and no teachers. Instead, *learners* fill the classrooms and project rooms and are supported in their work by *facilitators*. The school has adopted a new language to describe the new roles of both students and teachers. Students are now learners responsible for their own learning; teachers are now facilitators, responsible for designing projects and assessments and guiding and coaching learners and learner teams on their project work.

Learners at New Tech High @ Coppell have a vast array of technology tools and learning spaces in which to do their work. (See figure 6.4, a student project team at work in the open space media library at New Tech High @ Coppell; to view images in full color, visit go.solution-tree.com/21stcenturyskills.) Learners say it is "more professional here" and "we have a big advantage over students at other schools" (personal communication, June 1, 2009). Other learners made the following comments:

Figure 6.4: A student project team at work in the open space media library at New Tech High @ Coppell. Reprinted with permission.

Courtney: We have a big advantage going into the professional world.

Morgan: My brother-in-law does the same stuff at work.

Claire: My Dad really got into giving me ideas on my project on the green revolution and hybrid cars.

Coppell Independent School District worked with SHW Group architects to renovate an old elementary school into the New Tech High @ Coppell. The following text describes these renovations:

In order to maximize the potential of the learners in the project-based model, the design had to accommodate a radical shift from the classroom layout in the existing elementary school, while recognizing a very modest budget. By strategically removing walls in some locations and opening up others with glass, the spaces transformed from stand-and-deliver classrooms, to energized multi-use spaces for collaboration and teaming that allowed the learners to engage in a variety of activities using wireless internet and moveable furniture.

To build on the educational initiatives of collaboration and transparency in the learning process, certain rooms open out to hallways and, in some cases, glass was inserted into existing walls so that visitors, learners, and facilitators can see the processes at work. Visitors to New Tech High @

Coppell might feel more like they are in an art gallery or a high-end book store or café than a typical classroom building.[2]

SHW Group developed spaces throughout the building to provide settings for individual, small-group, and large-group interations. SHW called these settings small-group collaboration zones, project rooms, facilitator collaboration zones, single subject-matter learning environments, dual subject-matter learning environments, a digital media library, and large multigroup collaboration zones. (See figure 6.5, distinct activity zones at New Tech High @ Coppell.)

The designers took advantage of the planned robust wireless environment (both inside and outside) and the plan to issue every student a laptop for school and home use and made every space in the building external to the "classrooms" an extended learning area:

- Corridors—Learners and learner teams sit in the corridors to do their work.

- Alcoves—Student work groups use these little corner areas with soft furniture.

- Project planning rooms—Project teams plan their work and presentations in these small conference rooms with whiteboards. Learners call these spaces *workrooms*. New Tech High @ Coppell was the first New Tech High in the country to have small project planning rooms. Phase two of the construction added additional and bigger project planning rooms.

- Media library—Learners and learner teams do their work in this large area of open space with lots of comfortable furniture and some high-end equipment. (See figure 6.6, page 136, a picture of the digital media library at New Tech High @ Coppell.)

The single or dual subject-matter learning environments, which are characteristic of the New Tech model, provide spaces for large group, small group, or individual work, and can be repurposed for any working modality, or "interaction type," using flexible tables and

---

[2] From SHW Group's project narrative submission to the Council of Educational Facility Planners International for the 2009 James D. MacConnell Award.

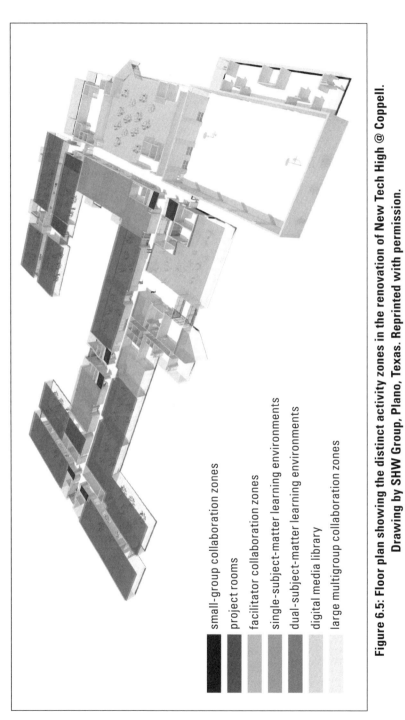

Figure 6.5: Floor plan showing the distinct activity zones in the renovation of New Tech High @ Coppell. Drawing by SHW Group, Plano, Texas. Reprinted with permission.

- small-group collaboration zones
- project rooms
- facilitator collaboration zones
- single-subject-matter learning environments
- dual-subject-matter learning environments
- digital media library
- large multigroup collaboration zones

Figure 6.6: Student collaborative project teams working in the digital media library at New Tech High @ Coppell. Reprinted with permission.

chairs. Because New Tech High @ Coppell is fully wireless, with 100 percent laptop and battery bays in every room, the rooms have few dangling power cords or other obstructions.

The Metropolitan Regional Career and Technical Center

The Metropolitan Regional Career and Technical Center (The Met) was founded in 1996 in Providence, Rhode Island, by Dennis Littky and Elliot Washor. The initial school site for one hundred students was housed in a downtown building. A second small Met of one hundred students opened in 1999 in a remarkable facility that includes classroom workrooms, project rooms, advisory rooms, and a large common room. Four additional small schools opened in 2002 on a common campus using a similar facility design for each small school.

Each one-hundred-student site (small school) at the Met has eight teachers in four learning groups and eight advisory groups. The small size is aimed at personalizing student learning. A key slogan and practice at the Met is "One kid at a time." Students are organized into advisories of fifteen individuals at the same grade level, led by an advisor who stays with them through their four years.

At the Met, the curriculum is Learning Through Interests/ Internships (LTIs). Students work with expert mentors in the real world, two days a week, in internships that are based on the students' interests, and come to school the other days to reflect on what they are learning on the job and work on their projects. Students work with their parents, teacher/advisor, and workplace mentor to develop their own personal learning plan. Popular LTI sites include the Audubon Society, New England Aquarium, hospitals, theater companies, law firms, architecture firms, multimedia companies, and more. To the Met, LTI sites are part of their facilities. The school site is designed to support students working on their LTIs.

Classrooms/workrooms have state-of-the-art computers, peripherals, and presentation technologies for students to do their work and exhibit it. Workrooms also have tools for making scale models, structures, and products for exhibition. Students do projects related to their LTIs. One student worked on a team to develop a 2,400-square-foot museum exhibit, another developed a brochure for new mothers in the neonatal unit at a hospital, and another student did a video project that documented the work of the radiology department at a local hospital.

There are now more than sixty Met schools across the United States and many more internationally. Big Picture cofounder Elliot Washor has been the conceptual architect of the Met design. He identified key elements and functions of the school building: "We needed spaces for individual work, one-on-one, small group, advisory, large space, to make stuff, and to display student work," Washor recalled (personal communication, June 8, 2009). The second Met building was then designed to include a commons, advisory rooms, project rooms shared by two advisories, conference rooms, meeting rooms, and wet lab space for art and science.

At the Public Street Met Campus, four distinct Met schools, each in their own distinct two-story building, share facilities (theater performance center and fitness center) across a campus. In the separate two-story buildings, the commons resides on the first floor and doubles as a cafeteria and an informal workspace. The advisory rooms are larger, now incorporating much of what the separate project rooms served in the past (see figure 6.7, a Met advisory room, on page 138). In addition, the second-story commons serves as an informal and purposeful workspace. (See figure 6.8, a floor plan of the Public Street Met buildings, on page 139.)

Learning environments are characterized by demountable walls, advisory rooms, project rooms, commons, meeting rooms, and more storage space for student projects. These spaces are intended to provide a variety of options for students: quiet space, meeting space, commons space, and advisory space.

Furniture also supports individual and group work. Soft, cushioned seats are dispersed throughout. Chairs move up and down, conform to the contours of the body, and feature sled bottoms or gliders.

Future Met schools, says Washor, will likely include garage-door openings to workrooms and rooms for artists in residence in blacksmithing, metallurgy, pottery making, and other arts, crafts, and specialized technologies. Currently, Met schools find comfortable settings for these activities in the community.

Figure 6.7: Advisory room at the Met doubles as project room for Met students. Reprinted with permission.

High Tech High

High Tech High, San Diego, California, is a public charter high school launched in 2000 with a diverse student population of four hundred students that mirrors the San Diego Unified School District. High Tech High brings to life its design principles of personalization, intellectual mission, adult world immersion, and performance-based student work and assessment through its size and school organization, facilities, program, and technology.

High Tech High is now nine schools in the San Diego region, six in a family of schools (elementary, middle, and high school) in San

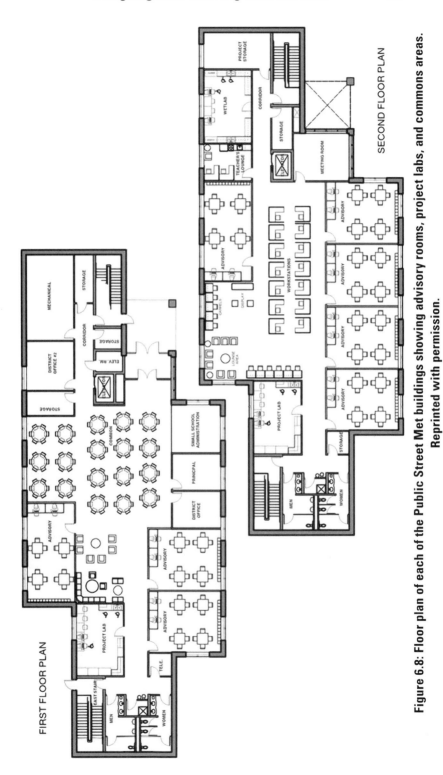

Figure 6.8: Floor plan of each of the Public Street Met buildings showing advisory rooms, project labs, and commons areas. Reprinted with permission.

Diego, a high school and middle school in North County, California, and a new high school in Chula Vista, California.

David Stephen, the conceptual architect for High Tech High, San Diego, working with the Stickler Group and Carrier Johnson, notes that "the original design sought to provide students with personal and small-group workspaces, use of technology, and a high-performance workspace. Key functions were inquiry-based learning, content delivery plus independent investigation, and building and fabricating things" (personal communication, June 8, 2009).

High Tech High originally featured seminar rooms, labs, project studios, small and large conference rooms, a commons area, and a great room. The great room had workstations and collaborative spaces for students. Stephen notes that "we moved away from the great room concept very quickly" because:

> We needed the student workstations and workspaces to be much nearer the classrooms. Now our basic model is a set of four to six classrooms with glass walls clustered around a centralized studio work area for multipurpose activities, including presentations, student project work, fabrications, and so on. (personal communication, June 8, 2009)

In the middle school, says Stephen, classrooms are clustered in a neighborhood concept (see figure 6.9, a cluster area studio surrounded by four flexible classrooms at High Tech Middle).

Figure 6.9: Cluster area studio surrounded by four flexible classrooms at High Tech Middle, San Diego, California. Photo by Bill Robinson. Reprinted with permission.

Wireless technologies and laptops have made a difference. In the new High Tech High in Chula Vista, four classrooms are clustered around a common studio work area (see the video of the new Chula Vista campus at www.hightechhigh.org/dc/index.php). Each classroom is separated by a removable wall to another classroom to enable team teaching by two teachers. (See figure 6.10, a floor plan of High Tech Middle, which is now common in High Tech High buildings as well.) Each classroom has thirteen laptops for student use, and students can bring their own laptops to school.

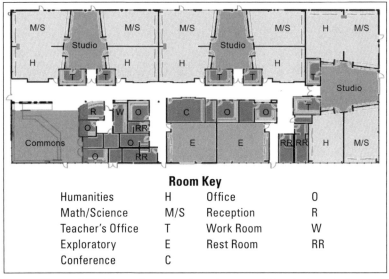

Room Key

Humanities	H	Office	0
Math/Science	M/S	Reception	R
Teacher's Office	T	Work Room	W
Exploratory	E	Rest Room	RR
Conference	C		

Figure 6.10: Floor plan showing clusters of four integrated classes surrounding a studio area at High Tech Middle. Drawing by David Stephen. Reprinted with permission.

"It's all about ownership," says Stephen. "Kids and teachers need a sense of place . . . where everyone knows one another." The commons provides a place for whole-school gatherings, student presentations, and an informal student work area.

Project studios have also evolved over the years. Originally these were separate from the seminar rooms; now every classroom includes the functionality of a project room. Specialized labs, what High Tech High calls "exploratories," include biotechnology, engineering or "fabrication," art, music, multimedia, and digital arts. "Furniture is really key," says Stephen. "It helps to turn atriums, corridors, and alcoves into work areas for individual students and for project teams."

New Line Learning Academy

One of the most interesting new learning environments comes from school innovator Chris Gerry, executive principal of the South Maidstone Federation in Maidstone, Kent, England. The county of Kent, which lies east of London and runs all the way to the English Channel, is the largest local authority in the country, with over six hundred schools. Gerry was formerly principal at Hugh Christie Technology College, where he first grouped ninety students engaged in project-based learning in a large open space, which he now calls a learning plaza.

Gerry is opening new buildings for New Line Learning (NLL) Academy and Cornwallis Academy in 2010 and refining his ideas in a pilot site developed by architect Philip Gillard of Gensler, a global architecture, design, planning, and consulting firm. The heart of the design is a learning plaza large enough to house ninety or 120 students. (See the animated plaza video at www.newlinelearning .com/new-builds/view/146/New-build-at-NLL-Academy or visit go.solution-tree.com/21stcenturyskills for direct links and full-color graphics.) Modular and mobile lecture-style seating is used to accommodate larger groups and divide plaza space. Each academy will house eight learning plazas. (See figure 6.11, the learning plaza prototype at New Line Learning Academy.) According to Gensler (2009):

> The "Plaza" concept was devised with the Academy to provide a higher degree of collaboration between teachers and pupils through an IT rich, flexible environment that promotes and enables a variety of static and fluid learning settings to occur simultaneously within the physical fabric—from individual personalised learning, to group based activities and a whole plaza scenario of 120 pupils—whilst providing a safe and secure home base. [The concept utilizes] technology such as 360° projection and large display areas, biometric lighting techniques to control and vary the ambience of individual spaces, and flexible and adaptable furniture to allow a variety of work mode settings orientated around sizes of user groups and activities being undertaken.

Figure 6.11: The learning plaza prototype at New Line Learning Academy shows the plaza divided in multiple ways for large-group, small-group, and individual learning. Reprinted with permission.

Gensler adopted a new language, adapted from Nair, Fielding, and Lackney (2005), to describe the different activity modes that take place in each environment and the degree of collaboration involved:

- Multiple intelligence—Allows for different work modes
- Studio—Allows for a mix of different work modes
- Campfire—Allows for class work
- Watering hole—Allows for small-group work
- Cave—Allows for self-study

Due to the pervasive technology and the flexible furniture, the plaza can be set up in many different configurations to aid the learning process. Furniture includes modular tables and mobile lecture-style amphitheater seating to accommodate larger groups and divide plaza space. The learning plaza incorporates a ground floor, a mezzanine, and an outdoor area. The plaza ground floor provides spaces for project-based learning, group work, lectures, and has breakout areas and a vestibule. The plaza mezzanine provides spaces for independent learning, small-group work, a balcony for spectators of project-based learning, and an outdoor classroom. In addition to the learning plaza, there are specialist plazas that contain specialty equipment for art, technology, and science.

New Learning Environments for Students at Work

What do all have these new learning environments have in common? There is much in common among the physical designs discussed here. All these schools do PBL, though the practice is different in all. Each design seeks to provide spaces for individual work, small-group work, large-group work, lectures, presentations, breakouts, and whole-school or cluster meetings. Table 6.1 summarizes the main features of each school.

Linking Pedagogy and Space

Most new school building construction in the United States and the United Kingdom today is still pouring "old wine into new bottles," replicating the 30-student, 900-square-foot classrooms that both support and often dictate teacher-directed whole-group instruction. These environments will not support student learning of 21st century skills and will be seen in the coming years as outmoded learning spaces requiring a building retrofit.

As school planners look to implement 21st century skills, they will increasingly link pedagogy and space and look to exemplars like Columbus Signature Academy, New Tech High @ Coppell, the Met, High Tech High, and New Line Learning Academy. These designs will be widely emulated and the experience of students, or learners, in these environments will inform the next generation of 21st century learning environment design.

Table 6.1: New Learning Environments in U.S. and U.K. Innovative Schools

	Columbus Signature Academy	New Tech High @ Coppell	The Met	High Tech High	New Line Learning Academy
Primary Student Work Area	Learning studio	Dual subject-matter learning environment	Advisory/project room	Clustered classroom/common studio	Learning plaza
Presentation Space	Presentation room	Large multigroup collaboration zones	Commons	Commons	Learning plaza
Large-Group Space	Multipurpose room	Large multigroup collaboration zones	Commons	Commons	Learning plaza
Extended Learning Spaces	Breakout area and project conference room	Corridor alcoves, project planning rooms, media library, and outdoor benches	Conference rooms, meeting rooms, and commons	Small and large conference rooms, common studios, and commons	Learning plaza, watering holes, and caves
Specialty Labs	Graphic, media, and science labs	Science	Fabrication	Biotech, engineering, art, music, multimedia, and digital arts	Art, technology, and science
Furniture	Rolling tables and chairs, and flip-up tables	Mix-and-match tables, office chairs, lounge chairs, and sofas in extended learning spaces	Cushioned seats, contour chairs, and flexible tables	Benches in extended learning spaces	Modular tables and mobile lecture-style amphitheater seating

References

Birkett, D. (2001, January 16). The school I'd like. *The Guardian.* Accessed at www.guardian.co.uk/guardianeducation/story/0,3605,422486,00.html on January 3, 2009.

Blishen, E. (Ed.). (1969). *The school that I'd like.* Baltimore: Penguin.

Buck Institute of Education. (2003). *Project based learning handbook.* Accessed at http://www.bie.org/index.php/site/PBL/pbl_handbook_introduction/#standards on January 3, 2009.

Burke, C., & Grosvenor, I. (2003). *School I'd like: Children and young people's reflections on an education for the 21st century.* London: RoutledgeFalmer.

CSO Architects. (2008). *K–12 Education: Columbus Signature Academy New Tech High. Episode one, two, and three.* Accessed at www.csoinc.net/?q=node/172 on December 18, 2009.

Davidson, J. (2001). Innovative school design for small learning communities. *Horace, 18*(1). Accessed at www.essentialschools.org/cs/resources/view/ces_res/208 on January 3, 2009.

Fielding, R. (1999). The death of the classroom, learning cycles, and Roger Schank. Accessed at www.designshare.com/index.php/articles/death-of-the-classroom/ on January 3, 2009.

Fisher, K. (2005). *Linking pedagogy and space.* Melbourne, Victoria, Australia: Department of Education and Training. Accessed at www.eduweb.vic.gov.au/edulibrary/public/assetman/bf/Linking_Pedagogy_and_Space.pdf on January 3, 2009.

Gensler design firm. (2009). *Brief, design, and prototype: South Maidstone Academies, Kent, UK.* London: Author.

Hertfordshire Grid for Learning. (2009). *Building schools for the future—Introduction.* Accessed at www.thegrid.org.uk/leadership/bsf/intro.shtml on January 3, 2009.

Kelly, F. S., McCain, T., & Jukes, I. (2009). *Teaching the digital generation: No more cookie-cutter high schools.* Thousand Oaks, CA: Corwin Press.

Long, G. (n.d.). Schools of the future. *Gareth Long—Education blog.* Accessed at http://garethl.com/29501.html on January 3, 2009.

Long, G. (2009, February 14). Student voice—thinking about learning environments. *Gareth Long—Education blog.* Accessed at http://blog.garethl.com/2009/02/student-voice-thinking-about-learning.html on December 18, 2009.

Nair, P., Fielding, R., & Lackney, J. (2005). *The language of school design: Design patterns for 21st century schools* (2nd ed.). Minneapolis, MN: DesignShare. Accessed at www.designshare.com/index.php/language-school-design on May 1, 2005.

Open Architecture Challenge. (2008). *2009 open architecture challenge: Classroom.* Accessed at www.openarchitecturenetwork.org/competitions/challenge/2009 on December 18, 2009.

Partnership for 21st Century Skills. (2003). *Learning for the 21st century.* Tuscon, AZ: Author.

Paul Hamlyn Foundation and the Innovation Unit. (2008). *Learning futures: Next practice in learning and teaching.* London: Authors. Accessed at www .innovation-unit.co.uk/images/stories/files/pdf/learningfutures_booklet .pdf on January 3, 2009.

Pearlman, B. (2006). 21st century learning in schools: A case study of New Technology High School. *New Directions for Youth Development, 110.* Accessed at www.bobpearlman.org/Articles/21stCenturyLearning.htm on January 3, 2009.

Prensky, M. (2001, October). Digital natives, digital immigrants. *On the Horizon, 9*(5), 1–6. Accessed at www.marcprensky.com/writing/Prensky - Digital Natives, Digital Immigrants - Part1.pdf on January 3, 2009.

Prensky, M. (2008, November/December). The role of technology in teaching and the classroom. *Educational Technology, 48*(6), 64.

Secretary's Commission on Achieving Necessary Skills. (1991, June). *What work requires of schools: A SCANS report for America 2000.* Washington, DC: U.S. Department of Labor.

School Works. (2005). *Knowsley school design festival: Learning centres for the future—Final report.* Accessed at www.knowsley.gov.uk/PDF/Design _Festival_Report.pdf on January 3, 2009.

Tapscott, D. (1998). *Growing up digital: The rise of the net generation.* New York: Mcgraw-Hill.

Wagner, T. (2008). *The global achievement gap: Why even our best schools don't teach the new survival skills our children need—and what we can do about it.* New York: Basic Books.

Washor, E. (2003). *Innovative pedagogy and school facilities.* Minneapolis, MN: DesignShare.

Watson, S. L., & Reigeluth, C. M. (2008, September/October). The learner-centered paradigm of education. *Educational Technology, 38*(5), 42–48.

Jay McTighe

Jay McTighe, Ed.D., is the coauthor of ten books, including the best-selling *Understanding by Design* series with Grant Wiggins. He has written more than thirty articles and book chapters and published in a number of leading journals, including *Educational Leadership* and *The Developer*. He served as director of the Maryland Assessment Consortium, a state collaboration of school districts developing formative performance assessments. McTighe is well known for his work with thinking skills, having coordinated statewide efforts to develop instructional strategies, curriculum models, and assessment procedures for improving the quality of student thinking.

Elliott Seif

Elliott Seif, Ph.D., is currently an educational consultant, a member of the ASCD faculty and the Understanding by Design (UbD) cadre, and a UbD trainer. He also conducts program reviews for school districts. He has an MA in social science education from Harvard University and a Ph.D. in curriculum research from Washington University in Saint Louis. Seif was a social studies teacher, a professor of education at Temple University, and a director of curriculum and instruction services for the Bucks County (PA) Intermediate Unit. He is well known for his books, book chapters, articles, and studies on effective school practices, curriculum renewal, thinking skills development, standards-based education, and understanding-based approaches to teaching and learning.

In this chapter, McTighe and Seif examine how to infuse 21st century outcomes into the curriculum with an approach that takes advantage of the principles and practices of Understanding by Design.

Chapter 7

An Implementation Framework to Support 21st Century Skills

Jay McTighe and Elliott Seif

A growing number of voices within and outside the educational establishment are calling for an enhanced emphasis on "21st century outcomes"[1] that include "the knowledge, skill and expertise students should master to succeed in work and life in the 21st century" (Partnership for 21st Century Skills, 2009, p. 2). This call for a comprehensive focus on 21st century outcomes raises two important and practical questions for educators to ask:

1. How might we effectively infuse these outcomes into an already over-crowded curriculum?

2. Which current educational practices and school structures are likely to support the attainment of 21st century outcomes, and which may inhibit it?

To answer, we propose a framework for supporting 21st century learning that presents a systemic approach to educational reform, adapted from one found in *Schooling by Design* (Wiggins & McTighe, 2007). Figure 7.1 (page 150) shows a graphic representation of this

---

[1] For clarification of 21st century outcomes, see Kay (page xiii in this volume) and Dede (page 51 in this volume). These outcomes are also examined in some detail in *The Intellectual and Policy Foundations of the 21st Century Skills Framework* (n.d.), developed by the Partnership for 21st Century Skills (www.21stcenturypartnership.com).

framework, with essential questions linked to its five major, interrelated components: (1) the mission of schooling, (2) principles of learning, (3) a curriculum and assessment system, (4) instructional programs and practices, and (5) systemic support factors. We will examine each of these components and suggest ways that schools and districts can transform themselves to implement a viable approach to teaching and learning that results in 21st century skills acquisition for all students.

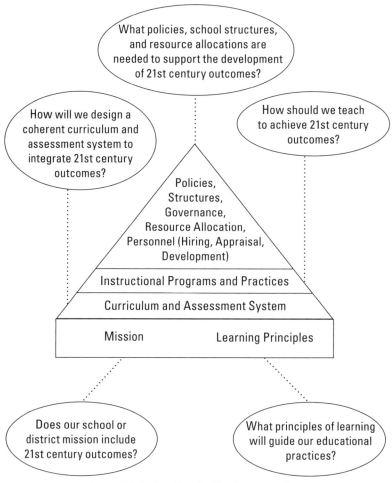

Figure 7.1: Schooling by Design organizer.

The Mission of Schooling

Does the school or district mission include 21st century outcomes?

A mission statement identifies the overall purpose of schooling and the kinds of graduates a school strives to develop. The best mission statements describe educational goals that are outcome—not input—oriented. Rather than specifying what the curriculum, learning environment, or extracurriculars will offer, a school or district mission should *overtly* articulate the 21st century knowledge, skills, habits of mind, and personal qualities to be cultivated in its learners.

In addition to their lack of focus on key learner outcomes, many district and school mission statements were crafted long ago and remain dormant, residing in a binder, on a website, or displayed through wall art. Such statements are empty words that have little or no impact on the daily operations of schooling. Even in cases where the educational mission is alive and influential, it may not identify a full range of 21st century outcomes. Given the centrality of a mission for an educational organization, we recommend that schools and districts, with the involvement of major constituencies, carefully examine and infuse key 21st century outcomes into their mission. These targeted capabilities and skills (for example, entrepreneurial literacy and global awareness) should be operationally defined, since precise outcomes will be needed to guide the development of appropriate curricula, assessments, and instructional practices to achieve them.

Principles of Learning

What principles of learning should guide educational practices in the 21st century?

Education is an enterprise devoted to learning. Thus, our work as educators should be guided by the most current understandings about the learning process. Since the last decade of the 20th century, research in cognitive psychology and neuroscience has significantly expanded our understanding of how people learn (see Bransford, Brown, & Cocking, 2000; Willis, 2006). Yet educational practice has not always kept pace with this new knowledge.

As a means of better aligning theory and practice, we recommend that schools and districts develop or adopt a set of learning principles based on research and best practices. Once in place, these principles provide a conceptual foundation for all school reform initiatives. As educators move to incorporate 21st century outcomes, learning principles will guide the development of the curriculum/assessment system and inform instructional practice and the selection of learning resources (such as textbooks and technology).

Figure 7.2 describes our own view of research-based learning principles, along with some of the implications of each principle for sound educational practice. We will use these learning principles to guide further discussion of the changes in curriculum, assessment, and instructional practices necessary to accommodate 21st century outcomes.

These first two components of the framework are foundational and linked. The mission defines the *what* of schooling, while the learning principles inform the *how*.

A Curriculum and Assessment System

How will we design a coherent curriculum and assessment system to integrate 21st century outcomes?

In a meta-analysis of the many factors that influence learning, noted educational researcher Robert Marzano (2003) found that the most important school-level factor impacting student achievement is a "guaranteed and viable curriculum." Marzano highlights the importance of building a curriculum that organizes a coordinated learning pathway *across* classrooms. This is especially important for the infusion of 21st century outcomes. Without an orchestrated design, the incorporation of designated skills, processes, and habits of mind will be predictably haphazard and unlikely to lead to the desired results. In other words, well-intentioned teachers working behind closed doors won't be able to guarantee a coherent curriculum of 21st century learning.

1. Learning is purposeful and contextual. *Therefore, students should be helped to see the purpose in what they are asked to learn. Learning should be framed by relevant questions, meaningful challenges, and authentic applications.*

2. Experts organize or chunk their knowledge around transferable core concepts ("big ideas") that guide their thinking about the domain and help them integrate new knowledge. *Therefore, content instruction should be framed in terms of core ideas and transferable processes, not as discrete facts and skills.*

3. Different types of thinking, such as classification and categorization, inferential reasoning, analysis, synthesis, and metacognition, mediate and enhance learning. *Therefore, learning events should engage students in complex thinking to deepen and apply their learning.*

4. Learners reveal and demonstrate their understanding when they can apply, transfer, and adapt their learning to new and novel situations and problems. *Therefore, teachers should teach for transfer, and students should have multiple opportunities to apply their learning in meaningful and varied contexts.*

5. New learning is built on prior knowledge. Learners use their experiences and background knowledge to actively construct meaning about themselves and the world around them. *Therefore, students must be helped to actively connect new information and ideas to what they already know.*

6. Learning is social. *Therefore, teachers should provide opportunities for interactive learning in a supportive environment.*

7. Attitudes and values mediate learning by filtering experiences and perceptions. *Therefore, teachers should help students make their attitudes and values explicit and understand how they influence learning.*

8. Learning is nonlinear; it develops and deepens over time. *Therefore, students should be involved in revisiting core ideas and processes so as to develop deeper and more sophisticated learning over time.*

9. Models of excellence and ongoing feedback enhance learning and performance. *Therefore, learners need to see models of excellent work and be provided with regular, timely, and user-friendly feedback in order to practice, retry, rethink, and revise their work.*

10. Effectively accommodating a learner's preferred learning style, prior knowledge, and interests enhances learning. *Therefore, teachers should pre-assess to find out students' prior knowledge, learning preference, and interests. They should differentiate their instruction to address the significant differences they discover.*

Figure 7.2: The principles of learning.

We believe that we need a different curriculum and assessment paradigm if 21st century outcomes are to be effectively integrated into the education system. This new curriculum and assessment system is built upon three operational guidelines:

1. Focus on the "big ideas" in core subjects and 21st century skills.

2. Assess valued outcomes in appropriate ways.

3. Map the curriculum backward from targeted transfer abilities.

Guideline One: Focus on "Big Ideas" in Core Subjects and 21st Century Skills

Nearly every teacher from preK to university level confronts the same challenge: too much content and not enough time to teach it all. The plethora of knowledge and skills identified in state and provincial standards documents can seem overwhelming, and the problem of content overload is exacerbated in many subject areas by "mile wide, inch deep" textbooks chock full of information.

The perceived expectation to teach to all of the standards and march through designated textbooks leads to superficial "coverage" of instructional content. Numerous studies have documented that coverage is the rule rather than the exception in American education. Many of these studies have noted the ill effects of coverage. For example, the Trends in International Mathematics and Science Study (TIMSS) International research studies document the fact that U.S. eighth-grade mathematics and science teachers cover far more content topics in mathematics and science than teachers in several other high-achieving countries (Schmidt, McKnight, & Raizen, 1997). TIMSS research also reveals that eighth-grade mathematics teachers in the United States focus more on applying algorithmic procedures to solving problems than on helping learners understand underlying mathematical principles (National Center for Education Statistics, 2003).

Similarly, a large-scale study by Pianta et al. (2007) revealed that much of elementary school instruction revolves around learning discrete skills taught through specific lessons and/or worksheets. In his study, approximately one thousand fifth graders in 737 science classrooms were observed across the United States. The study found that these fifth graders spend 91 percent of their time listening to the teacher or working alone, usually on low-level worksheets. Three out of four classrooms are "dull, bleak" places, the researchers report, devoid of any emphasis on critical reasoning or problem-solving skills.

We have observed similar circumstances in other core academic subjects. Why are these patterns so prevalent? The TIMSS research (Schmidt, McKnight, & Raizen, 1997) points out that it is not that teachers are disinterested in engaging student thinking and in-depth learning. Rather, the problem lies in what is to be taught. The current curriculum simply contains too many topics and is too fragmented, often without clear connections from one topic or one level to the next.

The costs of continuing with the current system are particularly germane when considering 21st century outcomes. The pressures of content coverage come at the expense of learner engagement and in-depth exploration of concepts and investigation of important questions. Thus, many of the very skills and processes needed to succeed in the modern world are blocked out of the curriculum.

> The current curriculum simply contains too many topics and is too fragmented, often without clear connections from one topic or one level to the next.

How then can we possibly add 21st century outcomes to an already overcrowded curriculum? Our proposal is straightforward: focus the curriculum around a core set of big ideas and essential questions within each subject area and across disciplines. Consider the popular 2003 film *Mona Lisa Smile*. The movie contains two scenes that illustrate the difference between a typical information-based learning experience in America's schools and an experience built around a less-crowded curriculum focused on big ideas and questions. In the first scene, Katherine Ann Watson, a beginning art teacher, uses a traditional art text and slide set to open an introductory art class with a lesson built around covering information about artists. She quickly discovers that her students have already read the text and have little to learn from her when she uses this approach. After agonizing over the situation, she comes to class with a different method. She begins with two essential questions that focus her teaching: "What is art?" and "What is the difference between 'good' and 'bad' art?" Next, she shows a new set of slides (including slides of her own artwork as a child) with these questions in mind, and begins to get thoughtful debate, discussion, disagreements, and even passion from her students. Her focus on differing perspectives of excellence in art causes her jaded students to become engaged and curious about the nature and meaning of art. As her students explore the questions, "What is art?" and "What is good art?" they think critically and creatively. They analyze and interpret paintings, communicate opinions, support their views, and develop creative ways of thinking about art. With time to think about and discuss provocative questions, her students realize deeper and more meaningful learning.

This example illustrates a key feature of the curriculum shift we advocate: a change in curriculum goals from broad surveys of too much academic knowledge and too many discrete skills to a focus on a few big ideas and essential questions, such as those illustrated in table 7.1. These are chosen because they are fundamental to the discipline, thought provoking, and support transfer of learning to new situations. Because the curriculum is more focused, there is greater opportunity for in-depth learning and infusion of 21st century skills.

> Curriculum goals change from broad surveys of too much academic knowledge and too many discrete skills to a focus on a few big ideas and essential questions, chosen because they are fundamental to the discipline, thought provoking, and support transfer of learning to new situations.

In summary, the key to unclogging a crowded content-driven curriculum is to create a clear conception of a few really important ideas and essential questions in order to focus on understanding and integrate 21st century skills. With a pared-down set of learning goals devoted to in-depth exploration and reflection, 21st century skills can be integrated into the curriculum and interdisciplinary themes can be developed over time within and among subject areas. Because the curriculum is more focused, teachers have time to "uncover" it by engaging students in analyzing issues, applying critical and creative thinking to complex problems, working collaboratively on inquiry and research investigations, accessing and evaluating information, applying technology effectively, and developing initiative and self-direction through authentic, long-term projects.

Table 7.1: Examples of Big Ideas and Essential Questions

Big Ideas	Essential Questions
History involves interpretation, and individuals may interpret the same events differently.	Whose story is this? How do we know what really happened in the past?
We can measure and represent the same thing in different ways.	How can we best show _____ (distance, quantity, size, rate of change, and so on)?
Scientists attempt to replicate experimental findings to verify claims.	How do we know what to believe about scientific claims?
Great literature explores common human themes and issues.	How are stories from other times and places about us? What truths can fiction reveal?

Guideline Two: Assess Valued Outcomes in Appropriate Ways

Educational assessments have a huge impact on teaching and learning, wherever they originate—be it in the classroom or at state and national agencies. Professional educators, parents, and students are well aware of the axiom that what is assessed signals what is valued. Students frequently ask, "Will this be on the test?" and allocate their attention accordingly. Schools and districts tend to emphasize those subjects that are assessed on high-stakes accountability tests, often at the expense of those that are not.

Moreover, how something is assessed signals how it should be learned. The increasing use of large-scale standardized assessments tied to the requirements of No Child Left Behind has influenced instructional practice. Most standardized tests used in the United States rely on selected-response and brief constructed-response items to assess knowledge and basic skills. These formats can become seductive, leading to multiple-choice/short-answer teaching and the belief that learning equals the ability to recall and recognize information and make low-level inferences. Even those standardized tests that include constructed-response items have encouraged the teaching of formulaic responses, such as the five-paragraph essay. Indeed, test preparation focused on the short-answer assessment format has assumed an increasing presence in many schools, displacing more meaningful learning that utilizes 21st century thinking skills.

If we genuinely value the infusion of 21st century skills with core academic goals, then assessments at all levels—classroom, district, and state—should be aligned accordingly. We do not deny that the traditional assessment formats have a place in determining whether students know vocabulary terms, procedures, algorithms, and basic facts. But we also believe that a balanced approach to assessments is critical if 21st century learning goals are to be appropriately assessed. The majority of assessments should be more open-ended and performance-based—designed to reveal whether students meet 21st century learning goals such as demonstrating an understanding of big ideas, formulating responses to essential questions, reflecting on and analyzing important issues, solving genuine problems, conducting research and inquiry, working collaboratively, and using technology. Assessments should also reveal whether students are able to transfer and adapt their learning to novel situations, since a fundamental goal of 21st century outcomes is to prepare students for a complex and rapidly changing world with unpredictable challenges. The use of assessments that measure student understanding of big ideas and promote thoughtful application, research and investigation, creativity, and the like will encourage concomitant curricular and instructional changes that support the attainment of 21st century skills.

> The use of assessments that measure student understanding of big ideas and promote thoughtful application, research and investigation, creativity, and the like will encourage concomitant curricular and instructional changes that support the attainment of 21st century skills.

Cornerstone assessment tasks. Cornerstone tasks, as characterized by Wiggins and McTighe (2007), represent a natural fusion of 21st century skills with the big ideas of academic content:

> The most basic flaw in the writing of conventional school curriculum is that it is too often divorced from the ultimate accomplishments desired. Thus, when we advise educators

to design the assessment system first, we are not referring to typical tests of mere content mastery. We are speaking of worthy authentic performances that embody the mission and program goals. Think of them as "cornerstone" performances—merit badge requirements—reflective of the key challenges in the subject, the essence of "doing" the subject with core content. Here are some examples of such challenges in a number of disciplines:

In science, the design and debugging of significant experiments

In history, the construction of a valid and insightful narrative of evidence and argument

In mathematics, the quantifying and solving of perplexing or messy real-world problems

In communication, the successful writing for specific and demanding audiences and purposes

In the arts, the composing/performing/critiquing of a sophisticated piece

Like the game in sports or the play in drama, these cornerstone performance demands are meant to embody key learning goals by requiring meaning making and transfer of prior learning. (pp. 42–43)

Cornerstone tasks have the following distinguishing qualities:

- They reflect genuine, real-world accomplishments and are set in authentic contexts. Unlike the majority of items found on standardized tests and textbook or worksheet drills, cornerstone tasks are contextualized. This means they establish a real or realistic situation to which students apply their knowledge and skill. Such tasks provide meaningful learning targets, while bringing rigor and relevance to the classroom. Accordingly, they help teachers answer those familiar student queries: "Why do we have to learn this?" "Who ever uses this stuff?"

- They require students to apply (in other words, transfer) their learning. If students truly understand a concept, they can apply their knowledge and skills to new situations. Cornerstone tasks require transfer, and thus provide a measure of understanding. They also signal to learners that a major goal of education is to enable them to *use* their learning in ways valued in the wider world beyond the classroom.

- They naturally integrate 21st century skills with the big ideas of academic content. Rather than simply requiring recall or recognition, such tasks call for the thoughtful use of knowledge and skills naturally integrated within authentic contexts. Thus, they call for genuine applications of thinking (such as creative problem solving), technology (such as information access), communication (written, oral, or graphic), collaborative teamwork, and habits of mind (such as persistence)—just like in the real world. By their very nature, cornerstone tasks require 21st century outcomes.

> Cornerstone tasks require transfer, and thus provide a measure of understanding. They also signal to learners that a major goal of education is to enable them to *use* their learning in ways valued in the wider world beyond the classroom.

- They recur across the grades, in increasingly sophisticated forms. Think of athletics and the arts. Six-year-olds play the same soccer game as high school, college, and professional players. Similarly, young children use crayons to draw pictures depicting their observations, thoughts, and feelings; professional artists do the same, although with more varied and sophisticated media. In both cases, the tasks (soccer and artistic creation) are recurring, with the students' performance becoming more skilled and mature over the years. We propose that cornerstone tasks should also recur *throughout* the curriculum, moving toward more sophisticated performances within and across the disciplines. As we systematically apply 21st century skills in recurring cornerstone tasks, we concurrently develop more sophisticated applications of critical and creative thinking, technology, communication, and collaboration.

What does a recurring task look like and sound like? Figure 7.3 first presents a cornerstone task frame (figure 7.3a) and then two recurring versions of the same basic task (figure 7.3b and c), one at the elementary level and one at the secondary level. Both of these tasks share common elements from the task frame. Notice that each task establishes a relevant context for actively involving students in gathering, analyzing, and displaying data. Both tasks call for some forecasting or prediction based on observed patterns. Both call for communication of findings to a target audience.

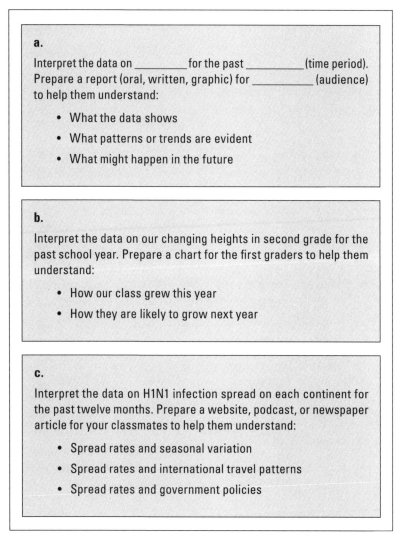

a.

Interpret the data on _____ for the past _____ (time period). Prepare a report (oral, written, graphic) for _____ (audience) to help them understand:

- What the data shows
- What patterns or trends are evident
- What might happen in the future

b.

Interpret the data on our changing heights in second grade for the past school year. Prepare a chart for the first graders to help them understand:

- How our class grew this year
- How they are likely to grow next year

c.

Interpret the data on H1N1 infection spread on each continent for the past twelve months. Prepare a website, podcast, or newspaper article for your classmates to help them understand:

- Spread rates and seasonal variation
- Spread rates and international travel patterns
- Spread rates and government policies

Figure 7.3: Cornerstone tasks: (a) sample task frame, (b) elementary example, and (c) high school example.

Elementary version. Second-grade students in three separate classes work in teams of four and take turns measuring the height of each member using tape measures affixed to the classroom walls. The height measurements are taken at the beginning of the school year and every seven weeks thereafter. When they begin, the second-grade teachers and classroom aides model the process and assist students with their measures and their recordings. As the year progresses, students require less help with the task, and by year end, many groups are working completely independently.

By mid-May, each second-grade class has obtained six height measures. The teachers demonstrate how to create a simple graph with height in inches plotted against the months of the school year, and the students plot their own data. Using rulers, they connect the dots to see "rise over run" (a visual representation of their growth over time).

The chart papers are posted throughout the room, and the students circulate in a gallery walk to view the changes in heights of the various groups. The teachers then ask the students to analyze the data by posing guiding questions: "In what months did we grow the most this year?" "Is there a difference between how boys and girls have grown in second grade?" "How does our class growth compare to that in the other second-grade classrooms?" (The teachers create an average class growth chart that they show to all second graders.) "What can we predict for next year's second graders about how they will grow based on our data?" Students are then asked to work in their groups to develop a presentation for the current first graders.

Secondary version. High school students use several Internet search engines to locate data from the World Health Organization, the National Institutes of Health, and at least two other sources on documented H1N1 (aka swine flu) cases. Working in teams, the students engage in the following task activities:

- Collect and record data from at least four sources on the spread of H1N1 virus in various countries.

- Compare and evaluate the four sources. (Which sources were the most thorough? Which were the most understandable? Which were the most credible?)

- Analyze the data. (What patterns did you notice with age and gender? What geographic patterns emerged? What about associated deaths? What was the impact of governmental policies, such as travel restrictions or quarantine, on the spread of infections? Do you have any predictions for future spread of the virus?)

- Prepare a summary report to effectively communicate the data and your analysis to a target audience (for example, a congressional committee, the general public, or teenagers) using an appropriate communications medium (such as a newspaper article, blog, website, podcast, or television news special). Include recommendations (such as for government policy or individual precautions) in the event of a future outbreak of a different flu strain.

Note that the secondary version of the task also incorporates the 21st century themes of global awareness and health/wellness, as well as critical thinking, information technology, and communication skills. All of the skills and processes in both tasks are transferable; they apply in mathematics, science, history, and a variety of real-world contexts.

Now imagine a recurring set of such tasks across the grades, emanating from the same task frame, but involving more sophisticated data from increasingly authentic situations. And imagine similar task frames established within and across all academic areas to guide other sets of recurring tasks. This is the type of *system* we advocate.

With such a system in place, students will become increasingly proficient and autonomous in their ability to apply core academic learning and 21st century skills, just as youth soccer or basketball players hone their knowledge and skills over the years. Cornerstone assessments have an added virtue—they become the source of documented accomplishments saved in a student's digital portfolio. The portfolio becomes a significant component of the curriculum/assessment system, since it creates a shift from an emphasis on Carnegie units and seat time to one favoring demonstrated achievement

> With such a system in place, students will become increasingly proficient and autonomous in their ability to apply core academic learning and 21st century skills, just as youth soccer or basketball players hone their knowledge and skills over the years.

on worthy tasks that incorporate 21st century outcomes. With this approach, students graduate from high school with a resume of authentic accomplishments that demonstrate their understanding of key ideas and their ability to apply 21st century skills, instead of merely a transcript of courses taken and a grade point average.

Guideline Three: Map the Curriculum Backward

Curriculum mapping offers a well-established process for orchestrating the scope and sequence of a curriculum to establish a coherent flow across grade levels, avoid unnecessary redundancies, and ensure that important knowledge and skills are not falling through the cracks. A more coherent and results-focused curriculum emerges when the curriculum is mapped according to the elements recommended in guidelines one and two (big ideas, essential questions, 21st century skills, and cornerstone assessment tasks) from grade 12 backward to kindergarten. By keeping the desired performances in mind (via the spiraling cornerstone assessment tasks), the curriculum maps remind teachers that their job is to uncover important ideas, explore critical questions, focus on learning and using 21st century skills, and prepare students to apply their learning to new situations.

> A more coherent and results-focused curriculum emerges when the curriculum is mapped according to big ideas, essential questions, 21st century skills, and cornerstone assessment tasks from grade 12 backward to kindergarten.

We encourage educators, as they map out a 21st century outcomes-based curriculum, to consider the fundamental concepts of the core disciplines along with the key, naturally recurring 21st century skills that grow out of the disciplines. We refer to subject areas as *disciplines* because they require disciplined ways of thinking and acting:

> Many people erroneously think of academic disciplines as the "content," but that is not what a discipline is. . . . Science is a "discipline" because the habit of jumping to conclusions based on prior beliefs runs deep in human beings (and novice scientists), and is overcome only through the "discipline" of trying to isolate key variables, and methodically testing for them. You have to learn the discipline of carefully observing, gathering apt evidence, and weighing its limited implications while remaining skeptical. The so-called scientific

method is not a "skill" but a set of dispositions, skills, and transfer abilities in the use of content, learnable only by doing. Similarly, the goal in learning to "do" history is to avoid present-centeredness and simplistic causal reasoning. One must learn to think and act like a journalist/curator/historian to learn the "discipline" of history. Learning only the factual "content" or highly-scripted "skills" is as little likely to make you "disciplined" as merely practicing discrete moves in basketball will equip you to be a successful game player. (Wiggins & McTighe, 2007, pp. 47–48)

Instructional Programs and Practices

How should we teach to achieve 21st century outcomes?

The ideas suggested so far—the development of a 21st century mission statement; the adoption of learning principles that emphasize deep understanding of subject matter and transfer of learning; and the "backward design" of a curriculum and assessment system focused around big ideas, essential questions, and open-ended, performance, and cornerstone assessments at all school levels—imply the need for major changes in day-to-day teaching behaviors. We have synthesized our instructional recommendations into a set of five indicators that suggest what students should experience as they achieve 21st century outcomes.

Indicator One: Interactive Strategies Actively Engage Students in Developing Understanding of Big Ideas and the Application of 21st Century Skills

Making sense of key ideas is central to the learning process as the teacher helps students make connections to prior knowledge, explore essential questions, and explain key ideas. The teacher uses engaging, interactive strategies to guide learners in developing and deepening their understanding and developing and applying critical 21st century skills, such as the following:

- Problem-based learning
- Science experimentation and historical investigation
- Socratic seminars

- Collaborative projects and communications
- Creative problem-solving strategies
- Visual learning tools that help students make connections (such as graphic organizers)
- Interactive notebooks
- Essential questions, with probes and wait time

The teacher and student work is conceptually rigorous, and learners are intellectually challenged; for example, students are often asked to conceptualize and make connections among information and ideas, summarize their learning, write cogent and coherent analyses, and/or support their ideas with substantive arguments.

Indicator Two: 21st Century Skills Are Explicitly Taught and Applied in the Academic Areas

Twenty-first-century skills and cornerstone tasks are integrated into academic learning areas and taught *explicitly* across the grades. As these skills are introduced in the younger grades, teachers break down the skills into critical components, and give students regular opportunities to practice and apply the skills while supported with coaching and feedback. Over time, we see students developing increased proficiency and the capacity to autonomously transfer these skills to new situations.

Indicator Three: Students Have Multiple Opportunities to Transfer Learning to New Situations

Students clearly understand that transfer is a major goal of their learning, and they are provided with many opportunities to apply their learning and understanding to novel situations. Students are regularly involved in relevant, real-life activities and assessments, such as writing letters to an editor, conducting research on problems of interest to students, examining current issues and controversies, and creating genuine products and performances. The teacher continually helps students to see the connections of ideas and skills to authentic experiences.

Indicator Four: Teachers Use Ongoing Assessments to Monitor Students' Level of Understanding of Ideas and Skills, and Adjust the Pace and Level of Instruction Accordingly

The teacher routinely uses pre-assessments to find out students' prior knowledge, interests, and preferred learning styles. As learning progresses, the teacher continually monitors the level of learning and understanding of targeted big ideas and 21st century skills for each student, and adjusts instruction as needed. Formative assessments, such as five-minute summaries at the end of a period, exit cards, no-fault quizzes, and informal observations are used to determine the level of learning and the needs of learners. The teacher provides timely and understandable feedback, along with opportunities for students to practice, rethink, and revise.

Indicator Five: Teachers Establish a Classroom Culture and Climate That Values Student Participation; Respects Student Ideas, Questions, and Contributions; and Encourages Students to Generate Ideas, Questions, and Conjectures

The climate of classrooms devoted to 21st century outcomes encourages intellectual risk taking and active meaning making. Mistakes are seen as growth opportunities, rather than failures. Students engage in the learning process in order to construct meaning, individually and collectively. They are encouraged to ask questions, offer their ideas, discuss their understanding of a principle, give feedback to each other, and create and share their thoughts and opinions. They are invited to regularly reflect on their learning, and their teachers are models of reflective practice.

Instructional Resources

Instructional resources have always had a significant influence on teaching practices. We believe this factor must be taken into account as we give greater attention to 21st century outcomes. Consequently, educators will need to carefully select instructional resources, including published programs and textbooks, technology, and software that are aligned with the recommended curriculum, assessment, and instructional practices we describe. To that end, we offer a set of review criteria (see table 7.2), built around the learning principles in figure 7.2 (page 153), that can be used to determine whether various resources will support 21st century learning.

Systemic Supports

What policies, school structures, and resource alloca-tions are needed to support the development of 21st century outcomes?

Our suggestions for revamping mission, learning principles, curriculum, assessment, and instruction will only be put into place in districts, schools, and classrooms where the system policies and structures support their implementation. While we cannot address all the various systemic factors required for educational reform toward 21st century outcomes, we wish to emphasize the importance of *alignment* among all the elements of a system. These questions will help secure that alignment:

- To what extent do current district and school policies, proce-dures, operations, and practices support or hinder efforts to achieve 21st century outcomes?

- To what extent do staff, parents, and students know that the district/school mission includes 21st century outcomes?

- To what extent does the district curriculum and assessment system emphasize 21st century outcomes?

- To what extent do classroom instructional and assessment practices reflect principles of learning and support achieve-ment of 21st century outcomes?

- To what extent do job descriptions and staff appraisal processes reference 21st century outcomes?

- To what extent do the grading and reporting systems include 21st century outcomes?

- To what extent do curriculum, assessment, and staff develop-ment consistently promote the development and use of 21st century outcomes?

Table 7.2: Review Criteria for Instructional Resources

Learning Principle	Review Criteria To what extent does this resource . . .
1	Support contextualized learning experiences (for example, frame learning with relevant questions, meaningful challenges, and authentic applications)? Incorporate 21st century interdisciplinary themes (such as global awareness and entrepreneurial literacy)?
2	Identify a limited number of big ideas—concepts, principles, themes, issues—and/or include provocative essential questions around which knowledge is examined?
3	Engage students in higher-order thinking and related 21st century skills and processes (such as problem solving, critical and creative thinking, issues analysis, and research investigation)?
4	Include opportunities for students to apply their learning in meaningful and varied contexts? Include performance-based assessments aligned with 21st century outcomes?
5	Contain effective and engaging activities to help students make connections and construct meaning? Include pre-assessments to help teachers check for prior knowledge and students' readiness for new learning?
6	Support collaborative and interactive learning?
7	Support opportunities for students to discuss attitudes toward learning? Develop self-directed attitudes and values?
8	Continually revisit and refine big ideas and 21st century skills? Spiral to develop and deepen student understanding and transfer ability?
9	Support teachers in providing students with models of excellence and timely feedback, along with the opportunity to use them to improve learning and performance?
10	Cater to the diverse abilities, interests, and needs of students? Support teaching to students' varied learning styles or intelligences?

Table 7.3: Framework for 21st Century Learning: Summary of Key Points

Mission Statement	• Outcome oriented • Specific focus on 21st century outcomes and teaching for understanding and transfer • Known by key stakeholders • Regularly reviewed and used to guide educational policy and practice
Learning Principles	• Explicit conception of learning based on latest research and best practice • Cognitive/constructivist view of learning
Curriculum	• Focus on fewer topics and transferable big ideas and essential questions in academic areas • Greater emphasis on in-depth learning, thinking, and understanding • Emphasis on infusing 21st century outcomes into the curriculum • Use of multiple resources including technology
Assessment	• Inclusion of more performance tasks involving the integration of big ideas of content areas with 21st century skills • Recurring cornerstone performance assessments anchor the curriculum around authentic transfer tasks • Use of ongoing assessments provide feedback to teachers and learners
Instruction	• Actions guided by a set of agreed-upon learning principles • Emphasis on active learning and the use of constructivist-based strategies • Emphasis of teaching and coaching on understanding and transfer
Systemic Factors	• Long-term commitment to the implementation of 21st century outcomes • Robust use of the backward design model for curriculum planning and school improvement • All major elements of the educational system (mission, learning principles, policies, procedures, resource allocation, curriculum and staff development practices, and so on) aligned in support of 21st century outcomes • Supportive federal and state guidelines, financial incentives, and content standards for implementation of 21st century outcomes and a teaching-for-understanding approach

- To what extent do the allocation of resources (including money and time) signal that 21st century outcomes are a priority?

- To what extent do agendas for staff meetings and professional development signal that 21st century outcomes are a priority?

A 21st Century Learning Framework

The changes to the current educational system proposed by this framework for 21st century learning are summarized in table 7.3. While the changes we advocate are not a quick fix, nor will they be easy to implement, such changes to educational missions and methods are necessary if schooling is to remain relevant and will adequately prepare our children to live and work in the 21st century.

References

Bransford, J. D., Brown, A., & Cocking, R. (Eds.). (2000). *How people learn: Brain, mind, experience, and school*. Washington, DC: National Academy Press.

Covey, S. R. (1989). *The seven habits of highly effective people: Restoring the character ethic*. New York: Simon & Schuster.

Marzano, R. J. (2003). *What works in schools: Translating research into action*. Alexandria, VA: Association for Supervision and Curriculum Development.

National Center for Education Statistics. (2003, March). *Teaching mathematics in seven countries: Results from the TIMSS 1999 video study*. Washington, DC: U.S. Department of Education. Accessed at http://nces.ed.gov/pubs2003/2003013 .pdf on October 12, 2008.

Partnership for 21st Century Skills. (2009). *P21 framework definitions document*. Washington, DC: Author. Accessed at www.21stcenturyskills.org/documents/ p21_framework_definitions_052909.pdf on August 14, 2009.

Partnership for 21st Century Skills. (n.d.). *The intellectual and policy foundations of the 21st century skills framework*. Washington, DC: Author.

Pianta, R. C., Belsky, J., Houts, R., Morrison, F., & the National Institute of Child Health and Human Development. (2007, March). Teaching: Opportunities to learn in America's elementary classrooms. *Science, 315*, 1795–1796.

Schmidt, W. H., McKnight, C. C., & Raizen, S. A. (with Jakwerth, P. M., Valverde, G. A., Wolfe, R. G., Britton, E. D., Bianchi, L. J., & Houang, R. T.). (1997). *A splintered vision: An investigation of U.S. science and mathematics education*. Boston: Kluwer Academic.

Weiss, I. R., & Pasley, J. D. (2004, February). What is high quality instruction? *Educational Leadership, 61*(5), 24–28.

Wiggins, G., & McTighe, J. (2007). *Schooling by design: Mission, action, and achievement.* Alexandria, VA: Association for Supervision and Curriculum Development.

Willis, J. (2006). *Research-based strategies to ignite student learning: Insights from a neurologist and classroom teacher.* Alexandria, VA: Association for Supervision and Curriculum Development.

John Barell

John Barell, Ed.D., is professor emeritus of Curriculum and Teaching at Montclair State University, Montclair, New Jersey, and a former public school teacher in New York City. Since 2000, he has been a consultant for inquiry-based instruction and creation of science/social studies networks at the American Museum of Natural History in New York City in collaboration with the International Baccalaureate Organization. For most of his educational career, he has worked with schools nationally to foster inquiry, problem-based learning, critical thinking, and reflection. He is the author of several books, including *Teaching for Thoughtfulness: Strategies to Enhance Intellectual Development*, *Developing More Curious Minds*, *Problem-Based Learning—An Inquiry Approach*, and *Why Are School Buses Always Yellow?*

In this chapter, Barell shows that problem-based learning is an ideal way to develop 21st century skills. He describes how teachers shift their standards-based curriculum from direct instruction of passive students to active engagement of problem solvers and question askers. His concrete examples illustrate ways problem-based inquiry can be adapted for meaningful use with students of all ages, talents, and challenges.

Chapter 8

Problem-Based Learning: The Foundation for 21st Century Skills

John Barell

Recently, I noticed several magazine advertisements that summarized for me why it is so important to challenge today's students to become skillful problem solvers. The first advertisement depicted a serene Antarctic scene: an iceberg looking like a tall ship, high bowsprit facing into the winds, with surrounding ice in wonderful shades of blues and whites. The ad was by Kohler, a manufacturer of plumbing supplies, telling readers that if they substitute their usual shower head spraying 2.75 gallons of water per minute for one using only 1.75 gallons per minute, they can save 7,700 gallons of water per year (Kohler ad, 2009).

This advertisement led me to consider some current issues and critical problems that need solving in the wider world, such as conservation of natural resources, the United States' overreliance on foreign fossil fuels, and the need to develop alternative sources of clean, renewable energy.

In more ads for U.S. manufacturers, I noticed the following headlines:

- The word "inoperable" now applies to far fewer brain tumors. (Cleveland Clinic ad, 2008, p. 19)

- The world is growing by more than 70 million people a year. So is that a problem, or a solution? (Chevron ad, 2008, p. 36)

- How can we squeeze more food from a raindrop? (Monsanto ad, 2009, p. 3)

Obviously, these companies want us to purchase their products and services and may just be manipulating our concerns for profit. But they do urge us to recognize the significant challenges we all face in today's world, challenges requiring us to innovate, change, take risks, recognize problems, and imagine alternative futures.

In the 21st century, we need all of the skills that have marked humankind as the creators and sustainers of cultures, the innovators of technologies, and the designers of ways of living and governing. These skills, which are more crucial now than ever before, include "critical thinking, problem-solving, collaboration, creativity, self-direction, leadership, adaptability, responsibility [and] global awareness" (Walser, 2008, p. 2). To this list, I add the significant skill of inquiry.

But What Makes the 21st Century Special?

Yes, it is true; humans have always engaged in problem solving and critical and creative thinking. History is replete with examples:

- Early hominids figuring out how to capture, kill, and consume prey much larger than themselves while using only stone tools

- Socrates confronting the youth of Athens with what he called "perplexities" to challenge their thinking

- Leonardo da Vinci and Michelangelo creating masterworks that revolutionized the old, medieval ways of seeing

- Rosa Parks challenging segregationist practices by refusing to move to the rear of the bus in Montgomery, Alabama, on December 1, 1955

- Sally K. Ride, America's first woman astronaut, determining what failed during the *Columbia* shuttle flight on February 1, 2003

But what makes the 21st century special? What are the new and threatening problems we face, both domestic and foreign, that necessitate more attention to how we think and solve problems? In addition to the complexities of energy production and conservation, preserving the planet, and fighting terrorism, we face almost intractable situations when it comes to providing health care, ensuring equity within all of our educational and judicial systems, and figuring out how to preserve our financial markets after the worst economic meltdown since the Great Depression.

The increased complexity of these challenges makes it all the more important that we do a better job preparing our students as problem solvers. We must provide students with improved strategies to help them deal with problems—this is what holds the most promise in our education system. Problem-based learning (PBL) is one such strategy.

The PBL approach often raises serious questions among those who are first exploring this option:

1. What is PBL?

2. What are the key elements of PBL?

3. What does PBL look like in the classroom?

4. Why start with a problematic scenario?

5. Why is inquiry important within PBL?

6. How do we develop curricula for PBL?

7. How do we enhance PBL with 21st century technology?

8. What do we know about the effectiveness of PBL?

What Is PBL?

When discussing problem-based learning, we must first explore the meanings of the word *problem*. Problem-based learning is something different, but not wildly so, from what many students are experiencing today when they answer short-term "problems" at the end of textbook chapters. In math and science, students work on individual problems, often with answers in the back of the book. On a larger instructional scale, students sometimes contend with "problems" that call for them to find solutions, such as how to improve the school playground or the water quality of a neighborhood pond or stream.

Some teachers use problematic situations in literature and history to organize the curriculum. For example, in one third-grade classroom, I witnessed two excellent teachers read *Franklin in the Dark* by Paulette Bourgeois (1986). This is the story of a little turtle, Franklin, who is afraid of "small, dark places" like his shell. So he goes on a quest searching for solutions. Before the end of the story, the teachers asked the students, "What do you think Franklin's problem is?" and "How would you solve it?" These "problem" questions engaged the students in thinking about Franklin's solutions as well as their own.

Problem-based learning goes well beyond these short-term instructional instances or simple questions. It encompasses a rethinking of the entire curriculum so that teachers design whole units around complex, "ill-structured" problematic scenarios that embody the major concepts to be mastered and understood. By "ill-structured" or "ill-defined" I mean the realistic, authentic problems—such as pollution of the planet and feeding the hungry—that are so complex, messy, and intriguing that they do not lend themselves to a right or wrong answer approach; on the other hand, "How far does an automobile travel in 3.5 hours going 60 mph?" would be an example of "well-defined" problem because there is a right answer.

Problem-based learning goes well beyond these short-term instructional instances or simple questions. It encompasses a rethinking of the entire curriculum so that teachers design whole units around complex, "ill-structured" problematic scenarios that embody the major concepts to be mastered and understood.

While engaged in the unit, students will ask good questions, conduct purposeful investigations, think critically, draw conclusions, and reflect until they arrive at a meaningful solution. In addition, such units no longer are limited in use to children with high aptitudes, but are used with students of all ages and abilities, including those with special needs.

From this perspective, PBL challenges teachers to reconstruct their understanding of problem solving. It takes them from solving homework problems in a single lesson to using advanced thinking skills throughout a unit designed around in-depth problem solving. To accomplish this, PBL requires a complete rethinking of the roles of teachers and students, as well as the goals of educational programs. PBL teachers not only present information, but they also learn along with students and help them become more skillful problem solvers. In this capacity, students are no longer passive recipients of knowledge; they are decision makers about the nature and structure of their own learning as they work their way through the problem-based unit.

What Are the Key Elements of PBL?

Cheryl Hopper—a former ninth-grade teacher in Paramus, New Jersey, who will be discussed in more detail in the following section—designed a sample unit that includes ten key elements of problem-based learning:

1. Real-world problems that foster inquiry and embody key concepts like change, equality, and environment

2. Choices about content as well as ways to learn and share understandings

3. Objectives reflecting the highest of intellectual challenges, including the need to pose questions, conduct purposeful research, think critically, make decisions, and draw reasonable conclusions supported with evidence

4. Experiences in small-group collaboration such as listening, reasoning together, and building upon each others' ideas

5. Feedback students receive from classmates and teachers during rehearsals of final findings; such feedback—"What we liked and our questions"—is most helpful and reflects what occurs in actual life experiences

6. Occasions to revise, modify, and elaborate on findings

7. Engagement in planning of, monitoring of, and self-reflection on work, progress, and results

8. Opportunities to obtain pre-, formative, and summative assessment information

9. A clear and easy-to-follow curricular structure centered on authentic problems and inquiry

10. Teachers and students sharing control of decision making, teaching, and learning

What Does PBL Look Like in the Classroom?

Cheryl Hopper's ninth-grade classroom was no ordinary experience for her students. Cheryl was the kind of teacher who announced on the first day, "There are no rules here. There are very high expectations." Students knew immediately that they were in for an exciting and challenging journey through world history and geography. What they didn't know was that they would soon experience the key elements of problem-based learning, especially real-world problems, inquiry, and assessment feedback—elements that would fully engage them in their learning.

The Problem Scenario

At the beginning of an interdisciplinary unit exploring the geography, politics, economics, history, art, and religion of Africa, Cheryl put her students into the roles of problem solvers. She used this scenario:

> You are an African nation that desires a substantial loan from the World Bank. Your goal is to convince the World Bank that your country's needs are great and you deserve a loan. The World Bank has a limited amount to lend and many other countries are asking for loans. Therefore, you must prepare a strong case for receiving a loan and be able to defend your need for the money. (Barell, 2003, p. 145)

Imagine being a student confronted with this challenge of not only learning about an African nation of your choosing, but also conducting extensive research about the nation's natural resources, history, and culture. Imagine having to identify a country's most pressing economic, political, and health needs; devise a plan to meet them; and then present your plan to the World Bank—in this case, Mrs. Hopper herself. This is not passive learning.

Cheryl's Guided Inquiry

For this unit, Cheryl used a variation of the structured approach to inquiry known as KWHLAQ (figure 8.1). This organizing framework provides a tool to guide student-generated questions within the unit.

K	What do we think we already *know*? Explore prior knowledge.
W	What do we *want* and need to find out?
H	*How* will we proceed to investigate our questions? *How* will we organize time, access to resources and reporting? *How* will we self-assess our progress (such as with a scoring rubric)?
L	What are we *learning* (daily)? And what have we *learned* at the end of our investigations?
A	How and where can we *apply* the results of our investigations—to this and other subjects/to our daily lives?
Q	What new *questions* do we have now? How might we pursue them in our next units?

Source: Barell, 2007a, p. 85.

Figure 8.1: The KWHLAQ approach to inquiry.

After two days of showing students slides featuring different aspects of African culture, geography, and government, Cheryl asked them to identify what they thought they already knew about Africa. They made a graphic web of the comments that reflected their prior knowledge as well as what they saw in the slide show. For example, the graphic organizer students created ("What do we *think* we already know?") included concepts such as "language (linked to diversity), apartheid (Nelson Mandela), deserts (Kalahari), art (music), poaching, and second largest continent." Cheryl used the slides to awaken their background knowledge about Africa and, most likely, to create new knowledge and a heightened sense of curiosity and awareness.

After the students webbed out what they *thought* they knew, Cheryl challenged them to identify what they needed to know if they were to understand the continent, its countries, and the varied cultures.

Here are some of Cheryl's students' questions:

- How and why did powerful kingdoms emerge in Africa, especially West Africa?
- How do geographical features account for the cultural diversity of the continent?
- What were the effects of European rule? Of apartheid?

- How have traditional patterns of life stayed the same and how have they changed?

- How does the art of Africa reflect its cultural diversity?

- What is imperialism?

- Why did Europe carve up Africa into colonies?

- What were the effects of European rule? (Barell, 2003, p. 139)

When we afford students opportunities to respond to "What do we want and *need* to find out?" we are challenging them to think of themselves as young professionals, in this case historians, cultural anthropologists, linguists, artists, social scientists, geographers, and economists. Casting students in these roles lends more authenticity to the problematic scenario. It is possible, as one teacher mentioned to me, that "some students don't *want* to know very much!" Thus, we challenge them to think of themselves as professionals in a situation requiring solutions.

Cheryl then helped students analyze and collate these questions, searching for commonalities and ways to connect one to another. One result of this process was that students' specific questions now more closely resembled some of the unit's general essential questions that focused on the history of colonialism ("How do colonial empires develop?"), the growth of different cultures ("What factors influence the growth of various and different cultures?"), and influences of geography ("How does geography affect the history and culture of a continent or country?"). When students finished these tasks, Cheryl used their responses to guide the development of the unit. Using questions from the KWHLAQ approach, she asked, "How will we go about finding answers to our questions?" and "How will we structure and manage our class time and access to resources to solve the problem?" (see figure 8.1, page 181).

Once they classified and organized their questions, they selected questions to work on and formed themselves into different investigative groups. Working in teams, they conducted research, planned out daily lessons to teach the class, and involved the teacher in appropriate roles. Each team taught a lesson and designed a role within the lesson for Cheryl. She was still in charge of the entire unit, but her students assumed more ownership of the process. Through a variety of activities, like becoming docents at a local African art museum, the students gained more control of their own learning while discovering answers to their own—and to the unit's—essential questions.

When watching Cheryl interact with her students during the planning of their lessons, I saw another major benefit of the PBL inquiry approach: students collaborate as they decide how to best share their new knowledge with their peers. They learn what it takes to make knowledge meaningful. And one of the major positive effects of this approach is students' taking on more responsibility for their own learning. They are not merely sitting back and soaking up lots of factual knowledge to be repeated on a summative assessment at the end of the unit. Rather, they are collaborating, conducting research, analyzing findings critically, and drawing individual and group conclusions—all requisite life experiences.

Final Assessment

With a well-written problematic scenario like Cheryl's, teachers have the potential for a final assessment that provides students with multiple opportunities and ways to demonstrate their understanding of key ideas and concepts. Cheryl's unit culminated in small groups of "international developers" making their cases for setting up a hospital or constructing other needed buildings. They used written and oral reports, PowerPoint presentations, interviews, newspaper articles, and various art forms (pictures, maps, creative writings, and the like)—not merely five-paragraph expository essays.

After the students presented their initial group requests, Cheryl provided an opportunity for questions and direct feedback, which is an essential element in authentic assessment (Wiggins, 1998). Cheryl also facilitated needed adjustments and improvements before final presentations. To guide her feedback, Cheryl used a rubric created with the students that stressed solving problems; making sound

> With a well-written problematic scenario like Cheryl's, teachers have the potential for a final assessment that provides students with opportunities and ways to demonstrate their understanding of key ideas and concepts.

decisions; organizing and presenting cases in a logical, convincing fashion; and responding to questions.

The feedback Cheryl provided did not coddle the students. For instance, after a student presentation about building a health facility, fellow students commented, "I think you're being rather unrealistic. I don't think you can build a hospital for the amount of money you're asking for. Have you considered other variables, such as the costs of cutting through the forest with the needed energy, supplies, and staffing?" These comments and responses reflected the deepening of their knowledge and understanding. As such, they served as assessments on what students did and did not understand during the entire process. And, again, this penultimate form of feedback provided the young urban planners with information and points of view they needed to culminate a final presentation.

After the final presentations, Cheryl asked all students to reflect on their learning processes (the Q of the KWHLAQ). Here are some of their responses:

- [When] I compared my country to a state in the U.S. or another developed country about the same size, it was easier for the World Bank to understand our problems.

- The information was easy to get, but we had to focus on the problems, and that was hard.

- I ended up with the question of why people continue to reproduce if their lives are so hard. (Barell, 2003, p. 146)

These examples show students completing the last two elements of the KWHLAQ approach (see figure 8.1, page 181). Here students are applying what they've learned as well as continuing on with questions about the future. In a well-designed PBL unit, further questions about such complex issues are always expected.

Cheryl's African unit presents the highest level of intellectual challenge. In six weeks, her students not only gathered significant information, but also made critical choices as they figured out the needs of a country and how best to resolve its problems. As she subsequently told me, "Their questions met all of my unit goals (in the form of essential questions)."

Imagine how different this unit would have been with the "Open your textbook and let's start reading and remembering" approach!

Why Start With a Problematic Scenario?

A well-designed problem scenario includes two important ingredients that ensure students learn from the PBL unit. The first is delineation of a complex problem embedding the core concepts the students will be studying. The second is an outline of the authentic assessment parameters that stipulate what students are to understand about the concept. Remember that the problems designed by the teacher (perhaps with students) will be clear but will also reflect the complex, ill-defined, and messy nature of real-world dilemmas.

A well-designed problem scenario includes two important ingredients that ensure students learn from the PBL unit. The first is delineation of a complex problem embedding the core concepts the students will be studying. The second is an outline of the authentic assessment parameters that stipulate what students are to understand about the concept.

A problematic scenario embodies the essential elements of the unit so that as students inquire and discern, they encounter the ideas and concepts the teacher wants them to think deeply about; this process introduces the core content of the scenario. Here are several other examples of problematic scenarios, each from a different grade level, that reflect these design principles.

Ocean Life: Grade 3

You are responsible for finding a way (or ways) to stop the destruction of the ocean so that the animal or plant life that you have chosen and researched can remain a part of the ocean community. You must find a way to show that your method of saving the ocean will help not only the species that you have chosen, but will also help to preserve all of the living and non-living things that the species is dependent on, and all of the things that are a part of the ocean community that depend on it (interdependence). (Catrupi, as cited in Barell, 2007b, p. 46)

This scenario could start several different units on ocean life, ecology, human actions, or the environment. Notice the charge in the first sentence: identify the core problem and figure out how to solve it. Students first become familiar with current conditions in the ocean—that life forms such as coral reefs are whitening and dying. Then they identify which problems to focus on and work toward resolving those problems.

In the second sentence of the scenario, the teacher challenges her students to present information that demonstrates their understanding of how all living things are interdependent. She sets the demands of authentic, summative assessment with reporting criteria that tell students from day one what she expects them to do and to learn.

Community Building: Grades 6–8, Special Needs

A major widget factory has announced that they are breaking ground within an undeveloped area. The factory will bring in a diverse population. You are a committee member that has the responsibility of determining and developing the community and the necessary facilities needed to make [the factory] functional . . . e.g. law enforcement . . . education . . . health . . . and emergency services. (Desotelle & Lierman, 2000, p. 2)

This community-building project for middle school students with special needs requires extensive research on what a community is, what services it provides, and what long-range planning is required. These students must develop their plans within a strict budget. After their presentations, their teacher and peers question the conclusions and provide feedback. How different is this from the usual special needs experience full of repetitious, boring worksheets?

High School: Literature

You are authors for a new publication on contributions of 19th century women authors. Readers are interested in the importance of the ideas of Anthony, Woolf, Austen, Chapin, the Brontës, Stanton, Stowe, and knowing what they might say about issues today. Readers will highly value your ability to state these 19th century authors' views clearly, analyze their importance, and make reasonable applications to and comparisons with one major current issue. Reasonable comparisons will be judged by logic, appropriateness, extensiveness of relationships, and drawing your own conclusions. (Adapted from Royer, 2000)

In this scenario, the teacher challenges students to conduct extensive research on one author, analyze her work, and predict (based on contextual evidence) what her stand on a contemporary issue might be. In the final sentence of the scenario, the student authors receive a set of criteria for reviewing each article. As in all well-formed scenarios, these criteria outline clear expectations for the treatment of the content.

Each of these problematic scenarios presents a significant and well-defined challenge requiring students to familiarize themselves with the subject, pose meaningful questions, think critically, and draw reasonable conclusions. According to Kim Nordin, these scenarios add "focus, drive and excitement to the unit" (personal communication, January 15, 2007).

Why Is Inquiry Important Within PBL?

We can have students solving problems, but to do so without a strong emphasis on inquiry as a curricular priority is a less than sound practice. As stated previously, inquiry is the driver of the complex thinking processes we have been engaged in since the dawn of consciousness: What lies beyond the hill? How will we feed, clothe, and protect ourselves? What do those lights in the sky mean? Today, with all the challenges we face in terms of providing equal access to education, employment, health, energy, security, nutrition, and growth opportunities, it seems logical that we highlight the role of inquiry.

The school board in Greenwich, Connecticut, has done just that. Their "Vision of the Graduate" proclaims that the following are the competencies students must have (assuming acquisition of content knowledge):

- Pose and pursue substantive questions
- Critically interpret, evaluate, and synthesize information
- Explore, define, and solve complex problems
- Communicate effectively for a given purpose

- Advocate for ideas, causes, and actions

- Generate innovative, creative ideas and products

- Collaborate with others to produce a unified work and/or heightened understanding. (Greenwich Public Schools, 2006)

If students graduate from this school system and others, they should be ready for college and life as responsible citizens.

Speaking on the nature of college education, Leon Botstein, president of Bard College in New York, made this statement about the importance of problem-solving skills for college students:

> The primary skills [learned in college] should be analytical skills of interpretation and inquiry. In other words, know how to frame a question. . . . You should not be dependent on the sources of information, either provided by the government or by the media, but have an independent capacity to ask questions and evaluate answers. (as cited in Flaherty, 2002, p. 4A27)

Botstein sees higher learning institutions focused on a single, clear goal: to empower their students to be thoughtfully inquisitive. He concluded by saying, "A college education has to engender a lifelong habit of curiosity, as opposed to becoming more convinced that you are an authority" (as cited in Flaherty, 2002, p. 4A27).

What Is the Role of Inquiry in PBL?

One of the benefits of a PBL approach using the kinds of scenarios outlined here is the opportunity for students to ask a starter question that checks their prior knowledge for accuracy: "What do I *think* I know about this situation?" The use of *think* calls for students to recognize that what they "know" might also include some information they aren't quite certain of. It is, therefore, important to acknowledge what is accurate as well as what is in doubt.

Author Arthur Costa, when discussing the importance of asking what we *think* we know, said, "It is my belief that what we have in our memories is a mixture of fact and fiction, of understandings in accordance with facts and down-right misunderstandings" (personal communication, June 25, 1998).

A second benefit comes with the *W* of KWHLAQ: "What do we want and need to find out?" This question asks students to identify gaps in their knowledge and understanding and taps into what they are genuinely curious about. It tells what they will need to know and find out in order to meet the challenge of the problematic scenario. Again, when asking our own questions, we are acting as young professionals, as scientists, literary critics, artists, historians, mathematicians, nutritionists, and physical educators.

Inquiry and Critical Thinking

The question "What do we need to determine?" demands that students step back, take a deep breath, and ask questions that give them important information as well as lead them toward generating viable solutions for their problematic scenarios. It is even more beneficial when PBL teachers generate lists of key questions and post them around the room for everybody to reference if they encounter a problematic scenario in other classes, in the news, or in their personal lives.

For example, consider these claims:

- We will have deficits as far as the eye can see.

- It is very likely that humans have largely caused global warming.

- "The artificial sweetener aspartame has been proved responsible for an epidemic of cancer, brain tumors and multiple sclerosis" (Mikkelson & Mikkelson, 2007).

What fundamental questions should we ask? What do we need to know about each in order to accept or believe it?

We should ask about sources, evidence, assumptions, definitions, and slant or bias. As students encounter more of these kinds of claims and judgments, they ask questions to learn more before drawing their own conclusions (Barell, 2009). In this way, PBL not only strengthens the students' question-asking skills, but also encourages the transfer of those skills beyond the immediate unit.

The question framework (figure 8.2) presents another questioning model used to promote inquiry skills with students from grade 4 upwards. The framework, similar to KWHLAQ, also provides a generic set of questions to pose about complex, perplexing situations. It allows the teacher to ask questions that help students examine a strange or puzzling situation. At the top, basic information is assessed; on the left, students search for causation; at the bottom, they compare; and on the right, they project into the future. To close, they clarify their tentative conclusions.

How Do We Develop Curricula for PBL?

Teachers often ask, "How can we prepare and plan for students' questions?" This question led me back to my own curriculum development roots. I formulated this step-by-step process to help clarify how teachers should organize units for problem solving and inquiry.

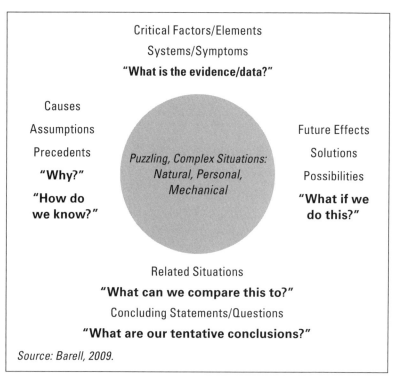

Critical Factors/Elements

Systems/Symptoms

"What is the evidence/data?"

Causes

Assumptions

Precedents

"Why?"

"How do we know?"

Puzzling, Complex Situations: Natural, Personal, Mechanical

Future Effects

Solutions

Possibilities

"What if we do this?"

Related Situations

"What can we compare this to?"

Concluding Statements/Questions

"What are our tentative conclusions?"

Source: Barell, 2009.

Figure 8.2: Question framework.

The following can be completed during planning time, alone, or with colleagues:

1. Identify a topic. Here teachers should refer to their district's curriculum as well as the state or provincial standards for what concepts and ideas they wish to present to their students.

2. Map out the concept. For example, if the topic is the U.S. Constitution, the teacher might map it as seen in figure 8.3.

3. Consult state and local standards to determine which of these subtopics you need and/or must include. Here in New York at the middle school level, students are expected to know and understand the origins and reasons for developing the Constitution; the forms and functions of three branches of the U.S. government; the Bill of Rights; and the concept of the Constitution as a "living document" (New York State Standards, n.d.).

4. Generate a set of intended outcomes or objectives for your unit, and specify essential questions. For instance, New York State considers the following to be essential questions for seventh and eighth graders engaged in the U.S. Constitution unit:

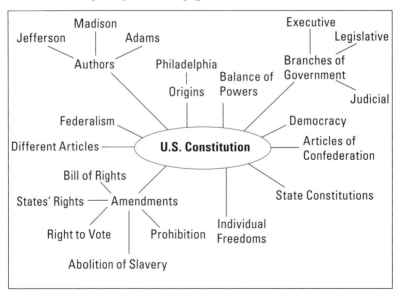

Figure 8.3: Concept map of the U.S. Constitution.

Why was the Constitution necessary? How does it embody the principles of the Declaration of Independence? How do federalism and the separation of powers promote the ideals within the Constitution and its various amendments? (New York State Standards, n.d.).

Specific outcomes that show how students understand the unit's content and can exercise their thinking include the ability to:

- *Define and explain* all major articles, the separation of powers, and similar concepts
- *Explain* reasons for the development of the Constitution
- *Compare* democracy with a republic/parliamentary system
- *Compare* our constitution with that of another country
- *Develop* a new constitution for your class/school/state and/or a fictitious country and be able to *compare/contrast* similarities and differences and *draw reasonable conclusions*

Having essential questions is splendid, but without specifically identifying what they expect students to be able to know and to do, teachers might not be able to determine the extent and quality of student understanding. These outcomes need to demand that students engage in the 21st century skills of questioning, problem solving, critical/creative thinking, hypothesizing, and reflecting. Note the emphasis on complex thinking with such phrases as "explain reasons," "compare," and "draw conclusions."

5. Design a problematic scenario that will spark students' interests and provide a structure for the entire unit. When creating such a scenario, teachers must incorporate knowledge and understanding of the essential concepts of the unit (in this case the U.S. Constitution) into the intended outcomes.

Here is one possible scenario:

You are a member of a delegation representing a new country in [name the geographical area]. You need to create your own constitution, but not copy the U.S. model. The constitutional committee of your home country wishes for you to present an explanation of the U.S. model, along with a critique and suggestions for modifications and improvements for your own country. You are not bound by the structure of the U.S. Constitution, but you need to demonstrate an understanding of key concepts such as federalism, balance/separation of powers, decision making, rights of states and citizens, and amendment powers. Furthermore, in your presentation to the constitutional committee in your home country you will need to justify the modifications and improvements you propose.

This scenario is designed to challenge students to not only learn as much as possible about the U.S. Constitution, but also to apply this new knowledge to crafting their own constitution. Of course, to do this properly they will need to know a good deal about U.S. history. Therefore, teachers could modify the scenario by challenging students to serve on a constitutional amendment committee charged with analyzing this "living document"—our U.S. Constitution—and make recommendations for altering it.

6. Formulate strategies that include inquiry approaches like KWHLAQ for observing artifacts and generating good questions. Students can help organize these questions in accordance with their needs, priorities, and ability level. In PBL, students conduct research and critically examine their findings for reliability, bias, verifiable assumptions, and so on. Then teachers collaborate with students on how to share the findings.

7. Use the problematic scenario as a summative assessment. There are many different ways for students to share what they know and understand about constitutions. They can engage in presentations as Cheryl's students did; share their ideas before a group of citizens; create videos and PowerPoints; engage in debates; write creatively; and, of course, reflect on their progress.

During the unit, the teacher should assess the quality of students' understandings using short-answer quizzes; essays; brief reports on research; and most importantly, writings in their inquiry journals. These journals will contain students' initial questions; research; subsequent questions; and daily, weekly, and/or final reflections on the important ideas they have learned, the process of inquiry, the application of ideas to other subjects, any new questions they have, and how these ideas correspond to their own lives.

How Do We Enhance PBL With 21st Century Technology?

We can enhance the problematic scenarios by using a wide array of 21st century technologies. Moreover, having students create their own connections among a variety of international points of view serves to enhance the significance of content as well as their understanding of what it means to live, survive, and prosper in a globalized world. Consider these examples:

> We can enhance the problematic scenarios by using a wide array of 21st century technologies.

- Daniel, the teacher of a Rosewood Elementary second-grade class in Rock-Hill, South Carolina, used a Promethean Activ-Board to help students understand concepts such as *climate* and *climate change*. The result was, in his own words, "a deluge of questions." As students became involved with the topic, Daniel was not only able to show Internet images of cold and warm fronts, but could also display several pages of a book he had previously scanned of polar ice floes (personal communication, January 15, 2009).

- Fifth-grade students in Charlotte, North Carolina, were planning their research questions for a final exhibit in an International Baccalaureate school. As they generated questions, the teacher was able not only to record them on the Promethean ActivBoard but also to save their jottings and discussions on their topics as well (personal communication, March 30, 2009).

- Middle school students in Van Nuys, California, and Winnipeg, Manitoba, Canada, communicated with each other across more than 1,500 miles "almost daily through blogs, wikis, Skype, instant messaging and other tools to share ideas about literature and current events" (Richardson, 2008, p. 37).

- Students in Webster, New York, used web-based social networking tools (blogs, wikis, Skype, and other tools) to "create their own networks" as they investigated the health of local streams around their schools (Richardson, 2008, p. 37). Through their efforts they learned about "global collaboration and communication," key elements for survival in the highly interdependent and competitive world of the 21st century (p. 37).

- At High Tech High in San Diego, California, students engaged in multidisciplinary projects that allowed them to communicate with experts within the community. For example, students in art, media, and biology came together to produce DVDs to solve problems on blood-related health issues. In a humanities, chemistry, and mathematics collaboration, students researched "African political struggles caused by a scarcity of natural resources," created documentary films, and modeled water-purification plants, which they then exhibited "before peers, teachers, parents and members of the community" (Rubenstein, 2008, p. 44).

What Do We Know About the Effectiveness of PBL?

Some researchers caution that we need to strengthen the conceptual foundations of PBL research (Belland, French, & Ertmer, 2009). There are others who tell us that challenging students to think through problematic situations can be "superior when it comes to long-term retention, skill development and satisfaction of students and teachers" (Strobel & van Barneveld, 2009, p. 44).

In terms of the efficacy of inquiry, however, we hear stronger support. A 2009 study concluded that "developmental research confirms the idea that curiosity drives intellectual development. . . . When a situation is designed to arouse curiosity, children display improved academic performance" (Engel & Randall, 2009, p. 184). Other studies indicate that when all students are challenged to "organize, synthesize, and explain" a complex problem or issue using the methods of inquiry and research, there is a positive impact on learning (Newmann & Associates, 1996, p. 29).

"Developmental research confirms the idea that curiosity drives intellectual development." (Engel & Randall, 2009, p. 184)

Other evidence of efficacy comes directly from teachers who have used these kinds of problematic scenarios with an emphasis on inquiry. Teacher Kim Nordin, for instance, tells us that this structure gave her students "focus, drive and excitement . . . allowing them to be inquirers . . . [who] felt like they had ownership of their projects" (personal communication, January 15, 2009). Suzy O'Hara, the International Baccalaureate coordinator, notes that the use of PBL "has provided our teachers with authentic and engaging ways to promote students' information gathering. It serves as the bridge connecting basic skills, with [the] problem solving and creative thinking needed to be successful in our ever changing world" (personal communication, July 16, 2009).

Enthusiasm for PBL is not limited to the lower grades. Ed Jernigan, the director of the Centre for Knowledge Integration at the University of Waterloo, Ontario, was focused on students solving authentic problems when he said:

> We have built our first-year curriculum around a sequence of real-world design challenges asking students to solve meaningful, open problems of societal and environmental concern. Their level of engagement and retention as assessed by case studies, their actual design presentations and their in-depth reflections is unique in my thirty-three years experience at Waterloo. (personal communication, July 20, 2009)

Obviously, more time and study of this real-world approach to teaching and learning is needed to provide deeper insight into its efficacy. As teachers develop expertise with PBL, however, I expect that the formal and informal results will give not only a clearer picture of its impact, but a positive one as well, showing that within such programs we liberate students' curiosity and imaginations to think boldly, innovate, and implement solutions to 21st century problems.

Final Thoughts

At this writing, the United States is struggling through the aftermath of the worst economic crisis since the Great Depression. With a warming planet, it is also striving to reach energy independence. Within this context, President Barack Obama laid out an educational challenge:

> I'm calling on our nation's governors and state education chiefs to develop standards and assessments that don't simply measure whether students can fill in a bubble on a test, but whether they possess 21st century skills like problem solving and critical thinking and entrepreneurship and creativity. (as cited in Henderson, 2009, p. 4)

To meet these intense and immediate challenges, we need educators like Kerry Faber in Edmonton, Alberta, Canada, whose sixth-grade students realize the importance of asking good questions to solve authentic problems. Some eagerly said, "When I ask good questions, I learn more. . . . Your mind will get stronger, sharper and prepare you for the real world. . . . You start thinking critically. . . . If you ask better questions, you get people thinking" (personal communication, March 15, 2009).

Our challenge in this new century is to help our students build upon their intrinsic curiosities about nature and our living, working, playing, creating and surviving therein. Posing and pursuing substantive questions is what we should all be doing, in schools and as good citizens of this republic. When asked what he and others had wrought at the Constitutional Convention in Philadelphia in 1787, Ben Franklin replied, "A republic. If you can keep it" (as cited in Platt, 1992).

To keep our republic, we need to educate for thoughtful engagement with all of its many challenges.

References

Barell, J. (2003). *Developing more curious minds.* Alexandria, VA: Association for Supervision and Curriculum Development.

Barell, J. (2007a). *Problem-based learning—An inquiry approach* (2nd ed.). Thousand Oaks, CA: Corwin Press.

Barell, J. (2007b). *Why are school buses always yellow? Teaching for inquiry, preK–5.* Thousand Oaks, CA: Corwin Press.

Barell, J. (2009). [Professional development materials]. Unpublished raw data.

Belland, B. R., French, B. F., & Ertmer, P. A. (2009). Validity and problem-based learning research: A review of instruments used to assess intended learning outcomes. *Interdisciplinary Journal of Problem-Based Learning, 3*(1), 59–89.

Bourgeois, P. (1986). *Franklin in the dark.* New York: Scholastic Press.

Chevron advertisement. (2008, September). *The Atlantic Monthly, 302*(2), 36.

Cleveland Clinic advertisement. (2009, November). *The Atlantic Monthly, 304*(4), 19.

Desotelle, J., & Lierman, L. (2000, Summer). *The lego community.* Paper submitted at the Facilitating the Future professional development workshop, Ashland, WI.

Engel, S., & Randall, K. (2009, March). How teachers respond to children's inquiry. *American Educational Research Journal, 46*, 183–202.

Flaherty, J. (2002, August 4). What should you get out of college? *The New York Times*, p. 4A27.

Greenwich Public Schools. (2006). *Vision of the graduate.* Accessed at www.greenwichschools.org/page.cfm?p=61 on December 4, 2009.

Henderson, J. (2009, June). Educating emerging entrepreneurs. *Education Update, 51*(6). Accessed at www.ascd.org/publications/newsletters/education_update/jun09/vol51/num06/Educating_Emerging_Entrepreneurs.aspx on December 30, 2009.

Kohler advertisement. (2009, May). *Vanity Fair, 585*, 20.

Mikkelson, B., & Mikkelson, D. P. (2007). *Kiss my aspartame.* Accessed at www.snopes.com/medical/toxins/aspartame.asp on December 5, 2009.

Monsanto advertisement. (2009, November 9). *The New Yorker*, 3.

Newmann, F. M., & Associates. (1996). *Authentic achievement: Restructuring schools for intellectual quality.* San Francisco: Jossey-Bass.

New York State Standards. (n.d.). *Social studies core curriculum.* Accessed at www.emsc.nysed.gov/ciai/socst/pub/sscore1.pdf on July 7, 2009.

Platt, S. (1992). *Respectfully quoted: A dictionary of quotations.* Accessed at www.bartleby.com/73/1593.htmlpn December 5, 2009.

Richardson, W. (2008, December). World without walls: Learning well with others. *Edutopia, 4*(6), 36–38.

Royer, C. (2000, Fall). *Undaunted—19th/early 20th century women writers, the need to be heard.* Paper submitted for Principles of Curriculum Development course, Montclair State University, Montclair, NJ.

Rubenstein, G. (2008, December). Real world, San Diego: Hands-on learning at High Tech High. *Edutopia, 4*(6), 40–44.

Strobel, J., & van Barneveld, A. (2009, Spring). When is PBL more effective? A meta-synthesis of meta-analyses comparing PBL to conventional classrooms. *Interdisciplinary Journal of Problem-Based Learning, 3*(1), 44–58.

Walser, N. (2008, September/October). Teaching 21st century skills: What does it look like in practice? *Harvard Education Letter, 24*(5), 2.

Wiggins, G. (1998). *Educative assessment: Designing assessments to inform and improve student performance.* San Francisco: Jossey-Bass.

David W. Johnson

David W. Johnson, Ed.D., is codirector of the Cooperative Learning Center at the University of Minnesota. In 2008, he received the Distinguished Contributions to Research in Education Award from the American Educational Research Association. He has coauthored more than five hundred research articles and book chapters, and more than fifty books. He is a former editor of the *American Educational Research Journal*. Johnson has also served as an organizational consultant to schools and businesses throughout the world.

Roger T. Johnson

Roger T. Johnson, Ed.D., is a professor in the Department of Curriculum and Instruction with an emphasis in Science Education at the University of Minnesota. Johnson has received several national awards, including the Exemplary Research in the Social Studies Award presented by the National Council for the Social Studies, the Helen Plants Award from the American Society for Engineering Education, and the Gordon Allport Intergroup Relations Award from the Society for the Psychological Study of Social Issues. He is codirector of the Cooperative Learning Center. In addition to numerous articles, he has coauthored more than fifty books on cooperative learning, conflict resolution, and positive negotiations.

In this chapter, Johnson and Johnson point out four important challenges of the 21st century and discuss how cooperative learning, constructive controversy, and problem-solving negotiations will play a central role in teaching students the competencies and values they need to cope with these challenges.

Chapter 9

Cooperative Learning and Conflict Resolution: Essential 21st Century Skills

David W. Johnson and Roger T. Johnson

When preparing to live in the tumultuous 21st century, it is essential that students learn how to function effectively in cooperative efforts and resolve conflicts constructively. Intentionally facilitating and teaching the skills of cooperation and constructive conflict resolution will raise the quality of collaboration students experience and deepen their learning, not only in face-to-face interactions in school, but also in their online relationships.

This chapter discusses four important challenges of the 21st century and how cooperation and constructively managed conflicts (constructive controversy and integrative negotiations) are at the heart of meeting these challenges.

The Tools for Meeting Four Important Challenges of the 21st Century

The 21st century brings four important challenges in which cooperation and constructive conflict resolution play a central role: (1) a rapidly increasing global interdependence that will result in increasing local diversity as well as more frequent and intense conflicts, (2) the increasing number of democracies throughout the world, (3) the need for creative entrepreneurs, and (4) the growing importance of interpersonal relationships that affect the development of personal identity. The tools for meeting these challenges include cooperative learning, constructive controversy, and problem-solving (integrative) negotiations.

Cooperative Learning

Cooperative learning is the instructional use of small groups so that students work together to maximize their own and each other's learning (Johnson, Johnson, & Holubec, 2008). Any assignment in any curriculum for any age student can be done cooperatively. When individuals cooperate, they work together to accomplish shared goals, and there is a mutual responsibility to work for one's own success. Three types of cooperative learning distinguish this type of learning from mere collaboration: formal, informal, and base groups.

Formal cooperative learning consists of students collaborating or working together, for one class period to several weeks, to achieve shared learning goals and complete jointly specific tasks and assignments. *Informal cooperative learning* consists of students working together to achieve a joint learning goal in temporary, ad hoc groups that last from a few minutes to one class period. *Cooperative base groups* are long-term, heterogeneous cooperative learning groups with stable membership in which students provide one another with support, encouragement, and assistance to make academic progress. They also help one another develop cognitively and socially in healthy ways, as well as hold one another accountable for striving to learn. Research since the early 1900s strongly indicates that cooperation (compared with competitive and individualistic efforts) results in the following (Johnson & Johnson, 1989, 2005):

- Greater effort exerted to achieve (for example, higher achievement and productivity, more frequent use of higher-level reasoning, more frequent generation of new ideas and solutions, greater motivation, greater long-term retention, more on-task behavior, and greater transfer of what is learned within one situation to another)

- Higher-quality relationships among participants (for example, greater interpersonal attraction, valuing of heterogeneity, and task-oriented and personal support)

- Greater psychological adjustment (for example, greater psychological health, social competencies, self-esteem, shared identity, and ability to cope with stress and adversity)

Because of the amount and consistency of research supporting its use, cooperative learning will always be present in 21st century educational practice. Any teacher who does *not* use cooperative learning or relies solely on telling students to "collaborate" may be considered not fully competent. As the research grows even stronger, the use of cooperative learning becomes more and more inevitable and foundational so that student achievement of content outcomes increases.

With cooperative learning comes conflict. The two types of conflict promoted most by positive interdependence are constructive controversy and integrative negotiations.

> Any teacher who does *not* use cooperative learning or relies solely on telling students to "collaborate" may be considered not fully competent.

Constructive Controversy

One of the central aspects of individuals promoting each other's success is disagreement and augmentation—that is, constructive controversy—among members of cooperative groups when they have to make a decision or come to an agreement. A controversy exists when one person's ideas, opinions, information, theories, or conclusions are incompatible with those of another, and the two seek to reach an agreement (Johnson & Johnson, 2007, 2009b). Constructive controversy involves what Aristotle called *deliberate discourse* (that is, the discussion of the advantages and disadvantages of proposed actions) aimed at synthesizing novel solutions (that is, creative problem solving).

With constructive controversy, teachers intentionally take time to enable students to become more efficient at resolving disagreements that threaten to waste students' time or to cause classroom disruptions. Teaching students how to engage in the controversy-resolution process begins with randomly assigning students to heterogeneous cooperative learning groups of four members (Johnson & Johnson, 1989, 2007,

2009b). Each group receives an issue on which to write a report and pass a test. Each cooperative group is divided into two pairs. One pair takes the con position on the issue; the other pair takes the pro position. Each pair receives the instructional materials necessary to define their position and point them toward supporting information. The materials highlight the cooperative goal of reaching a consensus on the issue (by synthesizing the best reasoning from both sides) and writing a quality group report. Students then (1) research, learn about, and prepare their assigned position; (2) present a persuasive case that their position is correct; (3) engage in an open discussion in which there is spirited disagreement; (4) reverse perspectives and present the best case for the opposing position; (5) agree on a synthesis or integration of the best reasoning from both sides; and (6) reflect on the process so that they may learn from the experience.

Overall, the research indicates that constructive controversies (compared with concurrence seeking, debate, and individualistic efforts) create higher achievement, greater retention, more creative problem solving, more frequent use of higher-level reasoning and metacognitive thought, more perspective taking, greater continuous motivation to learn, more positive attitudes toward learning, more positive interpersonal relationships, greater social support, and higher self-esteem (Johnson & Johnson, 1989, 2007, 2009b). Engaging in constructive controversy can also be fun, enjoyable, and exciting. The theory of constructive controversy, the supporting research, and the controversy procedure provide an empirical base for political discourse and collective decision making that can enhance student collaborations in a variety of situations both in and out of the classroom.

Integrative Negotiations

In order to function effectively in the 21st century, individuals must know how to negotiate constructive resolutions to conflicts of interest. A conflict of interest exists when the actions of one person attempting to maximize his or her wants and benefits prevents or interferes with another person maximizing his or her wants and benefits. Conflicts of interest occur frequently when people work together cooperatively. How conflicts are resolved has considerable influence on the quality of the cooperation and the long-term survival and health of the cooperative system. Twenty-first-century teachers can prepare students to mediate and to negotiate disagreements so that students resolve issues in a quality manner.

For example, teachers may use the program *Teaching Students to Be Peacemakers* (Johnson & Johnson, 2005b) to prepare students to solve problems. Students learn the following steps in their preparation to solve problems and mediate conflicts:

1. Recognize what is and is not a conflict, and the potential positive outcomes of conflicts.

2. Understand the basic strategies for managing conflicts (for example, withdrawal, forcing, smoothing, compromising, and engaging in problem solving and integrative negotiations).

3. Engage in problem solving and integrative negotiations by (a) describing what they want, (b) describing how they feel, (c) describing the reasons for their wants and feeling, (d) taking the other's perspective, (e) inventing three optional plans to resolve the conflict that maximize joint benefits, and (f) choosing one plan and formalizing the agreement with a handshake.

4. Mediate schoolmates' conflicts by (a) ending hostilities by breaking up hostile encounters and cooling off students, (b) ensuring disputants are committed to the mediation process, (c) helping disputants successfully use problem-solving negotiations with each other, and (d) formalizing the agreement into a contract.

5. Implement the Peacemaker Peer-Mediation Program. (Each day the teacher selects two class members to serve as official mediators. The role of mediator rotates so that all students serve as mediators for an equal amount of time.)

The outcomes of this program are manifold. The benefits of teaching students the problem-solving negotiation and the peer-mediation procedures include mastery of the negotiation and mediation procedures, retention of that mastery throughout the school year and into the following year, application of the procedures to their and other students' conflicts, and transference of the procedures to nonclassroom settings (such as the playground and lunchroom) and nonschool settings (such as the home). Trained students tend to use more constructive strategies, such as integrative negotiations, than do untrained students. Students' attitudes toward conflict tend to become more positive. Finally, when integrated into academic units, the conflict-resolution training tends to increase academic achievement and long-term retention of the academic material.

Four Crucial Challenges of the 21st Century

Cooperative learning, constructive controversy, and integrative negotiations are three essential approaches for meeting the four crucial challenges unique to the 21st century. These strategies provide students with the essential skills necessary to address each of these challenges in the more collaborative school and work environment.

> Cooperative learning, constructive controversy, and integrative negotiations provide students with the essential skills necessary to address 21st century challenges in the more collaborative school and work environment.

Challenge 1: Global Interdependence

The 21st century is characterized by increasing technological, economic, ecological, and political interdependence among individuals, communities, countries, and regions of the world. Thomas Friedman, in his book *The World Is Flat* (2005), argues that the world has to "connect and collaborate." British Prime Minister Gordon Brown stated that the nations and regions of the world urgently need to step out of the mindset of competing interests and instead find common interests and launch cooperative efforts to build new international rules and institutions for the new global era. Schools are the setting in which individuals will learn how to do so.

In a 2002 *Los Angeles Times* editorial, former U.S. President Bill Clinton asked whether this increasing world interdependence would be good or bad for humanity. Global interdependence accelerates the development of countries and increases incomes and living standards through heightened world trade. In contrast, global interdependence increases vulnerability of each country to all other countries. The economies of these countries are no longer autonomous. Internal economic disruptions in one country can affect the economy of many other countries. Inflation can spread across national borders. Drastic actions by one country can quickly translate into hardships for another. Thus, while interdependence creates greater worldwide prosperity and productivity, it also increases the capability of each country to influence the events within all other countries. The result is larger, more numerous conflicts that must be managed. Understanding the nature of interdependent systems, how to operate effectively within them, and how to manage conflicts are essential qualities of future citizens and leaders.

Global interdependence also means that the solution to most major problems individual countries face (for example, eradicating disease, world hunger, contamination of the environment, global warming, international terrorism, or nuclear proliferation) are increasingly ones that cannot be solved by actions taken only at the national level. This internationalization of problems blurs the lines between domestic and international problems. The international affairs of one country are the internal affairs of other nations. Countries are far more vulnerable to outside economic disruptions. Therefore, future citizens and world leaders must understand the nature of interdependent systems and how to operate effectively within them.

Diversity and pluralism. More intense global interdependence is increasing diversity and pluralism on the local level, due to advances in transportation and ease of moving from one country to another. Working cooperatively and resolving conflicts among diverse individuals will become a more commonplace need. Cooperative learning is especially helpful for capitalizing on the benefits of diversity (Johnson & Johnson, 1989) and ensures that all students are meaningfully and actively involved in learning. Active, involved students tend not to engage in rejecting, bullying, or prejudiced behavior. Cooperative learning ensures that students achieve their potential and experience psychological success so that they are motivated to continue to invest energy and effort in learning. Those who experience academic failure are at risk for paying no attention and acting up, which often leads to physical or verbal aggression against stereotyped classmates. Cooperative learning promotes the development of caring and committed relationships among

> Cooperative learning is especially helpful for capitalizing on the benefits of diversity.

students, including between majority and minority students. Students who are isolated or alienated from their peers and who have no friends are at risk for being targets or sources of physical or verbal aggression. The negative impact of isolation may be even more severe on minority students.

Cooperative learning groups provide an arena in which students develop the interpersonal and small-group skills needed to work effectively with diverse schoolmates. These interpersonal skills enable students to engage in discussions in which they share and solve personal problems. As a result, students' resilience and ability to cope with adversity and stress tend to increase. Children who do not share their problems and who do not have caring, supportive help in solving them are at more risk for physical or verbal aggression toward stereotyped classmates. Students in cooperative learning groups academically help and assist diverse groupmates and contribute to their well-being and quality of life. This behavior promotes a sense of meaning, pride, and self-esteem. Finally, the systematic use of cooperative learning provides the context for resolving conflicts in constructive ways, which is essential for positive relationships among diverse individuals.

International, national, intergroup, and interpersonal conflict resolution. As interdependence increases at the international, national, intergroup, and interpersonal level, so does the frequency and intensity of conflicts at all of these levels. These conflicts involve conflicts in collective decision making and conflicts of interest. *Destructive conflicts* tend to be competitive, where one party tries to win over another. *Constructive conflicts* tend to be cooperative, in which involved parties seek an agreement that benefits all. Conflict results when nations and organizations work together to solve mutual and/or global problems. Opposing groups can disagree about the nature and cause of the problems, have different values and goals related to outcomes and means, and disagree about how much each should contribute to the problem-solving efforts. How constructively such conflicts are resolved becomes a central issue in how effectively global interdependence is managed.

Disagreement about the care of the environment is one example of the need for understanding interdependence and applying that knowledge to resolving global conflicts constructively. Population estimates predict more than nine billion humans will inhabit the planet by 2050, and the ecosystems of the Earth will likely be unable to sustain such large numbers, especially if humans continue to deplete natural resources, pollute the environment, and reduce biodiversity. With increased population will come economic and social conflicts that could devastate the health and well-being of current and future human populations. The World Commission on Environment and Development recognized these difficulties in 1987 when it stated, "The Earth is one, but the world is not." The competencies students need to learn to effectively deal with such disagreement and conflict are those contained in constructive controversy and integrative negotiations. Teachers can help students learn from conflicts that arise in collective decision making and with conflicts of interest; rather than end these conflicts with punitive measures, teachers can teach the competencies and apply them to the higher-level conflicts students will experience outside the classroom.

Challenge 2: Increasing Number of Democracies

Due to increasing global interdependence, the spread of technology and information, and the increasing power of international organizations such as the United Nations, the number of democracies will increase throughout the world in the 21st century. In 1748, Charles de Secondat, Baron de Montesquieu, published *The Spirit of Laws* in which he explored the relationship between people and different forms of government. He concluded that while dictatorship survives on the fear of the people and monarchy survives on the loyalty of the people, a free republic (the most fragile of the three political systems) survives on the virtue of the people. Virtue is reflected in the way a person balances his or her own needs with the needs of the society as a whole. Motivation to be virtuous comes from a sense of belonging, a concern for the whole, and a moral bond with the community. The moral bond is cultivated by deliberating with fellow citizens about the common good and helping shape the destiny of the political community.

A number of important parallels exist between being an effective member of a cooperative learning group and being an effective citizen in a democracy (Johnson & Johnson, 2010). A cooperative learning group is a microcosm of a democracy. A *democracy* is, after all, first and foremost a cooperative system in which citizens work together to reach goals and determine their future. Similarly, in cooperative learning groups, individuals work to achieve mutual goals, are responsible for contributing to the work of the group, have the right and obligation to express their ideas, and are under obligation to provide leadership and ensure effective decisions. All group members are considered equal. Decisions result from careful consideration of all points of view. Group members adopt a set of values that include contributing to the well-being of their groupmates and the common good. All of these characteristics are also true of democracies.

Thomas Jefferson, James Madison, and the other founders of the United States of America considered the heart of democracy to be *political discourse*: the formal exchange of reasoned views on which several alternative courses of action could be taken to solve a societal problem. Political discourse is a method of decision making in a democracy. The intent of political discourse is to involve all citizens in the making of the decision, persuade others (through valid information and logic), and clarify what course of action would be most effective in solving the problem, such as poverty, crime, drug abuse, poor economic health, or racism. The expectation is for citizens to prepare the best case possible for their position, advocate it strongly, critically analyze the opposing positions, step back and review the issue from all perspectives, and then come to a reasoned judgment about the course of action the society should take. The clash of opposing positions is expected to increase citizens' understanding of the issue and the quality of decision making, given that citizens would keep an open mind and change their opinions when logically persuaded to do so. Engaging in political discourse involves both short-term and long-term positive interdependence. The short-term positive interdependence is the immediate creation of consensus among citizens as to which course of action will best solve the problem. The long-term interdependence is the improvement of the political process and the maintenance of the health of the democracy. Cooperative learning and constructive controversy have been used to teach elementary and secondary students how to be citizens in a democracy in such countries as Armenia, Azerbaijan, the Czech Republic, and Lithuania (Avery, Freeman, Greenwalt, & Trout, 2006; Hovhannisyan, Varrella, Johnson, & Johnson, 2005).

Digital citizenship skills. In addition to the citizenship skills needed to be productive and responsible citizens of a democracy, individuals need to develop digital citizenship skills. Digital citizenship skills enable individuals to use technology in safe and responsible ways. Like all skills, digital citizenship has corresponding attitudes about the responsible and productive use of technology, such as cooperativeness and the avoidance of competitiveness. In many ways, being a good citizen on the Internet is the same as being a good collaborator. Most technology is used to achieve mutual goals and is, therefore, a cooperative endeavor. Technology is aimed primarily at enabling members of a team, organization, society, or multinational entities to achieve mutual goals more effectively. Technology allows research teams from all over the world to coordinate their activities almost instantly. Members of the same organization in many different locations can receive simultaneously instructions on completing a joint task. It is technology that makes resources available to complete cooperative enterprises such as massively multiplayer online games. Technology also provides access to multitudes of potential collaborators and shared spaces in which to complete cooperative tasks. Furthermore, people's behavior online can define their identity in their online relationships. The next wave of social networking will move technology systems away from restricting users to walled-off membership in a few sites, such as Facebook, toward a more open and flexible sharing among numerous niche communities. This will help individuals to make visible their *social graph*, or the network of people they know, are related to, or work with, independent of any given address book or networking system. Digital citizenship skills will thus become an essential aspect of individuals' lives in the 21st century.

Challenge 3: The Need for Creative Entrepreneurs

The economic future of societies depends on their capability to grow, attract, and support talented, innovative, and creative entrepreneurs (Florida, 2007). Because creative entrepreneurs are highly mobile, countries with the highest quality of life will attract the highest number of creative entrepreneurs. The challenge for educational systems in each country is to produce creative entrepreneurs who will then contribute to the future economic health of the country.

Nations must first ensure their educational system is socializing students into being creative, productive people who believe that they can better their life through being entrepreneurs. Nations must also ensure that their quality of life is sufficient to attract and keep creative entrepreneurs. Two factors that largely determine quality of life are the absence of poverty and its resulting social problems and the ability of individuals to potentially better their lives through becoming entrepreneurs. Education is the key mechanism for individuals to rise from one social class to another. Thus, schools have the responsibilities to teach students how to be creative problem solvers and especially to maximize the achievement for students from lower socioeconomic groups, ensuring that they go on to universities and graduate programs.

Teaching students to be creative is not something many schools achieved in past eras. Creativity is the capability to create or invent something original or to generate unique approaches and solutions to issues or problems (Johnson & Johnson, 1989, 2005a, 2009a). Creativity is a social product advanced through mutual consideration of diverse ideas in a cooperative context; it does not emerge well in a competitive or individualistic context. Cooperative learning and constructive controversy (that is, students disagreeing with each other and challenging each other's conclusions and theories) tend to increase the number of ideas, quality of ideas, feelings of stimulation and enjoyment, and originality of expression in problem-solving tasks.

Research shows that cooperative learning, compared with competitive and individualistic learning, increases the number of novel solutions, results in the use of more varied reasoning strategies, generates more original ideas, and results in more creative solutions to problems. In addition, cooperative learning and constructive controversy encourage group members to dig into a problem, raise issues, and settle them in ways that show the benefits in a wide range of ideas and result in a high degree of emotional involvement in and commitment to solving the problems (Johnson & Johnson, 2005a).

In constructive controversies, participants tend to invent more creative solutions to problems, be more original in their thinking, generate and utilize a greater number of ideas, generate more high-quality ideas, analyze problems at a deeper level, raise more issues, experience greater feelings of stimulation and enjoyment, become more emotionally involved in and committed to solving the problem, and experience more satisfaction with the resulting decision (Johnson & Johnson, 2005a).

High-quality reasoning skills. In addition to creativity, more frequent discovery and development of high-quality cognitive reasoning strategies occurs in cooperative environments than in competitive or individualistic situations (Johnson & Johnson, 1989, 2005a). Studies from Jean Piaget's cognitive development theory and Lawrence Kohlberg's moral development theory indicate that cooperative experiences promote the transition to higher-level cognitive and moral reasoning more frequently than competitive or individualistic experiences. Furthermore, when members of a cooperative group express differences of opinion, according to Piaget as well as controversy theory, they enhance the level and quality of their cognitive and moral reasoning. Finally, in cooperative situations, students tend to engage in more frequent and accurate perspective taking than they do in competitive or individualistic situations. This accurate perspective taking enhances members' ability to respond to others' needs with empathy, compassion, and support.

Challenge 4: Changes in Interpersonal Relationships

In the 21st century, the emphasis on friendship formation and positive interpersonal interactions is increasing, as the rise in popularity of social networks already shows. These relationships will take place with increasing intensity in two settings: face-to-face interactions and online. Cooperation and constructive conflict resolution will play a vital role in building positive relationships in each setting, whereas competition and individualism will tend to result in negative relationships in each setting. Cooperative efforts promote considerably more positive regard among individuals. This is also true for relationships between majority and minority individuals, and for relationships between students with special needs and those without.

> In the 21st century, the emphasis on friendship formation and positive interpersonal interactions is increasing, as the rise in popularity of social networks already shows.

Online relationships. Current trends seem to indicate that in the 21st century, relationships may start and/or develop online with increasing frequency. Relationships developed and maintained through such avenues as email, websites such as Facebook and MySpace, blogging, texting, tweeting, and online multiplayer games facilitate connections among peers. Online interaction can supplement face-to-face relationships, maintain previous face-to-face relationships as people move to different geographic locations, or be the setting in which new relationships form.

Online relationships are usually built around mutual goals and a common purpose; they tend not to be random. People read a blog for a purpose, find people with similar interests for a reason, and engage in games to have fun and test their skills. The fact that online relationships are built on a common purpose makes them by definition cooperative. The more people know about cooperative efforts and the more skilled they are in cooperating, the more successful their online relationships will be.

It is important to realize that online relationships are real relationships. Actual people read email messages, respond to comments on a blog, receive and send Twitter messages, post messages on Facebook, and so on. Not only are they real, but they are important. Relationships are based on the time individuals spend interacting with one another. More and more relationship time may be spent online. More and more people are spending as much or more of their relationship time online compared to face-to-face.

Electronic media offer the opportunity to expand the number of relationships a person has very quickly and very easily. There are few barriers for entry into online relationships, and the opportunity to do so is high. A person can use the Internet to easily find other people who have similar interests and beliefs. Entering one website may provide access to dozens of people with whom to interact about an area of mutual interest. Having such immediate access to large numbers of potential friends is difficult if not impossible in face-to-face situations. The ease of creating relationships online enhances individuals' ability to find collaborators and identify people who have resources essential for completing cooperative projects.

In Internet relationships, personal geography tends not to be relevant. No matter where an individual lives, it is possible to find friends all over the world. Thus, diversity of community may be unimportant to many people because, regardless of who their neighbors are, they can find a community of like-minded people on the Internet. Or, if a neighborhood is too homogeneous for an individual's tastes, he or she can use the Internet to find diverse friends and a wide variety of perspectives. Because diverse perspectives and resources enhance cooperation and constructive conflict, Internet relationships can enhance the quality of cooperation and constructive conflict considerably.

It is easy to interact with lots of people simultaneously on the Internet. The same email can be sent to dozens, even hundreds, of people. What a person posts on a Facebook page can be accessed by friends from all over the world who can then respond. In contrast, most face-to-face relationships are one-on-one. The speed at which communication takes place online enhances cooperation and coordination of efforts in most cases as long as messages are phrased cooperatively. If competitive messages are sent, the speed of communication may alienate more people more quickly.

In online relationships, people primarily know others through what they disclose about themselves. There can understandably be much skepticism about what people say about themselves online. In cooperative situations, trust may be higher, as individuals tend to be open, accurate, and honest in their communications and disclosures. Generally, however, the 21st century will no doubt see the development of new ways for assessing individual's online personas and honesty, such as assessing speed of keyboarding and responding, cleverness in phrasing responses, patterns of wording in messages, sense of humor, creativity in writing, and so on.

Online relationships can be highly positive and fulfilling. The arrival of email can bring joy. The honest disclosure of thoughts and feelings can be liberating. Support from online friends can be quite powerful. Not all online relationships, however, are positive. Cyberbullying and other negative interactions occur online. Nonetheless, the vast majority of online relationships seem to be quite positive, resulting in laughter, good humor, cheerfulness, joy, and fun. Such behaviors reflect positive relationships.

Material posted on the Internet spreads rapidly and widely and may be available to interested parties for decades. That means people must concern themselves more with what they post on the Internet and its impact on their privacy in public and face-to-face relationships. For example, behavior with a friend can be recorded on a cell phone and sent to dozens of people, and even end up posted on YouTube. Pictures of a teenager at a party can show up on a company website twenty years later.

Finally, online relationships focus attention on ethics, manners, and values. When people develop online relationships, they develop new systems of ethics and manners due to the nature of the technology. What is polite and what is rude, for example, may be different online than in face-to-face relationships. Online relationships can also affect individuals' value systems. A recent study found that in the United States, Japan, Singapore, and Malaysia, the more people played a prosocial online game, the more they tended to engage in prosocial behavior afterward, and when they played a violent online game, they were more likely to behave in competitive, obstructive ways afterward.

The Impact of Online Interaction on Face-to-Face Relationships

The increasing ease of building and maintaining online relationships in the 21st century will have considerable impact on face-to-face relationships. First, the majority of face-to-face interaction individuals may experience will take place in school. Second, as the amount of time spent in face-to-face relationships declines, the face-to-face interactions that do occur will increasingly include touch. Online relationships developed through voice chat and video provide additional cues such as tone of voice and facial expressions, but they do not provide touch (although touch-technology is under development). Touch is central to human social life. At birth, touch is the most developed sensory modality, and it contributes to cognitive, brain, and socioemotional development through infancy and childhood. Individuals deprived of human touch may develop serious psychological and developmental problems. Touch is essential to the emotional experiences in a relationship, because it communicates and intensifies emotions. Touch is especially important in communicating positive emotions, such as love, affection, caring, gratitude, empathy, and sympathy. As a person has fewer face-to-face relationships, the amount of touch in each relationship may tend to increase. Touch is especially important in cooperative relationships and when conflicts have been resolved constructively.

Identity Formation

A person's *identity* is a consistent set of attitudes that defines "who I am" (Johnson & Johnson, 1989). It is a generalization about the self derived from a person's interactions and relationships with other people, and from memberships in certain groups, communities, and cultures. Identity is made up of the multiple views we have of ourselves, including our physical characteristics, social roles, the activities we engage in, our attitudes and interests, gender, culture, ethnicity, and age. In addition, our identity includes ideals we would like to attain and standards we want to meet. All of these aspects of identity are arranged in a hierarchy that is dynamic, not static. Each aspect of a person's identity has positive or negative connotations. The sum of a person's approval or disapproval of his or her behavior and characteristics is referred to as *self-esteem*.

Forming an identity involves seeing oneself as a member of a moral community that shares a joint identity and engages in prosocial actions. Moral communities tend to reflect egalitarianism (that is, a belief in the equal worth of all members) and mutual respect. Identity in a competitive context, in contrast, defines a person as a separate individual striving to win. A competitor may have a moral identity involving the virtues of inequality, being a winner, and disdaining losers.

Cooperative experiences tend to increase the frequency with which participants engage in prosocial behaviors, whereas competitive experiences tend to increase the frequency with which individuals engage in antisocial behavior such as bullying and aggression with the intent of harm. Being prosocial has its benefits. Prosocial children tend to build positive relationships and enjoy positive well-being. Engaging in prosocial behavior influences a person's identity.

> Forming an identity involves seeing oneself as a member of a moral community that shares a joint identity and engages in prosocial actions.

The identities of people who rescued Jews during the Holocaust, for example, were still enhanced more than fifty years later by their good deeds. Elementary school students who privately agreed to give up their recess time to work for hospitalized children saw themselves as more altruistic immediately and a month later (Cialdini, Eisenberg, Shell, & McCreath, 1987).

Online Identity

In the 21st century, people's identities will be tied to the way they are perceived by the people with whom they have online relationships. Online identities are different from the identities people develop in face-to-face situations. Online, physical appearance is usually arbitrary, and identity comes more from a person's cleverness in phrasing messages, how he or she writes, the quickness and insightfulness of his or her responses, and what is unique about his or her insights, views, and contributions. For the identities to be positive, however, the online interaction needs to be within cooperative efforts in which conflicts are managed constructively. It is under those conditions that positive, strong identities tend to develop.

Coping With the Challenges

The challenges facing citizens of the 21st century begin with the increasing economic, technological, and environmental global interdependence. With global interdependence will come increased diversity at the local level, and frequency and intensity of conflicts among nations and regions, as well as individuals and groups. More and more countries will become democracies. In order for a country to prosper economically, it must develop, attract, and hold onto creative entrepreneurs. High-quality relationships will continue to hold considerable importance, but online relationships formed around cooperative endeavors will become more and more dominant. The Internet will also affect individuals' formation of personal identities. In all of these challenges, cooperative learning, constructive controversy, and problem-solving negotiations will play a central role in teaching children, adolescents, and young adults the competencies and values they need to cope with challenges and lead productive and fulfilling lives during the 21st century.

References

Avery, P., Freeman, C., Greenwalt, K., & Trout, M. (2006, April). *The "deliberating in a democracy project."* Paper presented at the annual meeting of the American Educational Research Association, San Francisco.

Cialdini, R. B., Eisenberg, N., Shell, R., & McCreath, H. (1987). Commitments to help by children: Effects on subsequent prosocial self-attributions. *British Journal of Social Psychology, 26*, 237–245.

Florida, R. L. (2007). *The flight of the creative class: The new global competition for talent.* New York: Collins Business.

Friedman. T. (2005). *The world is flat.* New York: Farrar, Straus and Giroux.

Hovhannisyan, A., Varrella, G., Johnson, D. W., & Johnson, R. (2005). Cooperative learning and building democracies. *The Cooperative Link, 20*(1), 1–3.

Johnson, D. W., & Johnson, R. T. (1989). *Cooperation and competition: Theory and research.* Edina, MN: Interaction Book Company.

Johnson, D. W., & Johnson, R. T. (2005a). New developments in social interdependence theory. *Genetic, Social, and General Psychology Monographs, 131*(4), 285–358.

Johnson, D. W., & Johnson, R. T. (2005b). *Teaching students to be peacemakers* (4th ed.). Edina, MN: Interaction Book Company.

Johnson, D. W., & Johnson, R. T. (2007). *Creative controversy: Intellectual challenge in the classroom* (4th ed.). Edina, MN: Interaction Book Company.

Johnson, D. W., & Johnson, R. T. (2009a). An educational psychology success story: Social interdependence theory and cooperative learning. *Educational Researcher, 38*(5), 365–379.

Johnson, D. W., & Johnson, R. T. (2009b). Energizing learning: The instructional power of conflict. *Educational Researcher, 38*(1), 37–51.

Johnson, D. W., & Johnson, R. T. (2010). Teaching students how to live in a democracy. In F. Salidi & R. Hoosain (Eds.), Democracy and multicultural education (pp. 201–234). Charlotte, NC: Information Age Publishing.

Johnson, D. W., Johnson, R. T., & Holubec, E. (2008). *Cooperation in the classroom* (7th ed.). Edina, MN: Interaction Book Company.

de Montesquieu, C. (1748/2004). *The spirit of laws.* New York: Kessinger.

World Commission on Environment and Development. (1987). *Report of the World Commission on Environment and Development: Our common future.* New York: United Nations Documents.

Douglas Fisher

Douglas Fisher, Ph.D., is a professor of language and literacy education in the Department of Teacher Education at San Diego State University and a teacher leader at Health Sciences High & Middle College. He is the recipient of an International Reading Association Celebrate Literacy Award, the Farmer award for excellence in writing from the National Council of Teachers of English, and a Christa McAuliffe award for excellence in teacher education from the American Association of State Colleges and Universities. He has published numerous articles and books on reading and literacy, differentiated instruction, and curriculum design.

Nancy Frey

Nancy Frey, Ph.D., is a professor of literacy in the School of Teacher Education at San Diego State University and a teacher leader at Health Sciences High & Middle College. Frey was previously a teacher at the elementary and middle school levels in the Broward County (Florida) Public Schools. She later worked for the Florida Department of Education on a statewide project for supporting students with diverse learning needs in general education curriculum. She is a recipient of the Christa McAuliffe award for excellence in teacher education from the American Association of State Colleges and Universities. She has coauthored books on literacy.

In this chapter, Fisher and Frey describe three ways for teachers to respond to the extreme shifts in technological advancement and student needs for the 21st century: (1) considering functions rather than tools, (2) revising technology policies, and (3) developing students' minds through intentional instruction.

Chapter 10

Preparing Students for Mastery of 21st Century Skills

Douglas Fisher and Nancy Frey

"Does it work?" asked a curious adolescent as she stared at the chalkboard at the front of the classroom.

We don't like to think of ourselves as getting older, but the bewildered question of a teen who is flummoxed by the sight of an object "us old people" take for granted, a common blackboard, certainly makes us feel old. What led up to this question requires a bit of explanation.

Nancy was scheduled to speak to a group of school principals in a nearby community during a professional development meeting on quality instruction for all learners. It has become our practice to include students from the high school where we work in our presentations, whenever possible, to bring the audience a student's perspective. Three tenth-grade students, Coraima, Susana, and Mariana, accompanied Nancy to this presentation. As the four of them entered the room where the meeting would take place, the girls stopped and let out an audible gasp.

"Does it work?" asked Coraima.

Nancy looked to the front of the room to see what Coraima was referring to, and then silently contemplated her own mortality. Coraima was referring to the chalkboard.

Given that there was a piece of chalk in the tray, Nancy was able to answer in the affirmative. She watched as the three teenagers approached the board and took turns making tentative marks with the chalk. "It's soft," said Mariana.

Nancy realized at that moment that the girls had never had a chalkboard in their classrooms, only whiteboards and dry-erase markers. More recently, they have become acquainted with interactive Smart Boards and document cameras. Their only experiences with chalk were with the sidewalk variety, where the rough surface requires more pressure and a firmer stroke. And as members of a digital generation, their syntax reflected a worldview of communication tools as active, not passive.

We're not saying that whiteboards or Smart Boards represent the cutting edge of technology, but rather that these students have a scope of experiences that differs from that of their teachers. This in itself is nothing new, but it does serve as a reminder that educational technologies can prompt a sea change in teaching. For instance, the invention of chalkboards more than two hundred years ago revolutionized schooling because it made it possible to move from individual study to large-group instruction (Krause, 2000).

> These students have a scope of experiences that differs from that of their teachers.

The girls' use of technology throughout the day with Nancy illustrated how ubiquitous new forms of technology have become. They took photographs of themselves with their cell phones and sent them to one of their teachers to document their adventure. One of the girls also had a digital camera, and while Nancy finished her presentation, the girls recorded themselves lip-synching to popular songs, which they later uploaded to YouTube. They sent text messages to friends and parents and tweeted throughout the day to update them on their status and collected a few photos for possible use on their MySpace pages. What was most notable, however, was how ever-present these communication tools were in the hands of the girls. The point was not to use technology for its own sake. To these adolescents, these were tools to fulfill an ancient need to communicate, share, collaborate, and express. This evolution has even been captured in political cartoons. In figure 10.1, the artist and public commentator captures the fact that the need to communicate has remained consistent, yet the form has changed. At the same time, he raises a concern about the newer forms of communication and their potential limitations.

Figure 10.1: One person's view of the changing landscape of communication. Reprinted with permission from Mike Keefe, *The Denver Post*, and InToon.com.

Like the chalkboards of our school days, the best technologies fade into the background—they "weave themselves into the fabric of everyday life until they are indistinguishable from it" (Weiser, 1991, p. 94). The tools themselves evolve; our task as educators is to foreground communication while keeping abreast of the technologies that support it. If we focus on the tool but lose sight of the purpose, we are forever condemned to playing catch-up in a landscape of rapidly changing technology. Remember beepers? They enjoyed a brief popularity in the 1990s but became obsolete with the widespread use of cell phones. Few people use paging devices anymore because a new technology can fulfill a similar function more efficiently. Focusing on the tool at the expense of the purpose means that we shortchange our students. We risk failing to prepare our students to be 21st century learners who can adapt to new technology because they understand the collaborative, cooperative, and communicative purposes that underlie the tool. As architect Frank Lloyd Wright noted, "Form follows function."

When we keep the function in mind, the forms assume a "natural technology" so that they become a tool for our teaching repertoire (Krause, 2000, p. 6).

As urban educators, we are also concerned about the access students have to technology. The elementary school that the girls attended was a Title I school, with 100 percent of the students qualifying for free or reduced-price lunch. In addition, 72 percent of the students, including the three girls, were identified as English language learners. Yet even among students who come from low-income households, cell phones and cameras are ubiquitous. As well, they knew how to gain access to the Internet, even though none of them had laptops. What they did have going for them was a series of school experiences that ensured digital learning.

> As urban educators, we are also concerned about the access students have to technology.

Form and Function in the 21st Century

Others in this volume have noted that a major challenge facing educators is in preparing students for economies and technologies that do not currently exist. However, it is likely that they will be required to participate on an increasingly diverse and global playing field made possible by communication tools that allow them to respond to societal changes. A growing number of professional organizations have crafted position papers stating as much. For instance, the National Council of Teachers of English (NCTE) suggests that 21st century readers and writers will be able to:

Develop proficiency with the tools of technology;

Build relationships with others to pose and solve problems collaboratively and cross-culturally;

Design and share information for global communities to meet a variety of purposes;

Manage, analyze, and synthesize multiple streams of simultaneous information;

Create, critique, analyze, and evaluate multi-media texts; and

Attend to the ethical responsibilities required by these complex environments. (NCTE, 2009, p. 15)

We stated earlier that we try to include student perspectives in our work. Therefore, it seems only fair that we do so now. Consider the recommendations gathered in a survey (Project Tomorrow, 2009) of more than 280,000 students for how students would use stimulus package money to improve their schools:

- 52 percent recommended a laptop for each student.

- 51 percent asked for more games and simulations for teaching concepts.

- 44 percent requested use of digital media tools.

- 43 percent said they would like interactive whiteboards installed.

- 42 percent wanted online textbooks.

- 40 percent stated that email, instant messaging, and text-messaging tools would enhance their learning.

A superficial analysis of their feedback might conclude that it is no more than a shopping list of gadgets, but that would do a disservice to the student participants. They can't name the function, but they can name the form. It is our responsibility as educators to detect the functions that underlie the forms or tools. The students' requests connote a deep-seated need to communicate and collaborate, to access information at any time of the day or night, and to have the tools they need to synthesize, evaluate, and create information. Therefore, in our instruction, we must provide access to technology at the same time we are teaching the functions related to communication.

How Can Teachers Respond?

There are a number of ways we can join our students in their 21st century mindset. Thankfully, we are not the first group of educators who have had to make conceptual shifts in our approaches. Yes, it is true that these shifts are accelerating and technology is advancing at an alarming rate. Having said that, there are ways for teachers to respond. We focus on three here: (1) considering functions rather than tools, (2) revising technology policies, and (3) developing students' minds through intentional instruction.

Considering Functions, Not Tools

It's time for a confession: we feel stressed trying to keep up with the innovations of the 21st century. Not too long ago, we were asked to join a Ning, and we didn't know what it was. More recently, we were introduced to Twitter when a student wanted to tweet us. Our stress was reduced when we heard Marc Prensky, in his 2008 keynote at the National Council of Teachers of English conference, suggest that we have to stop thinking of technology in terms of nouns (PowerPoint, YouTube, or Twitter) and instead think in terms of verbs (presenting, sharing, and communicating). In other words, as teachers, we should focus on the functions of the technology rather than the tools or forms of technology. Thankfully, the functions are familiar to us. We'll never keep up with all of the tools (forms). We just need to understand the functions for which the tools are developed so that we can be smart consumers and pick and choose the tools that serve our instructional needs. This was a liberating realization.

Our list of functions, and some current tools associated with those functions, can be found in table 10.1. It is difficult to write this knowing that by the time this is printed, the tools will have likely changed. Think of the list, then, as a historical reminder, and feel free to add new tools to the functions on the list as you discover them. Hopefully, the acknowledgment that tools change yet functions remain will reduce stress and allow educators to select new tools for teaching that engage learners. Increasingly, these tools are moving away from an emphasis on the device and toward a sustained focus on the purpose.

Revising Technology Policies

Once we realized that the technology our students had could be used for good (learning) and not evil (distraction), we had to confront the technology policy. Like most schools, we initially banned technology. At this moment, most schools still ban technology. The week this chapter was written, Doug was in a school in which there were posters in every hallway that read, "If we see it, you lose it!" with pictures of

Table 10.1: Technology Functions With Current Tools

Functions	Tools
Communicating	Text messaging, Twitter, Digg, video conferencing
Listening	Podcasts, iTunes, streaming media, RSS feeds
Networking	MySpace, Facebook, Ning
Presenting	PowerPoint, Keynote, Wimba
Producing	GarageBand, iMovie
Searching	Google, Yahoo, Lycos
Sharing	YouTube, blogs, vlogs, Flickr, collaborating, wikis, VoiceThread, Google Docs
Storing	MP3 players, flash drives, servers, CD/DVD

MP3 players and cell phones. Of course, most of the teachers walking in the hallway had cell phones on their belts, but that's another story.

As we considered the impact of our technology prohibition, we realized that we were doing a disservice to students. They were not developing as global citizens who understood the power and responsibility that came with the technology. A common mobile phone today has more power than most computers a decade ago, yet most students do not know how to use one as a learning tool. In addition, people are routinely rude to one another with their technology. They talk during movies, interrupt dinner to take calls, text while driving, and engage in all kinds of other dangerous or inappropriate behavior. We asked ourselves what we were doing to combat this problem and teach young people to be courteous with their technology. After all, they are going to enter a world of work that is very different from ours—one in which technology is used to solve problems and locate information.

The result of our deliberation was an end to prohibition and a focus on courtesy. We now actively teach students how to use their technology in ways that are appropriate for the environment. A copy of our courtesy policy is shown in table 10.2 (page 229). After several years with this policy, we are pleased to say that technology is no longer an issue for us. We don't confiscate phones, and we don't spend valuable instructional minutes enforcing a policy that worked in the 20th century when few students carried these types of devices. Of course there are minor infractions from time to time, but they are addressed. Students understand that they will have a chance to use their technology in a time and place that is appropriate and that it is discourteous to listen to music or text friends while the teacher is talking or during productive group work.

Courtesy is a code that governs the expectations of social behavior. Each community or culture defines courtesy and the expectations for members of that community or culture. As a learning community, it is our responsibility to define courtesy and to live up to that definition. As a school community, we must hold one another and ourselves accountable for interactions that foster respect and trust. Discourteous behaviors destroy the community and can result in hurt feelings, anger, and additional poor choices.

In general, courtesy means that we interact with one another in positive, respectful ways. Consider the examples of courteous and discourteous behavior shown in table 10.2.

At our school, it is expected that students treat one another, the faculty, staff, and administration—indeed any adult—with respect, courtesy, and cooperation. Further, teachers are expected to treat one another, the students and their families, and the administration in courteous ways.

Discourteous behavior is recognized as an opportunity for learning. In general, students receive feedback, counseling, and guidance when they make mistakes and engage in discourteous behaviors. Repeated failure to engage in courteous behavior results in increasingly punitive consequences, including reparations, restoring the environment, meetings with faculty or staff, meetings with administrators, the development of a behavioral contract, removal of privileges, and/or suspension or expulsion from the school.

Today, students are routinely invited to use their technology to find information. For example, an English teacher we were visiting said to her students, "Who has unlimited service? Can you look up *progeny* for Andrew and talk about what it means?" This two-sentence exchange demonstrates the conceptual shift schools can make in the

Table 10.2: Courtesy Policy

Courteous	Discourteous
Saying please and thank you	Using vulgar, foul, abusive, or offensive language
Paying attention in class	
Socializing with friends during passing periods and lunch	Listening to an iPod during a formal learning situation such as during a lecture or while completing group work
Asking questions and interacting with peers and teachers	
Asking for, accepting, offering, or declining help graciously	Text messaging or talking on a cell phone during class time
Allowing teachers and peers to complete statements without interruptions	Bullying, teasing, or harassing others
	Hogging bandwidth and/or computer time
Throwing away trash after lunch	Not showing up for your scheduled appointments or not completing tasks
Cleaning your own workspace	
Reporting safety concerns or other issues that require attention to a staff member	Failing to communicate when you're not coming to school

21st century. First, technology can be used at school. Second, technology can be used for learning and finding information. And third, we should help each other be productive and learn.

Of course, the school technology policy is not the only thing that needs to change. We need to change Internet-access policies as well. Consider the greatest collection of free video content ever created—YouTube—and the fact that it is banned in most schools. In our school, we use YouTube on a daily basis. In fact, we're not sure that we could plan a lesson that doesn't involve a video clip. And we have yet to look for something and not find it—the collection is simply amazing. For example, we wanted to talk with students about memory formation and how they could use current understandings of the human brain to learn more efficiently. We searched YouTube and found several great sources of information to include.

But we can't get hung up on the tool. YouTube is great, but there will be other tools that eventually come along to meet this need. Our issue is the fact that most teachers can't access this treasure trove of information. We believe that this will change as educators become increasingly savvy in terms of both advocacy and use.

Developing Students' Minds Through Intentional Instruction

A significant part of our work has focused on developing students' thinking skills through intentional instruction (Fisher & Frey, 2008b). Our goal is to release responsibility for learning to students, yet still provide them with the support required to be successful. We have found the *gradual release of responsibility model* most appropriate to accomplish this goal. The gradual release of responsibility model suggests that teachers move purposefully from providing extensive support to using peer support and then no support. Or as Duke and Pearson (2002) suggest, teachers have to move from assuming "all the responsibility for performing a task . . . to a situation in which the students assume all of the responsibility" (p. 211).

The role of instruction in providing access to technology is vital in this regard. Many of our students don't have laptops or other expensive tools, but nearly everyone has a mobile phone, camera, or MP3 player. However, they may lack the opportunity at home to perfect their skills in using Web 2.0 features. That means that they need instruction and opportunities for using these tools to fulfill the functions of literacy learning during their school day. A gradual release model allows for students to gain expertise in the company of teachers and peers who can model, guide, and collaborate.

Unfortunately, in too many classrooms, releasing responsibility is too sudden and unplanned and results in misunderstandings and failure. Consider the classroom in which students hear a lecture and are then expected to pass a test. Or the classroom in which students are told to read texts at home and come to class prepared to discuss them. Or the classroom in which students are assigned a problem set twenty minutes after the teacher has demonstrated how to do the problems. In each of these cases, students are expected to perform independently but are not well prepared for the task. In addition, in each of these classrooms, modern technology tools are not mobilized to develop students' thinking.

Our interpretation of the gradual release of responsibility model includes four components: focus lessons, guided instruction, collaborative tasks, and independent learning (Fisher & Frey, 2008a). Our work, in terms of both teaching and research, suggests that implementation of this instructional framework leads to significant improvement in student engagement and achievement. However, we also want to emphasize that this is not a linear process and that teachers can implement the components in ways that are effective for their outcomes. Our criteria, however, are that all four are present each time students and teachers meet. Let's explore each of the components. Note that table 10.3 (page 232) contains a list of things to look for in a classroom using this framework.

Focus lessons. A typical focus lesson lasts from ten to fifteen minutes. It is designed to do two things: (1) establish a purpose and (2) provide students with a model. Often the purpose is written on the board and briefly discussed with students. Some teachers require that students include the purpose in their notes. Others make a verbal reference to the purpose several times during the class meeting. We aren't too concerned with where and how the purpose is listed, but rather that the students know what is expected of them and why they're learning what they're learning.

The second part of the focus lesson is the model. While volumes can and have been written on modeling, it's rarely done in the secondary classroom. Instead, middle and high school teachers tend to provide procedural explanations, emphasizing the *how*, but not the *why*. Modeling, on the other hand, is metacognitive and includes the thinking behind the thinking. When students get a glimpse inside the thinking of an expert, they begin to approximate that behavior. Imagine the science student who gets to hear her teacher's understanding of an atom or the history student who witnesses the internal debate his history teacher has about sources of information, including the search for corroborating evidence via the Internet. The models we provide students allow them access to academic language and academic thinking as well as information about expert problem

Table 10.3: Elements of a Gradual Release of Responsibility Lesson

Focus Lessons
The teacher uses "I" statements to model thinking.
The teacher uses questioning to scaffold instruction, not to interrogate students.
The lesson includes a decision frame for when to use the skill or strategy.
The lesson builds metacognitive awareness, especially indicators of success.
Focus lessons move to guided instruction, not immediately to independent learning.

Guided Instruction
The teacher uses small-group arrangements.
Grouping changes throughout the semester.
The teacher has an active role in guided instruction; he or she does not just circulate and assist individual students.
There is a dialogue between learners and the teacher as they begin to apply the skill or strategy.
The teacher uses cues and prompts to scaffold understanding when a student makes an error, and he or she does not immediately tell the student the correct answer.

Collaborative Tasks
The teacher uses small-group arrangements.
Grouping changes throughout the semester.
The concepts students need to complete collaborative tasks have been modeled by the teacher.
Students have received guided instruction of the concepts needed to complete collaborative tasks.
Students are individually accountable for their contributions to the group.
The task provides students with an opportunity for interaction.

Independent Learning
Students have received modeled, guided, and collaborative learning experiences related to concepts needed to complete independent tasks.
Independent tasks extend beyond practice to application and extension of new knowledge.
The teacher meets with individual students for conferencing about the independent learning tasks.

Source: Adapted from Better Learning Through Structured Teaching: A Framework for the Gradual Release of Responsibility, *Fisher & Frey, 2008a, pp. 127–128. Reprinted with permission. Learn more about ASCD at www.ascd.org.*

solving and understanding. Daily modeling is critical if students are going to understand complex content.

We have witnessed amazing examples of teacher modeling using technology to address functions and needs. For example, we observed a history teacher modeling his thinking about word solving. When he got to the word *ratify*, he took out his cell phone and sent a text message to a friend to clarify the meaning of the term. We observed a science teacher modeling her thinking about chemical reactions using an interactive website in which variables can be manipulated with different outcomes. We saw an art teacher model his understanding of light and perspective using a digital camera and computer, and we observed an English teacher modeling questions she had for an author by using iChat to send her questions directly to the author. In each of these cases, the teacher modeled his or her *thinking*, and that thinking provided an authentic reason to access 21st century technology, the technology our students use on a daily basis.

Guided instruction. Having a purpose and a model is not enough to ensure enduring understanding. Learners also need to be guided in their thinking. We define guided instruction as the strategic use of cues, prompts, or questions to encourage students to do some of the cognitive work. The latter part of the definition is critical—guided instruction is intended to result in greater student understanding and is not simply a restatement of the information provided during a focus lesson. Guided instructional events, whether with the whole class or small groups of students, are planned strategically such that teachers understand student thinking and can provide a precise scaffold.

We have been very impressed with our teaching colleagues who have used technology to support their guided instruction. We regularly see a biology teacher send instant messages and text messages to students who need scaffolding. We know a history teacher who uses Twitter to send messages to his students, providing them with cues about the tasks at hand. And we have a colleague in English who digitally records her writing conferences with students and then loads them on a course website (password

> Guided instruction is intended to result in greater student understanding and is not simply a restatement of the information provided during a focus lesson.

protected for each student) so that students can use the content from their individual interviews while writing their essays. Again, the technology tools are serving a specific instructional purpose; they are facilitating the transfer of responsibility from teacher to student and are providing the scaffolding necessary for students to develop their thinking skills.

Collaborative tasks. In order to learn—to really learn—students must be engaged in productive group tasks that require interaction. They have to use the language and thinking of the discipline with their peers to really grasp it. And they have to be accountable for their individual contributions to the group task so that the teacher knows which students understand the content and which need additional instruction. There are any number of collaborative tasks that are effective, including the following.

Collaborative writing tasks. We have an English colleague who uses Google Docs to provide students with opportunities to write and receive feedback from peers. We have another English teacher colleague who uses wiki technology (www.writingwiki.org) to provide students with a public outlet for their work. In both of these forums, students learn to collaborate with others, to share feedback in constructive ways, and to think critically about what they read because the writing has not been verified, censored, or edited in any formal way.

Internet reciprocal teaching. During Internet reciprocal teaching (for example, Castek, 2006), each member of the group is responsible for an aspect of comprehension (predicting, questioning, summarizing, or clarifying) and reads from websites while evaluating the information located on the site. A science teacher we know provides topics, and students find articles to read related to the topic. Donald Leu and his colleagues in the New Literacies Research Team at the University of Connecticut (n.d.) have developed a rubric (see table 10.4) for evaluating the quality of the discussions students have while in Internet reciprocal teaching groups.

Graphics production. Our history colleague invites students to create iMovies or digital comic books to demonstrate their understanding of differing perspectives in history. We were most impressed with a twenty-page graphic novel created using Comic Life that

Table 10.4: Internet Reciprocal Teaching Dialogue Rubric

Reciprocal Teaching Strategy	Beginning (1 Point)	Developing (2 Points)	Accomplished (3 Points)	Exemplary (4 Points)	Score
Questioning	Generates simple recall questions that can be answered directly from facts or information found within the website's home page.	Generates main idea questions that can be answered based on information gathered by accessing one or more links to the website's content.	Generates questions requiring inference. Facts and information must be synthesized from one or more links to the website's content and combined with prior knowledge.	Generates questions flexibly that vary in type, based on the content read and the direction of the dialogue.	
Clarifying	Identifies clarification as a tool to enhance understanding and initiates clarification dialogue when appropriate.	Identifies appropriate words for clarification with the dialogue's context.	Assists group in clarifying identified words based on context clues.	Uses strategies for word clarification that can be applied generally across reading contexts.	

continued on next page →

Reciprocal Teaching Strategy	Beginning (1 Point)	Developing (2 Points)	Accomplished (3 Points)	Exemplary (4 Points)	Score
Summarizing	Summary consists of loosely related ideas.	Summary consists of several main ideas but also many details.	Summary synthesizes main ideas, is complete, accurate, and concise.	Summary is accurate, complete, and concise and incorporates content vocabulary contained in the text.	
Predicting	Demonstrates knowledge of predictions as an active reading strategy.	Directs group predictions to set a clear purpose for reading.	Articulates predictions that build logically from context.	Provides justification for prediction and initiates confirmation or redirection based on information located in the text.	

Source: Reprinted with permission. Jill Castek, New Literacies Research Team, Protocol for Internet Reciprocal Teaching (IRT), n.d., pp. 6–7.

depicted life during the French Revolution. The students who created this included a blog on each page, which served a narration function as well as providing historically accurate information describing these events of the time. A sample page can be found in figure 10.2.

Regardless of the instructional routine used for collaborative tasks, there are two keys to making this component effective. First, it must provide students an opportunity to interact with one another using the language and content of the discipline. Second, students must be individually accountable for their contributions to the group. Together, these factors increase engagement and provide teachers with formative assessment information useful in planning future instruction.

Independent learning. As part of instruction, students have to apply what they have been taught. Ideally, this occurs under the guidance of the teacher as part of class time before homework is ever assigned. There are a number of in-class independent tasks that help

**Figure 10.2: Graphic novel page created using Comic Life.
By Marina Bautista. Reprinted with permission.**

students master content. For example, quickwrites allow students to clarify their thinking on a subject. Of course, students can complete these on their laptops. Quickwrites also provide teachers a glimpse into student understanding. Out-of-class independent learning—homework—should be saved until students have a firm grasp of the content. Simply said, students need practice before being asked to complete tasks on their own. But in many classrooms, students are assigned tasks for homework that have not yet been taught. As the MetLife (2008) survey documented, secondary teachers confessed that they "very often or often" assigned homework because they ran out of time in class. The practice of assigning homework for missed class content will not result in student understanding. In fact, it is more likely to reinforce misunderstanding because in many cases students are practicing ineffectively and incorrectly.

In terms of technology-enhanced independent learning tasks, we regularly see podcasts used to facilitate understanding. For example, English teachers can use the Classic Tales podcast (www .theclassictales.com), which makes narrated classic works of fiction available free of charge. There are thousands of free podcasts available online that can extend students' understanding of content, such as those from the History Channel, National Geographic, 60 Second Science, Scientific American, the Museum of Modern Art, and the Smithsonian, to name a few. In addition, discussion boards provide students an opportunity to independently engage in content. For example, a discussion board on *Romeo and Juliet* allows students in different English classes at the same school, or across many schools, to share their thinking and questions about the play.

We witnessed one student's learning using "old" and "new" literacies in a project for her tenth-grade English class. Edith is an English language learner and does not have a computer in her home. However, she has access to technology and instruction at school. Our students address a schoolwide essential question each quarter, and the one that focused Edith's study asked, "Does age matter?" Her English teacher modeled her thinking each day as she read aloud portions of J. M. Barrie's *Peter Pan* (2003). In addition, Edith met with other students to discuss and write about the related text she selected to read, *A Long Way Gone: Memoirs of a Boy Soldier* (Beah, 2007). The author's moving account of a childhood spent as an unwilling recruit in a rebel army in Sierra Leone prompted her to learn more about the plight of child soldiers and victims throughout the world. In addition to writing a traditional essay addressing the essential question, she completed an alternative assignment to represent similar ideas. Edith collaborated with another student to learn GarageBand in order to compose an original piece of instrumental music. Her English teacher showed her how to search Flickr for photographic images licensed under Creative Commons that would allow her to legally use them in an iMovie she made with the help of the technology coordinator at the school. She asked another faculty member to proof her draft presentation and gathered feedback from several trusted peers. The result was a four-minute video that addressed war, child soldiers, and corruption across nearly one hundred years and examined the heavy cost paid by children in the Middle East, Central America, Africa, and Asia when war is waged on civilians. What was most remarkable to us was the way Edith took leadership of completing this project. She gathered resources, both human and digital, to craft a very personal and individual response to an issue of global importance. Simply making technology available to her would have been insufficient. She needed the instruction that comes from a talented teacher, as well as access to peers and adults with whom she could collaborate. The technology became the tool for her to fulfill the timeless need to create and express her viewpoint about a complex topic.

An Invitation

Given that our attempts to ban technology have failed and technological innovation is accelerating, it's time that we consider the use of 21st century tools that serve long-standing functions. Humans need to communicate, share, store, and create. As a species, we've engaged in these functions for centuries. There's really nothing new about them. What is new are the forms, or tools, that students use to meet these needs. As their teachers, it is our responsibility to meet them halfway. We have been entrusted to guide the next generation, and doing so requires that we apprentice them in the functions they will need to be successful. And this success will involve tools that we haven't yet imagined. We're no longer stressed about this; we're excited to learn alongside students as they teach us tools and we help them understand functions.

References

Barrie, J. M. (2003). *Peter Pan* (100th anniversary ed.). New York: Henry Holt.

Beah, I. (2007). *A long way gone: Memoirs of a boy soldier.* New York: Farrar, Straus and Giroux.

Castek, J. (2006, April). *Adapting reciprocal teaching to the Internet using telecollaborative projects.* Symposium presented at the annual meeting of the American Educational Research Association (AERA), San Francisco.

Duke, N. K., & Pearson, P. D. (2002). Effective practices for developing reading comprehension. In A. E. Farstrup & S. J. Samuels (Eds.), *What research has to say about reading instruction* (3rd ed., pp. 205–242). Newark, DE: International Reading Association.

Fisher, D., & Frey, N. (2008a). *Better learning through structured teaching: A framework for the gradual release of responsibility.* Alexandria, VA: Association for Supervision and Curriculum Development.

Fisher, D., & Frey, N. (2008b, November). Releasing responsibility. *Educational Leadership, 66*(3), 32–37.

Krause, S. D. (2000, Spring). Among the greatest benefactors of mankind: What the success of chalkboards tells us about the future of computers in the classroom. *The Journal of the Midwest Modern Language Association, 33*(2), 6–16.

Leu, D., & the University of Connecticut New Literacies Research Team. (n.d.). *Protocol for Internet reciprocal teaching (IRT).* Accessed at www.newliteracies .uconn.edu/carnegie/documents/IRT.pdf on November 10, 2009.

MetLife. (2008). *The MetLife survey of the American teacher: The homework experience.* Accessed at www.ced.org/docs/report/report_metlife2008.pdf on August 29, 2008.

National Council of Teachers of English. (2009, March). Literacy learning in the 21st century: A policy brief produced by the National Council of Teachers of English. *Council Chronicle, 18*(3), 15–16.

Prensky, M. (2008, November). *Homo sapiens digital: Technology is their birthright.* Keynote presentation at the annual meeting of the National Council of Teachers of English, San Antonio, TX.

Project Tomorrow. (2009). *Speak up 2008 congressional briefing.* Accessed at www .tomorrow.org/speakup/speakup_congress.html on April 5, 2009.

Weiser, M. (1991, September). The computer for the 21st century. *Scientific American, 265*(3), 94–104.

Cheryl Lemke

Cheryl Lemke, M.Ed., is president and CEO of the Metiri Group, a consulting firm dedicated to advancing effective uses of technology in schools. Under her leadership, school districts across North America are using Metiri's innovative Dimensions21 system to benchmark their progress with 21st century learning. Prior to launching the firm, she was the executive director of the Milken Exchange on Education Technology for the Milken Family Foundation. Lemke specializes in public policy for K–12 learning technology, working at many levels with governors, legislators, superintendents, business leaders, and teachers. As an associate superintendent for the Illinois State Board of Education, Lemke managed a center for learning technology with over one hundred staff members, translating the fifty-million-dollar annual budget into a new statewide network, professional development centers, community-based technology planning processes for Illinois schools, and online curriculum projects designed to help students learn. She also oversaw the development of state learning technology plans in both Illinois and Washington. Recognized nationally as a proactive leader in learning technology, and sought after as a consultant, speaker, and writer, Lemke has designed policy in the state house that translates into sound educational practice in the schoolhouse.

In this chapter, Lemke introduces three important innovations of 21st century learning: visualization, democratization of knowledge, and participatory cultures for learning. She provides an impressive demonstration of ways technology permits greater balance between a visual approach and traditional language-based communication.

Visit **go.solution-tree.com/21stcenturyskills** to view the graphics in this chapter in full color and to access live links to tools and materials.

Chapter 11

Innovation Through Technology

Cheryl Lemke

There is no turning back. The Internet has become integral to life in the 21st century—a place for work, play, communication, and learning. It is easy to lose sight of just how integral it has become, and how knowledge-based the world economy has become. The combination of human ingenuity and digital tools has led to innovations that have, in some cases, become viral (Foray & Lundvall, 1998). The statistics are staggering: in 2009, the mobile world celebrated its four billionth connection (Global System for Mobile Communications, 2009); over one trillion unique URLs have been registered in Google's index (The Official Google Blog, 2008); there have been nearly sixty-one million views to date of the YouTube most-watched video, *Guitar* (Jeong-hyun, n.d.; Shah, 2005); on average, nine hundred thousand blogs are posted every twenty-four hours (Singer, 2009); over 2.5 billion tweets have been sent (Reed, 2008); YouTube was sold to Google in 2006 for $1.65 billion (Associated Press, 2006); over one hundred million users are logging onto Facebook every day; and approximately 2.6 billion minutes globally are dedicated to using Facebook daily, in thirty-five different languages (Singer, 2009).

Regardless of whether you find these statistics energizing or overwhelming, there is no question that the line between our digital and physical lives is blurring.

Outside of school, 96 percent of nine- to seventeen-year-olds embrace the Web 2.0 culture of social networking, blogging, twittering, GPS mapping, or interactive gaming at some level (National School Board Association, 2007). These youth communicate in real time through texting, instant messaging, and sharing of media files. According to the National School Board Association (2007), they typically spend about nine hours per week outside of school using social networking and ten hours watching television. But the reality is that there are significant variations among youth across the country with respect to the type and frequency of such digital media use (Jenkins, 2007). That holds true in schools as well, with significant differences in the type and frequency of technology use across states (*Education Week* and the Editorial Projects in Education Research Center, 2009b). A June 2009 Nielsen publication reported that, while children and youth do use electronic media in excess of six hours per day, using more than one medium simultaneously 23 percent of that time, they also enjoy reading books, magazines, and newspapers. Nielsen found that 77 percent of U.S. teens have their own mobile phone, 83 percent text message, and 56 percent use picture messaging. Teens average 2,899 text messages per month, which is fifteen times the average number of voice calls (191) they log each month. It would seem that email and phone calls are now considered their "father's mode of digital communication," not theirs (Nielsen Company, 2009).

The responsibility of educators is to ensure that today's students are ready to live, learn, work, and thrive in this high-tech, global, highly participatory world. To that end, U.S. school systems are conspicuously out of sync with the culture of today's society (U.S. Department of Education, 2009).

> The responsibility of educators is to ensure that today's students are ready to live, learn, work, and thrive in this high-tech, global, highly participatory world. To that end, U.S. school systems are conspicuously out of sync with the culture of today's society.

While the more progressive educators are seizing this moment in history to launch a quiet Web 2.0 revolution in preK–12 education, the majority have yet to act. A 2009 national survey conducted by the Consortium on School Networking (CoSN) suggests that the majority of American school districts are at a crossroads with Web 2.0. While school district administrators clearly acknowledge the potential of Web 2.0

tools for learning, the majority of school districts have yet to turn that potential to their students' advantage. According to administrators who responded to the CoSN survey, the top three reasons for using Web 2.0 in school are to (1) keep students interested and engaged in school, (2) meet the needs of different kinds of learners, and (3) develop the critical-thinking skills of students. To date, that potential remains untapped. Instead, many school districts are checking student technologies (such as smartphones, cell phones, iPods, and iTouches) at the schoolhouse door (Lemke, Coughlin, Garcia, Reifsneider, & Baas, 2009).

At the same time, U.S. Secretary of Education Arne Duncan is calling for school districts to innovate using technology. At a national institute in 2009, he said, "Technology presents a huge opportunity . . . good teachers can utilize new technology to accelerate learning and provide extended learning opportunities for students." He went on to say, "We must take advantage of this historic opportunity to use American Recovery and Reinvestment Act funds to bring broadband access and online learning to more communities" (U.S. Department of Education, 2009).

Nationally, there is a call to action for smart, innovative, and informed leadership in 21st century learning in preK–12 education. The combination of crisis and vision has served America well more than once in its two-hundred-year history as it has evolved as a nation. A crisis is now before the United States in the form of the global economic downturn. The question is whether policy leaders will create an informed, collective vision for 21st century learning to turn that crisis into opportunity, and thus turn a new page in American education.

Innovation: The Fuel for a Knowledge-Based Economy

Economists claim that innovation is the fuel for today's global, knowledge-based economy and for its recovery. As such, innovation must play a dual role in America's preK–12 education system: as a foundational principle to the new educational system, and as a 21st century skill acquired by professionals and students alike. *Innovation* is defined here as a creative idea that has achieved sufficient social and/ or professional acceptance so as to become the impetus for ongoing ripples of creativity and change (Drucker, 2002). To build upon the ideas of author Malcolm Gladwell (2000), an innovation is an idea that has tipped and is viral, influencing the system within which it spreads.

21st Century Learning and Student Engagement

In a significant turn of events, business and government leaders are now acknowledging the critical importance of preK–12 education to the economic future of the United States. To that end, policy leaders are advocating for the transformation of preK–12 schools into 21st century learning environments. For the purposes of this chapter, *21st century learning* is defined as the combination of a set of discrete 21st century skills (for example, critical thinking, collaboration, information literacy, and so on), and academic standards to be implemented through digital innovations in the context of emergent research from the cognitive sciences on how people best learn.

> In a significant turn of events, business and government leaders are now acknowledging the critical importance of preK–12 education to the economic future of the United States.

The intent of this chapter is to discuss three of the innovations rippling through our society that must inform America's bold new vision for 21st century learning. A key driver for this new vision is the current lack of student engagement in American schools that has contributed to an extremely high dropout rate nationally; nearly 30 percent of students who begin their ninth-grade year of high school do not graduate (*Education Week* and the Editorial Projects in Education Research Center, 2009a). Some of the disconnect to learning is explained through the concept of *flow*, which is defined as learning with the intensity cranked up—when the learner is at the top of his or her game (Csikszentmihalyi, 1990). Teachers create opportunities for students to get into that flow by balancing the complexity of the task with the students' current repertoire of learning strategies. Too much complexity without the requisite strategies results in frustrated students unable to do the work. On the other hand, if highly capable students with strong learning strategies are given too simple a task, they rapidly become bored. Figure 11.1 depicts the concept of flow (adapted from Csikszentmihalyi, 1990; Schwartz, Bransford, & Sears, 2006).

The research by Csikszentmihalyi (1990, 2002) shows that when that balance is perfected, students enter a flow experience in which

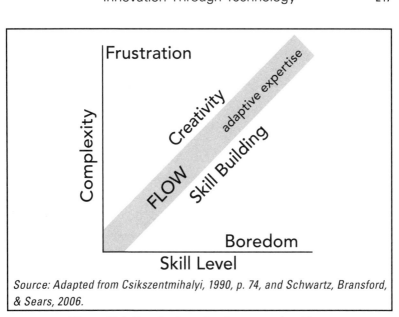

Figure 11.1: Developing adaptive expertise: Flow.

they are fully engaged, intrinsically motivated, and 110 percent invested in their learning. During flow experiences, many students report the sensation of time seeming to stand still as they engage in the experience. Leading cognitive science researchers suggest that the optimal flow experience balances skill level (that leads to efficiency in learning) with the level of task complexity (that leads to creativity and innovation). They contend that a balance between the two will lead to adaptive expertise in learners, which is necessary in dealing with the complexities of life in the 21st century.

The diagram in figure 11.2 (page 248) represents a framework for engaging students deeply in learning (Fredricks, Blumenfeld, & Paris, 2004; Lemke & Coughlin, 2008; Schlechty, 2002). In order to engage students fully in deep learning, they need to be motivated, curious learners who are in classrooms that scaffold that engagement through visualization, democratization of knowledge, and participatory learning.

Innovation One: Visualization

The link between visualization and learning can best be described as sense making. Physiologically, we are wired to swiftly process visuals, albeit differently than we process sound and text. Recent

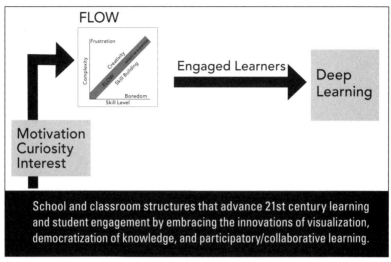

Figure 11.2: A framework for engaging students deeply in learning. Reprinted with permission from Metiri Group.

technological advances through functional magnetic resonance imaging (fMRI) scans confirm a dual coding system through which visuals and text/auditory input are processed in separate channels, presenting the potential for simultaneous augmentation of learning. Our working memory, which is where we do all our thinking, processes visuals and text/sound differently. Both of these channels are extremely limited in their capacity.

The implications of this for education are many. First and foremost, it is important to acknowledge that people learn better from combining visuals with text and sound than through using either process alone, provided the design of learning resources follows certain multimedia principles (Mayer & Moreno, 2003).

This set of seven principles related to multimedia and modality is based on the work of Richard Mayer, Roxanne Moreno, and other prominent researchers (Chan & Black, 2006; Ginns, 2005; Mayer, 2001; Mayer & Moreno, 2003).

1. **Multimedia Principle:** Student retention is improved through a combination of words (verbal or text) and visuals, rather than through words alone, provided it doesn't introduce redundancy of content.

2. **Spatial Contiguity Principle:** Students learn better when corresponding text and visuals are physically integrated rather than separated.

3. **Temporal Contiguity Principle:** Students learn better when corresponding text and visuals are temporally synchronized rather than separated in time.

4. **Split-Attention Principle:** Students learn better when extraneous words, pictures, and sounds are excluded rather than included.

5. **Modality Principle:** Students learn better when text is presented auditorily as speech rather than as on-screen text.

6. **Individual Differences Principle:** Design effects from these principles are higher for low-knowledge learners than for high-knowledge learners, and they are higher for high-spatial learners than for low-spatial learners.

7. **Direct Manipulation Principle:** As the complexity of the materials increases the impact of direct manipulation of the learning materials (animation, pacing) on transfer also increases.

Students engaged in learning that incorporates high-quality multimodal designs outperform, on average, students who learn using traditional approaches with single modes. This was borne out by a recent meta-analysis that revealed multimodality (the use of text or sound and visuals together) can positively shift achievement—provided the multimedia principles are followed. The meta-analysis found that, with noninteractive multimodal learning, such as text with illustrations or lectures with graphics, a student performing at the 50th percentile would, on average, increase performance to the 71st percentile (a gain of 21 percentiles). With interactive multimodal activities, such as simulations, modeling, and real-world experiences, a student at the 50th percentile would, on average, increase performance to the 82nd percentile (a gain of 32 percentiles) (Lemke, 2008).

> Students engaged in learning that incorporates high-quality multimodal designs outperform, on average, students who learn using traditional approaches with single modes.

Outside the classroom, the 21st century brings us a myriad of visual images in multimedia through a host of technology devices, at a rapid pace unparalleled in the history of mankind. Examples abound (for live links to the following examples, and to see a full-color version of this chapter, visit go.solution-tree.com/21stcenturyskills).

- *The New York Times* provides interactive media on the economic crisis that enables users to explore the recessions of past years and compare them to that of 2009 (Quealy, Roth, & Schneiderman, 2009).

- *The New York Times* also provided an interactive graphic during the 2008 presidential debates that innovatively displayed the candidate names mentioned by other presidential candidates during the series of debates leading up to the Iowa caucuses (Corum & Hossain, 2007).

Another interactive venue for learning through visualization is online gaming. It enables participants to join multiuser groups from around the world to interact competitively and cooperatively in games, such as *Civilization* and *World of Warcraft*, or interact via an avatar in *Second Life*. Visual media also enables us to exercise with interactive videos on the Wii; link up with friends via GPS mappings; capture and post visuals and video on YouTube; and access news in real time across the globe. A prime example of this last use was the coverage of recent protests and governmental reactions following the 2009 Iraqi elections. Real-time access occurred through Twitter posts, CNN news, and YouTube video and visuals from the smartphones of those present at the scene.

Every day, student users are exposed to visuals, videos, and animations embedded in television commercials and programming, multimedia sites, communications, interactive games, Web 2.0 tools, and presentations. Contrary to popular belief, students are not born with the full range of abilities required to interpret, think with, and build simple or complex multimedia communications that involve visuals, text, and/or voice and sound. They need to learn to become informed viewers, critics, thinkers, and producers of multimedia. Just as there is a grammar and syntax for text literacy, so there is for visual/multimodal literacy. The use of visualization is yet another way in which teachers can scaffold their students' learning.

Three strategies teachers might consider in using technology to capitalize on the power of visualization and build students' visual literacy are as follows:

1. Develop students as informed consumers of information.

2. Engage students in thinking critically and creatively using visuals.

3. Engage students in communicating using visuals.

Develop Students as Informed Consumers of Information

Students need to be informed consumers of visuals. One of the ways to achieve this is to help students analyze how advertisers manipulate images. KCTS Channel 9 in Seattle has produced a website that provides middle school students with opportunities to see the process in action. One of the offerings on the Don't Buy It: Get Media Smart site—Secrets of a Magazine Cover Model Revealed!—offers glimpses into the making of a "girl next door" into a fashion model (KCTS Television, 2004; http://pbskids.org/dontbuyit/entertainment/covermodel_1.html). Figure 11.3 shows screen captures from the process. These and other programs provide teens with an understanding of the digital manipulations routinely done in advertising. This is especially important given the pervasiveness of the idealization of models' bodies by consumers, which can lead to low self-esteem and

Source: KCTS Television, 2004, and PBS Kids. Reprinted with permission from Stephanie Malone, Drew Ringo, and KCTS Television.

Figure 11.3: From "girl next door" to fashion model.

eating disorders among children, teens, and adults. This recognition of the potential for manipulation of media is an important first step in media literacy. An informed consumer recognizes that people are impacted emotionally, psychologically, physiologically, and cognitively by visuals and, thus, interpret media accordingly.

Engage Students in Thinking Critically and Creatively Using Visuals

Visualization can also be an extraordinary tool in a student's repertoire for critical and creative thinking. The more authentic the work, the better. Teachers and students alike can use readily accessible public datasets to engage in authentic investigations of open-ended questions concerning a range of topics. Examples abound. One digital tool that is particularly compelling for schools is free of charge on a website called Gapminder (www.gapminder.org). This visualization tool is built around a dataset from the United Nations. The dataset includes worldwide demographics, health, energy, politics, security, and other key elements (Gapminder Foundation, 2009). Each country is represented by a dot on the screen. Each continent has a unique color. The user determines the dataset to be charted on each of the axes and then watches as the tool shows the shifts in countries' positions across the years. For example, the two charts in figure 11.4 display the percentage of adults with HIV charted against the income per person for the countries of the world in 1983 and then in 2007. Students can use the visualization tool to track HIV infection in specific countries, with options for looking at specific demographics and/or income brackets within those countries. The full datasets are available for export to further analyze the data (Gapminder Foundation, 2009; visit go.solution-tree.com/21stcenturyskills for live links and to see full-color versions of the graphics in this chapter).

The teachable moments that can be created with this tool are unlimited. Take a look at our second example in figure 11.5 (page 254). It is three screen shots of a data run in which the average life expectancy of citizens in South Africa is charted in relationship to the average income per person over time. This chart shows a strong, steady increase for income and life expectancy in South Africa from 1932 to 1980. Then, in 1980, the income began slipping backward,

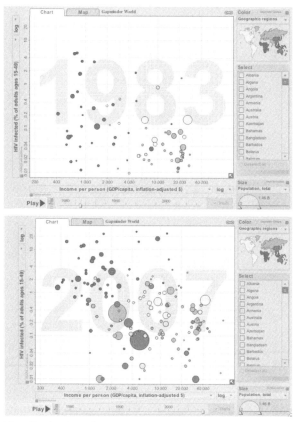

Source: Visualization from Gapminder World, powered by Trendalyzer from www.gapminder.org.

Figure 11.4: Charting the relationship over time between the percentage of adults with HIV in countries throughout the world in relation to the average income per person.

but the life expectancy continued to climb. In 1991, the upward trend in life expectancy reversed and began slowly decreasing; while at the same point in time, the income per person began slowly increasing. Those trends continued through 2007. Students exploring this data visualization quickly begin asking why the reversals happened in those specific years, and what factors caused the reversals. They might speculate that it was caused by a war, a natural disaster such as a famine or a tsunami, or perhaps industrialization. Students can rerun the scenario adding neighboring countries, zeroing in on

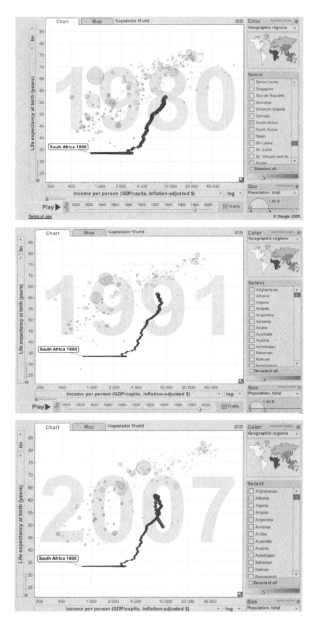

Source: Visualization from Gapminder World, powered by Trendalyzer from www.gapminder.org.

Figure 11.5: Life expectancy at birth by income in South Africa, 1800–2007.

particular years, charting new data elements, and, of course contextualizing their search through the use of other Web, print, and expert resources. This represents an extremely rich opportunity for critical thinking and problem solving with students.

Engage Students in Communicating Using Visuals

In addition to interpreting visuals, students should also understand how to create original visuals to communicate their ideas, represent their data, and tell their stories. Teachers can tap into websites that provide insight into which types of charts are most effective in displaying various types of datasets (see www.juiceanalytics.com/chartchooser/; visit go.solution-tree.com/21stcenturyskills for live links and to see a full-color version of the graphics in this chapter). As with any visual product, students need to adhere to the principles of multimodal design as described on pages 248–249. For example, in following the Spatial Contiguity Principle, charts should, where possible, integrate text into the design rather than using legends. In figure 11.6 (page 256), the cognitive load on working memory is higher for the nonintegrated example because the viewer has to look back and forth between the circle chart and the legend. In the integrated example, the load is reduced because the text is inside the chart.

A key strategy for scaffolding learning through visualization is the establishment and use of a set of guidelines that set high standards for the visual quality of student work. Many designers use a minimum of four key standards for design: contrast, repetition, alignment, and proximity (Williams, 2003) in concert with the multimedia principles listed previously. The visual design of digital products can increase or decrease the effectiveness of the communication:

- **Contrast**—The idea behind contrast is to ensure that each element of the visual design is *significantly different* from the others. The eye is attracted to differences; it is the element that attracts the reader to the work. For example, if two or more different sizes of fonts are used, use two that are very different, such as these:

9 point 18 point

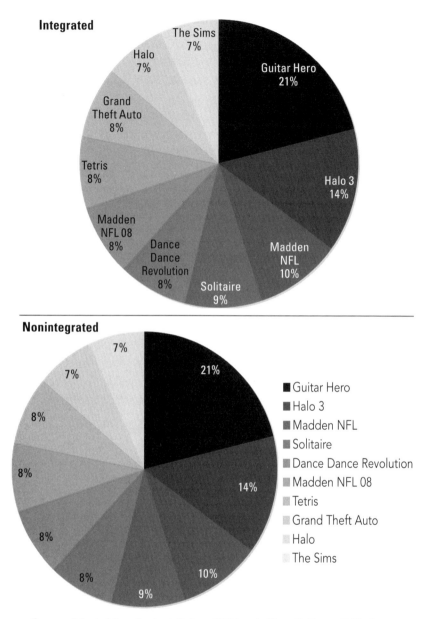

Integrated

The Sims 7%

Halo 7%

Grand Theft Auto 8%

Tetris 8%

Madden NFL 08 8%

Guitar Hero 21%

Halo 3 14%

Madden NFL 10%

Solitaire 9%

Dance Dance Revolution 8%

Nonintegrated

7%

7%

8%

8%

8%

8%

9%

10%

14%

21%

- Guitar Hero
- Halo 3
- Madden NFL
- Solitaire
- Dance Dance Revolution
- Madden NFL 08
- Tetris
- Grand Theft Auto
- Halo
- The Sims

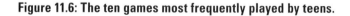

Source: Adapted from Lenhart, Kahne, Middaugh, Macgill, Evans, & Vitak, 2008. Data is from the Gaming and Civic Engagement Survey of Teens and Parents, November 2007–February 2008. Margin of error is ±3%.

Figure 11.6: The ten games most frequently played by teens.

- **Repetition**—Repeating elements of the design strengthens the unity of the piece. Repetition can be used with fonts, shapes, colors, thicknesses, spatial relationships, and so on. An example is shown in figure 11.7 (page 258) from the Technology Entertainment Design (TED) webpage (www.ted .com/talks/list), where each entry has the same style heading and format.

- **Alignment**—The way each element is placed on the page directs the order in which the reader's eye will move through the page. Thus, each element should have a visual connection with another element. In the example in figure 11.7, the eye is immediately drawn to the top headline and then drops to the visuals representing the six talks. For each talk, the proximity of the visual and text to its right causes the eye to flow to that text next, following the natural habit (in reading English) to move across the page, left to right. The natural inclination of the eye is to return to the visual but because the eye moves left to right, it returns to the text, and may repeat that eye movement several times. (The design thus creates eye movement that ensures all of the information in the text and visual will be processed.)

- **Proximity**—The eye prefers simple landscapes. Where possible, items that are related should be grouped close enough together to suggest to the eye that they are one visual element. This provides a clean structure, organizes information for the reader, and reduces visual noise. In the case of the Education Commission of the States Web heading in figure 11.8, there are four main elements, as outlined in the gray shading in the bottom portion of the graphic.

Visual literacy is a critical component of what it means to be literate in the 21st century. It can augment and extend students' critical thinking; deepen their understanding in science, math, social studies, and other core subjects; establish strong ties between the arts and sciences; provide a range of opportunities for expressions of what they know and are able to do; and help to ensure that they will be informed consumers of media.

> Visual literacy is a critical component of what it means to be literate in the 21st century.

Source: Technology Entertainment Design, n.d., www.ted.com. Reprinted with permission.

Figure 11.7: Example of repetition and alignment.

Source: Education Commission of the States, 2010, http://www.ecs.org.
Reprinted with permission.

Figure 11.8: Example of proximity.

Innovation Two: Democratization of Knowledge

The Internet has opened up a new opportunity for people to learn throughout their lives in both formal and informal environments, individually and in groups. Low-cost access to technology devices connected to high-speed broadband is now available to the majority of the population. Many communities are seeking broadband solutions to ensure equitable access for all members of the community. Despite this rapid growth of broadband in communities and homes, schools continue to play a role in ensuring that all students have robust access—at least within the school day.

The very ecology of learning is evolving. People are informally learning based on personal, professional, family, work, and community needs, interests, or responsibilities. Bridget Barron, a researcher from Stanford, has suggested that adolescent learning should be reconsidered in light of the informal learning opportunities now available to students (Barron, 2006). The diagram in figure 11.9 (page 260), based on Barron's work, identifies a host of formal and informal learning situations in which preK–12 students may be involved.

The implications for schools are significant. School is just one node among the learning contexts available to students; educators should be actively considering how to extend the formal learning launched in schools into other nodes. In addition, educators should seek to

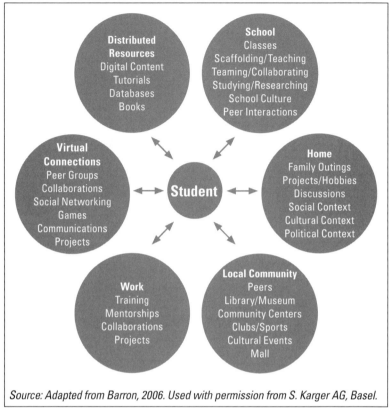

Figure 11.9: Contexts for 21st century learning.

become sufficiently familiar with the informal learning students are actively engaged in outside of school in order to integrate student interests with formal learning experiences. The intent would be to bring added relevancy and student interest to the formal work within the classroom and to integrate, to some degree, students' formal and informal learning. Another responsibility of schools is to ensure that students gain knowledge and expertise in navigating, interacting, and learning within digital environments. The taxonomy that one might consider in thinking about the democratization of knowledge includes:

- **Browsing the Net**—The universal adoption of *google* as a verb says it all. Information is truly at the fingertips of the informed Internet navigator. The key word is *informed*. While information is available, it is critical that schools provide intensive work with students on informed searching, navigating the visible and invisible Web, critiquing websites to check for reliable sources, and persevering to ensure comprehensive, balanced searches.

- **Learning objects**—A learning object is a self-contained resource, usually digital and/or web-based, that can be used and reused to support learning. Many of the first learning objects were in the form of virtual manipulatives—dynamic objects through which students could explore properties to further their knowledge (Utah State University, 2007). Today, learning objects take the form of YouTube videos, iPod audio and/or video files, interactive websites, scripted slide shows, and so on. That means that twenty-four hours a day, seven days a week, these objects are available to interested learners. Learning objects can be used to supplement face-to-face classrooms, can be embedded in virtual classes, and can easily be accessed by students who are studying, but have not yet mastered the topic. For example, the National Council of Teachers of Mathematics Illuminations website provides many virtual manipulatives, including one that enables students to manipulate the areas that represent each element of the equation $(a + b)^2 = a^2 + 2ab + b^2$ (National Council of Teachers of Mathematics, 2009; visit http://illuminations.nctm.org/ Activity/Detail.aspx?ID=127 to view this manipulative). A second example is a calculator students can use to determine the emissions of their homes. The program enables them to manipulate entries to see the results on carbon emissions (U.S. Environmental Protection Agency, n.d.; visit http://www.epa .gov/CHP/basic/calculator.html to view this manipulative).

- **Simulations**—The depth of student learning increases when students are able to experiment with the parameters behind a visual simulation. For example, in a new generation of tools called Yenka, a U.K. firm enables students to learn some rudimentary steps in programming by controlling a dancer's onscreen actions through their creation and running of a flowchart. These resources are available, free of charge, for use by individuals in their homes, and can also be licensed for a fee by schools (Crocodile Clips, 2009; visit www.yenka. com/en/Yenka_Programming/ to view the simulation). A free-of-charge simulation, SimCalcMathWorlds, enables students to experiment with rate, linear functions, and proportionality through graphing calculators and computers that generate math functions. For example, students are able to determine speed and rate of acceleration of two fish along a linear path while simultaneously watching the functions charted on a grid (see www.kaputcenter.umassd.edu/projects/simcalc/).

- **University courses available to the public**—In the first decade of the 21st century, many universities in the United States have made their courses available online. Currently, MIT Courseware (Massachusetts Institute of Technology, 2009) and Rice Connexions (Rice University, n.d.) have made thousands of courses available. Another digital access point for thousands of free university courses, lectures, and interviews is iTunes University.

- **Online courses for K–12 students and teachers**—According to a meta-analysis on online learning released by the U.S. Department of Education in May of 2009, online learning for both K–12 students and teachers is one of the fastest growing trends in educational technology (Means, Toyama, Murphy, Bakia, & Jones, 2009). The report indicated that the number of K–12 students enrolled in technology-based distance learning courses had increased by 65 percent from the 2002–2003 school year to the 2004–2005 school year. A recent report by the Sloan Consortium (Picciano & Seaman, 2009) estimated that more than one million U.S. K–12 students were engaged in online courses in 2007–2008, which represents a 47 percent increase since 2005–2006. The authors of that study reported a wide range of needs that were fulfilled through online courses, from those seeking advanced placement and college-level courses, to those needing credit recovery or remediation. This access provides a tremendous opportunity for students who are seeking an alternative to the local offerings in terms of courses available, timing of courses, and mode of learning.

The Florida Virtual High School (FVHS) is an example of one of the largest virtual high schools. In the 2007–2008 school year, FVHS enrolled approximately one hundred thousand students nationally (diplomas are granted by the student's local community school). FVHS announced in the summer of 2009 a new American History, full-credit high school course to be conducted completely within the gaming environment Conspiracy Code (Nagel, 2009).

- **Online course units**—Many school districts and individual teachers are leveraging online learning as a supplement to classroom work. In some cases, teachers are using online units as an integral component of their courses. One example of online units is from the federally funded web-based Inquiry Science site hosted at the University of California, Berkeley (http://wise.berkeley.edu). The science inquiry units offered on this site are free of charge to participating schools. Four of the self-contained units are as follows: Airbags: Too Fast, Too Furious? (Grades 11–12); Global Climate Change: Who's to Blame? (Grades 6–9); TELS: Mitosis and Meiosis (Grades 9–12); and Wolf Ecology and Population Management (Grades 7–12). The units are typically four to five days (one class period) in length, are aligned to standards, include lesson plans, and are highly interactive for student teams through the website.

The democratization of knowledge provides the opportunity for lifelong individual and group learning. For students to leverage that opportunity fully requires critical thinking, information literacy, and a measure of self-direction, all of which need to be developed in part by our school systems. The democratization of knowledge also provides tremendous opportunities for educators to begin transforming their schools into physical and virtual places of 21st century learning. One of the critical differences from conventional education is a solid foundation in inquiry learning that is student-centered and authentic. Educators are at a crossroads. They can embrace this democratization of knowledge by authentically connecting their students' formal and informal learning. Or they can ignore it and run the risk of obsolescence, becoming certification mills for the interactive learning that takes place out of school.

The democratization of knowledge provides the opportunity for lifelong individual and group learning. For students to leverage that opportunity fully requires critical thinking, information literacy, and a measure of self-direction, all of which need to be developed in part by our school systems.

Innovation Three: Participatory Learning

Today's schools are focused on individual acquisition of knowledge, student by student, despite the fact that, increasingly, society, community, and work emphasize teaming, collaboration, and participatory learning.

While the Internet of the 1990s gave previously underrepresented groups a public voice, the Web 2.0 tools of the 21st century have given rise to a participatory culture. The advent of Facebook, YouTube, Flickr, Twitter, RSS feeds, GPS tracking, smart mobile devices, and robust international broadband networks have enabled millions to interact in real time twenty-four hours a day, seven days a week. Web 2.0 tools have enabled everyone with sufficiently robust Internet access to post, exchange, and comment on video, audio, and text files; share tagging perspectives through sites such as Delicious.com; interact on social networking sites; participate in live chats; interact and share perspectives within communities of interest/practice; use GPS tracking and texting to connect in real time; participate in interactive, online games and gaming communities; and stay connected and informed through RSS feeds, Flickr, and Twitter.

New social patterns are emerging at unprecedented rates. People now expect to be active participants in theses virtual communities, not just passive observers. At the heart of these communities is the evolutionary nature of community norms, content, discourse, and life cycle. Yes, someone establishes the foundational tools, but the community is seldom carefully and strategically planned. Rather, it evolves over time, shaped by dialogue, discussion, shared resources, responses to inquiries, commentary and critique, and levels of participation based on perceived value. An innovative example is the use of Facebook by a teacher to engage students in learning about the periodic table. (Visit go.solution-tree.com/21stcenturyskills for live links and to see full-color versions of the graphics in this chapter.)

At High Tech Middle School in San Diego, students used social networking to personally identify with the elements in the periodic table (see figure 11.10; http://staff.hthcv.hightechhigh.org/~jmorris/period%20table%20page.html). Students were asked to list personal characteristics, identify the attributes of elements, and then select which elements' attributes most closely aligned to their personal

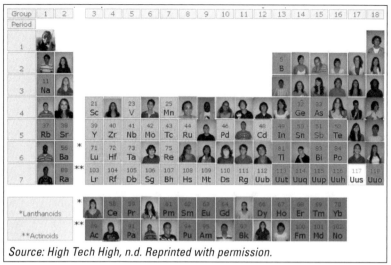

Source: High Tech High, n.d. Reprinted with permission.

Figure 11.10: The Periodic Table: Students' Facebook pages on the elements.

characteristics. Once their Facebook page was established for their element, they proceeded to "friend" other elements in alignment with their elements' attributes.

By clicking on the live site, each student's Facebook page reveals the characteristics of attributes they share with the element they believe aligns most closely to him or her. See figure 11.11 (page 266) for an excerpt.

That participatory culture is reflected in today's economic globalization. Multinational corporations in particular epitomize this participatory culture, where the success of an individual is directly tied to the success of the teams within which they work. Often the effectiveness of the teams lies in the social and emotional maturity of the members, the diversity of members' expertise, and members' leadership and commitment. This is indicative of Web 2.0 participatory cultures where the power lies in the quality, frequency, expertise, backgrounds, and commitment of the participants.

From an educational perspective, it is important to note that participation is not synonymous to collaboration. A participatory culture can range from the harmonious to the acrimonious. The topic of interest that brings a community together may range from social justice to the intellectual, the political, the social, the economic,

Student Entry: What I have in common with Hydrogen.

Gets Along Well With Others: I have an easy-going nature about me and would consider myself to have a go-with-the-flow personality. Just like Hydrogen, I like to be near others and hanging out with friends any chance I get. In this fast-paced world we live in, sometimes it's nice to just spend some time relaxing with friends.

Low Boiling Point (-252.87 C): Generally, I am a calm and collected individual. As is true of anyone, I have my moments of high stress and low patience, but for the most part I am a calm and caring individual. I share my cool nature with Hydrogen.

Just like Hydrogen, I am little but powerful. I have always thought of myself as someone who is small but mighty. I am a strong individual who can take care of herself and others. I am someone you can depend on for strength and dependability. I share this strength and usefulness with Hydrogen.

Source: High Tech High, n.d. Reprinted with permission.

Figure 11.11: Student's Facebook page on Hydrogen.

a community perspective, or simply entertainment and personal interest. The size of the community, its purposes, its longevity, and the norms within those communities vary considerably.

As the three innovations (visualization, democratization of knowledge, and participatory learning) introduced in this chapter ripple through society, people are using their ingenuity to use those innovations for their own purposes. In doing so, they continually influence and redefine the very ecology of the society—hence the ripple effect. This same phenomenon is true of learning. Researcher Kai Hakkarainen and his colleagues discuss how educators think about learning in three distinct ways (Hakkarainen, Palonen, Paavola, & Lehtinen, 2004). The first is an acquisition model, which emphasizes what the individual knows and is individually able to learn. The second model is participation. In this case, the educator goes beyond the acquisition model to acknowledge the social aspect of learning. While students in this model might engage in collaborative work, the measure of success is still largely focused on how much the individual is able to learn, accompanied perhaps by a measure of the student's ability to work within a group, community, network, or culture. The third model is knowledge creation. In this model, the output of the group or community is a valued asset, complemented by a measure of the individual's contributions to the team and acquisition of knowledge. The reality is that educators should be encompassing all three perspectives on learning.

Today's schools are out of sync with society—they are still operating on the acquisition model. They do register some forays into the participation model through collaborative learning, but they neither regularly establish structures that measure and value the group or community's collective knowledge construction, nor document the contributions of the student to that work. This translates into a need to restructure learning, teaching, and assessment to increasingly emphasize and value the participation in groups and the group's knowledge creation, in addition to the individual's acquisition of knowledge. This is necessary if schools are to graduate students who are ready to thrive in this new participatory culture.

Implications of the Three Innovations

Students who are learning in schools influenced by the innovations of visualization, democratization of knowledge, and participatory cultures need different skills than prior generations. Tremendously important to these students are the skills discussed throughout this book, including critical and creative thinking, self-direction, collaboration, multimodal learning, and adaptability. The ecology of learning will itself evolve over time, with students taking stronger, more active roles in shaping their learning trajectories, often blending informal and formal learning in face-to-face, virtual, and hybrid learning never before possible. One of the immediate ways in which schools can immerse students in such learning is through authentic learning. Such learning is defined by Fred Newmann as learning that has three key elements: (1) deep inquiry (Higher Education Academy, 2009) into the subject matter (as opposed to surface learning), (2) relevancy beyond the school day (students are working with teams outside of the school on projects that matter), and (3) knowledge construction (students are producing

> Students who are learning in schools influenced by the innovations of visualization, democratization of knowledge, and participatory cultures need different skills than prior generations.

and constructing actual products to contribute to the community of interest as they demonstrate what their team now understands and what they individually understand).

Getting There From Here

To ensure U.S. students are ready to thrive in today's global, knowledge-based society, our schools need to embrace the innovations of visualization, democratization of knowledge, and participatory cultures for learning. This begins through leadership's creation of a culture of openness, risk taking, and adaptability within schools, where learners, teachers, and their communities can investigate how these innovations will change, grow, and adapt learning inside and outside of school. A first step is to gauge your school's readiness for 21st century learning. Metiri Group's Dimensions of 21st Century Learning (D21) provide a framework for gauging such readiness (Metiri Group, 2008):

- **Vision**—Does your school system have a forward-thinking, common vision for 21st century learning that represents societal innovations to serve as a unifying and energizing force of change?

- **Systems thinking/leadership**—Are all educators and staff thinking and acting systemically to embrace innovation in ways that advance the vision?

- **21st century skills/learning**—Has your school system adopted 21st century skills in the context of research-informed learning strategies?

- **21st century learning environments**—Is the vision of 21st century learning coming to life in your schools?

- **Professional competencies**—Are your teachers, administrators, and other staff ready to facilitate, lead, and assess 21st century learning among students, the community, and parents?

- **Access and infrastructure**—Is the access to technology devices and the infrastructure sufficiently robust to support 21st century learning?

- **Accountability**—Are learners, educators, and the system held accountable for making progress, while also provided with the data and support for achieving results?

For educators, this framework translates into a need for leadership that (1) establishes a culture of openness to new ideas in and outside of education, (2) encourages calculated risk taking, and (3) is sufficiently insightful to establish a process that accelerates the spread of powerful, creative ideas that have the potential to "tip and ripple." Authors from the *Harvard Business Review* suggest such leaders should be strategists, those who generate organization change in highly collaborative ways that, at times, challenge and change current assumptions (Rooke & Torbert, 2005).

It is time to challenge assumptions in today's preK–12 school systems and embrace the ripple effects of these three innovations: visualization, democratization of knowledge, and participatory learning.

References

Associated Press. (2006, October 10). Google buys YouTube for $1.65 billion. *MSNBC online.* Accessed at www.msnbc.msn.com/id/15196982 on July 1, 2009.

Barron, B. (2006). Interest and self-sustained learning as catalysts of development: A learning ecology perspective. *Human Development, 49*(4), 193–224.

Chan, M. S., & Black, J. B. (2006, April). *Learning Newtonian mechanics with an animation game: The role of presentation format on mental model acquisition.* Paper presented at the American Education Research Association Annual Conference, San Francisco.

Corum, J., & Hossain, F. (2007, December 15). Naming names. *The New York Times.* Accessed at www.nytimes.com/interactive/2007/12/15/us/politics/ DEBATE.html on October 10, 2008.

Csikszentmihalyi, M. (1990). *Flow: The psychology of optimal experience.* New York: Harper and Row.

Crocodile Clips. (2009). *Yenka programming.* Accessed at www.yenka.com/en/ Yenka_Programming/ on July 7, 2009.

Education Week and the Editorial Projects in Education (EPE) Research Center. (2009a, June 11). *Diplomas count 2009: Broader horizons: The challenge of college readiness for all students.* Bethesda, MD: Authors.

Education Week and the Editorial Projects in Education (EPE) Research Center. (2009b). *National technology report: Breaking away from tradition.* Bethesda, MD: Authors.

Drucker, P. F. (2002, August). The discipline of innovation. *Harvard Business Review, 80*(8), 95–103.

Foray, D., & Lundvall, B. D. (1998). *The knowledge-based economy: From the economics of knowledge to the learning economy.* In D. Need, G. Siesfeld, & J. Cefola, *The economic impact of knowledge* (pp. 115–122). New York: Butterworth-Heinemann.

Fredricks, J. A., Blumenfeld, P. C., & Paris, A. H. (2004). School engagement: Potential of the concept, state of the evidence. *Review of Educational Research, 74*(1), 59–109.

Gapminder Foundation. (2009). *Gapminder: Unveiling the beauty of statistics for a fact based world view.* Accessed at www.gapminder.org on June 5, 2009.

Ginns, P. (2005). Meta-analysis of the modality effect. *Learning and Instruction, 15*(4), 313–331.

Gladwell, M. (2000). *The tipping point: How little things can make a big difference.* Boston: Little, Brown.

Global System for Mobile Communication. (2009, February 11). *Mobile world celebrates four billion connections. GSM Association press release.* Accessed at www.gsmworld.com/newsroom/press-releases/2009/2521.htm on June 20, 2009.

Hakkarainen, K., Palonen, T., Paavola, S., & Lehtinen, E. (2004). *Communities of networked expertise: Professional and educational perspectives.* Amsterdam: Elsevier Science.

High Tech High. (n.d.). *We are the periodic table of elements.* Accessed at http://staff.hthcv.hightechhigh.org/~jmorris/period%20table%20page.html on January 28, 2010.

The Higher Education Academy. (2009). *Deep and surface approaches to learning.* Accessed at www.engsc.ac.uk/er/theory/learning.asp on October 1, 2008.

Jenkins, H. (2007, December 5). *Reconsidering digital immigrants. Confessions of an aca-fan: The official weblog of Henry Jenkins.* Accessed at www.henryjenkins.org/2007/12/reconsidering_digital_immigran.html on June 8, 2009.

Jeong-hyun, L. (n.d.). In *Wikipedia, the free encyclopedia.* Accessed at http://en.wikipedia.org/wiki/Jeong-Hyun_Lim on July 5, 2009.

KCTS Television. (2004). *Don't buy it: Get media smart.* Accessed at http://pbskids.org/dontbuyit/entertainment/covermodel_1.html on May 20, 2009.

Lemke, C. (2008). *Multimodal learning through media: What the research says.* Accessed at www.cisco.com/web/strategy/docs/education/Multimodal-Learning-Through-Media.pdf on June 6, 2008.

Lemke, C., & Coughlin, E. (2008). *Student engagement.* Culver City, CA: Metiri Group.

Lemke, C., Coughlin, E., Garcia, L., Reifsneider, D., & Baas, J. (2009, March). *Leadership for Web 2.0 in education: Promise and reality.* Culver City, CA: Metiri Group.

Lenhart, A., Kahne, J., Middaugh, E., Macgill, A. R., Evans, C., & Vitak, J. (2008). *Teens, video games, and civics.* Washington, DC: Pew Internet & American Life Project.

Massachusetts Institute of Technology. (2009). *MIT OpenCourseWare.* Accessed at http://ocw.mit.edu on June 9, 2009.

Mayer, R. (2001). *Multi-media learning.* Cambridge, UK: Cambridge University Press.

Mayer, R. E., & Moreno, R. (2003). Nine ways to reduce cognitive load in multimedia learning. In R. Bruning, C. A. Horn, & L. M. PytlikZillig (Eds.), *Web-based learning: What do we know? Where do we go?* (pp. 23–44). Greenwich, CT: Information Age Publishing.

Moreno, R., & Mayer, R. E. (2005). *A learner-centered approach to multimedia explanations: Deriving instructional design principles from cognitive theory.* Accessed at http://imej.wfu.edu/articles/2000/2/05/index.asp on October 8, 2008.

Means, B., Toyama, Y., Murphy, R., Bakia, M., & Jones, K. (2009, May). *Evaluation of evidence-based practices in online learning: A meta-analysis and review of online learning studies* (Report No. ED-04-CO-0040 Task 0006). Washington, DC: U.S. Department of Education. Accessed at www.ed.gov/rschstat/eval/ tech/evidence-based-practices/finalreport.doc on June 30, 2009.

Metiri Group. (2008). *Dimensions of 21st century learning.* Accessed at http:// D21.metiri.com on July 7, 2009.

Nagel, D. (2009, June 2). Virtual school begins rolling out game-based courses. *THE Journal.* Accessed at http://thejournal.com/Articles/2009/06/02/Virtual-School-Begins-Rolling-Out-GameBased-Courses.aspx on June 8, 2009.

National Council of Teachers of Mathematics. (2009). *A geometric investigation of (a + b)².* Illuminations. Accessed at http://illuminations.nctm.org/ ActivityDetail.aspx?ID=127 on July 7, 2009.

National School Board Association. (2007). *Creating and connecting: Research and guidelines on online social—and educational—networking.* Alexandria, VA: Author.

Nielsen Company. (2009). *How teens use media: A Nielsen report on the myths and realities of teen media trends.* New York: Author. Accessed at http://blog .nielsen.com/nielsenwire/reports/nielsen_howteensusemedia_june09.pdf on July 6, 2009.

Official Google Blog. (2008, July 25). *We knew the Web was big.* Accessed at http://googleblog.blogspot.com/2008/07/we-knew-web-was-big.html on June 20, 2009.

Picciano, A. G., & Seaman, J. (2009). *K–12 online learning: A 2008 follow-up of the survey of U.S. school district administrators.* Newburyport, MA: The Sloan Consortium. Accessed at www.sloanconsortium.org/publications/survey/ pdf/k-12_online_learning_2008.pdf on April 4, 2009.

Quealy, K., Roth, G., & Schneiderman, R. M. (2009, January 26). How the government dealt with past recessions. *The New York Times*. Accessed at www.nytimes.com/interactive/2009/01/26/business/economy/20090126 -recessions-graphic.html on May 10, 2009.

Reed, N. (2008). *GigaTweet*. Accessed at http://popacular.com/gigatweet on July 7, 2009.

Rice University. (n.d.). *Connexions*. Accessed at http://cnx.org/ on June 6, 2009.

Rooke, D., & Torbert, W. R. (2005, April). Seven transformations of leadership. *Harvard Business Review, 83*(4), 67–76.

Schlechty, P. C. (2002). *Working on the work: An action plan for teachers, principals, and superintendents*. San Francisco: Jossey-Bass.

Schwartz, D. L., Bransford, J. D., & Sears, D. (2006). Innovation and efficiency in learning and transfer. In J. P. Mestre (Ed.), *Transfer of Learning from a Modern Multidisciplinary Perspective* (pp. 40–59).

Shah, J. A. (2005, December 20). *Guitar* [YouTube video]. Accessed at www .youtube.com/watch?v=QjA5faZF1A8 on July 5, 2009.

Singer, A. (2009, January 12). Social media, Web 2.0 and Internet stats. *The Future Buzz*. Accessed at http://thefuturebuzz.com/2009/01/12/social-media-web -20-internet-numbers-stats on July 2, 2009.

Technology Entertainment Design. (n.d.). *TED: Ideas worth spreading—Talks page*. Accessed at www.ted.com/talks/list on February 18, 2010.

U.S. Department of Education. (2009, June 8). *Robust data gives us the roadmap to reform*. [Speech Secretary Arne Duncan gave at the Fourth Annual IES Research Conference]. Accessed at www.ed.gov/news/speeches/2009/06/06082009 .html on June 19, 2009.

U.S. Department of Education. (2009, June 26). *U.S. Department of Education study finds that good teaching can be enhanced with new technology*. U.S. Department of Education Press Release. Accessed at www.ed.gov/news/ pressreleases/2009/06/06262009.html on May 10, 2009.

U.S. Environmental Protection Agency. (n.d.). *Household emissions calculator*. Accessed at http://epa.gov/climatechange/emissions/ind_calculator2.html #c=transportation&p=reduceOnTheRoad&m=calc_WYCD on July 7, 2009.

Utah State University. (2007). *National Library of Virtual Manipulatives*. Accessed at http://nlvm.usu.edu/en/nav/grade_g_2.html on May 20, 2009.

Williams, R. (2003). *The non-designers design book*. Berkeley, CA: Peachpit Press.

Alan November

Alan November, M.Ed., is recognized internationally as a leader in education technology. He began his career as an oceanography teacher and dorm counselor at an island reform school for boys in Boston Harbor. He has been a director of an alternative high school, computer coordinator, technology consultant, and university lecturer. As practitioner, designer, and author, Alan has guided schools, government organizations, and industry leaders as they plan to improve quality with technology. His writing includes dozens of articles and the best-selling book, *Empowering Students With Technology* (2001). November was cofounder of the Stanford Institute for Educational Leadership Through Technology and is most proud of being selected as one of the original five national Christa McAuliffe Educators.

In this chapter, November reinforces Pearlman's rationale for redesigned schools. He cautions against using expensive technology to continue the trend of schools as managers of student learning. It's time, he says, to redesign not only the physical structure but the culture of schools. Technology makes it possible for students to become less dependent on schools and take more responsibility for managing their own learning.

Chapter 12

Technology Rich, Information Poor

Alan November

Yesterday, I was in one of the most beautiful and caring independent schools I have ever visited. It had resources that took my breath away. When I addressed the combined junior and senior class, many of whom would be attending top-ranked universities upon graduation, I asked them if they knew why my website was ranked third out of more than seven hundred million results when I typed the word *November* into Google. Their responses were immediate and confident:

- "You have the most important content."

- "You paid Google."

- "Your site has the most visits."

All of these answers are incorrect. The students were so overly confident that they knew what they actually did not know—it was frightening. The teachers were shocked at what their students did not know. The Web has become the dominant media of our society, yet we are not teaching our children critical-thinking skills in this media. Calculate how easy it would be to manipulate people who believe the most important information is at the top of their search results. Also consider how many students (and adults) only look at the top page of results when they do a search. Or, how many only use one search engine when they are doing research. Why do we teach students to use PowerPoint and build wikis before we teach them to be literate in the most powerful information media ever invented by society?

"Houston, we have a problem."

Most educators agree that we need 21st century schools and that we need to prepare students for the information economy. However, what does this really mean, and what are the essential questions and planning processes needed to prepare our students to have a global work ethic?

> Most educators agree that we need 21st century schools and that we need to prepare students for the information economy. However, what does this really mean, and what are the essential questions and planning processes needed to prepare our students to have a global work ethic?

What it does not mean is giving every student a laptop without fundamentally changing our concept of curriculum, assessment, and the role of the teacher and learner. This chapter will focus on designing a planning process to help us manage the transition from paper as the dominant technology for storing and retrieving information (a static technology) to digital (a dynamic technology).

From Static to Digital Technology

Up until now, due largely to an initial lack of digital technology in our schools, the traditional planning paradigm has been to launch a technology planning committee. The driving questions in this approach are as follows: How much technology do we need? Where do we need it? And, what technical skills do our teachers and students need? However, technology is only the digital plumbing. Of course we have to ask how many computers/interactive boards/PDAs we need, where to put them, and how to train teachers and students to use them. But simply doing a really good job with the technology planning paradigm is not sufficient. What will distinguish our use of technology in our education system is preparing children to have a global work ethic. Technical skills are necessary, but they are not enough.

One of my clients, an executive in a high-tech company, calls what schools do with technology planning akin to "spray and pray" planning. The spray-and-pray model invests in a technocentric process that leads to bolting technology on top of traditional work instead of rethinking the work. In other words, students are usually given the same kinds of assignments and roles they had before the technology was implemented. For example, I have walked into many laptop schools and watched every student in a classroom taking notes with what amounts to a $2,000 pencil. As the famous quote goes, "The process whereby the lecture notes of the instructor get transferred to the notebooks of the students without passing through the brains of either" does not describe a 21st century practice, regardless of the tool used for the transfer. When I ask students to describe the most useful application of their laptops, the standard answer is "taking notes."

The saddest outcome of the spray-and-pray model of planning is that, in some cases, we have actually lowered the quality of student work in our rush to add technology. Plagiarism has significantly increased. Many students are looking for the easiest way to finish an assignment, and there has been a loss of deep understanding of concepts as students whip together their homework and projects. Students are using Web 2.0 tools (often blocked by filters in schools) to collaborate over social-networking sites to "share" homework. As more handheld devices, such as smartphones, come to school, the potential for distraction escalates. Read *The Dumbest Generation: How the Digital Age Stupefies Young Americans and Jeopardizes Our Future (Or, Don't Trust Anyone Under 30)* by Mark Bauerlein (2008) to learn more.

We are now in a cycle of constant change and innovation. We are approaching the handle curve of the hockey-stick pattern of change—straight up. There will be an explosion of new technologies (have you seen the Smartpen?), and we will continue to see the price of the hardware plummet and a plethora of new software tools emerge. We will see the end of textbooks and the explosion of online learning. It is up to us to take this historic time of change and to think

> We have a chance to redesign the culture of teaching and learning to a more empowering authentic model of learning. This is the time to think big and to expand our boundaries of what we believe our children can achieve.

deeply about the implications of these powerful new learning and teaching tools and global connectivity. We have a chance to redesign the culture of teaching and learning to a more empowering authentic model of learning. This is the time to think big and to expand our boundaries of what we believe our children can achieve.

Big Idea Assumptions

While nearly impossible to predict, in the middle of this explosion of innovation, educators have to sort out what skills we teach today that will have a chance of outlasting the changes in the technology. Currently, schools are not designed for constant adaptation to innovations from society.

Let's start with the big picture trends that should guide our thinking about preparing our students to have a global work ethic:

- Immediate access to an over-abundance of information—How do we make sense of it all? YouTube serves up one billion videos per day. As of November 2009, there were 27.3 million tweets on Twitter per day.

- Essentially free global communications—We already have a range of tools such as Skype that provide essentially free global communication. Every one of our classrooms can become a global communications center.

- Job markets flowing to the people who can provide the highest quality at the lowest price wherever they happen to live—In his book *The World Is Flat,* Thomas Friedman (2005) explains that the Web creates opportunities for people around the world to earn a living without the need to immigrate. Are we preparing our children to have a global work ethic?

In direct response to the big picture trends are these specific skills, our students must learn:

- How to make meaning with overwhelming amounts of information

- How to work with people around the world (empathy)

- How to be self-directed, interdependent, and a superb lifelong learner

If we wanted to prepare our students for the global economy, we would immediately turn every classroom into a global communications center linking students to authentic audiences around the world. We would be providing professional development for teachers to redesign their assignments to be more rigorous and authentic. We would

Our students must learn:
- How to make meaning with overwhelming amounts of information
- How to work with people around the world (empathy)
- How to be self-directed, interdependent, and a superb lifelong learner

be laser-beam focused on redefining what it means to be literate. Learning to read from books is essential but no longer sufficient. Where we now teach the grammar of paper, we will need to teach the grammar of the Internet as well. Too many adults read the Internet as if it were paper shoved down a wire. The Internet has its own grammar and syntax and architecture of information. It is amazing how many people are being manipulated by a media they mistakenly believe they understand.

Most importantly, we would be redefining the role of the learner, the teacher, and even the family.

When my work takes me overseas to developing countries such as China or Singapore, there is a clear sense of urgency by educators to connect their students to people around the world and to empower students to take more ownership of their own learning. For example, Singapore has crafted a national vision called "Thinking Schools, Learning Nation." One of the basic design elements is to "teach less, learn more." There is a clear understanding that the role of the teacher and the learner must fundamentally change if the country wants to prepare students to have a global work ethic. Students who are taught to be dependent upon the teacher managing learning for them will not necessarily develop the lifelong learning and problem-solving skills that are required in the global economy.

Re-engineering our planning process from technology planning to global work-ethic planning requires that we ask questions

Re-engineering our planning process from technology planning to global work-ethic planning requires that we ask questions that focus on the results of our investment.

that focus on the results of our investment. The real revolution is not the laptops and the wiring. The laptops we buy today will soon be replaced. What will not go away is access to the overwhelming amounts of shifting (and growing) information and global communications. Our planning focus must shift to clearly define what it means to be Web literate and to link our students to authentic audiences around the world and across the curriculum.

Currently, how many of our students graduate from school with a global work ethic? How many students have the discipline to manage their own learning? How many students understand how to organize teams of people from around the world to solve increasingly complex problems? Questions like these should be driving our planning.

Once we have the infrastructure (network, hardware, software) in place, we should be asking what information does everyone need in order to be the most effective teacher, learner, administrator, or parent. For example, with a computational knowledge engine such as Wolframalpha (www.wolframalpha.com), students can take responsibility for correcting their own math homework as they generate the graph and the solution set for any equation. While it may sound counterintuitive to ask students to correct their own homework, research suggests that immediate feedback while learning is very important. In his book *Flow: The Psychology of Optimal Experience*, Mihaly Csikszentmihalyi (1990) lists immediate *feedback* as critical to optimal learning. Again, while the technology is essential, a computational knowledge engine basically provides students with access to information they have never had before. It also places the learner in a more powerful position of managing his or her own learning.

With access to dynamic tools such as Wolframalpha, we can raise our expectations that our students can design their own homework. Further, if we add another free tool such as Jing (www.jingproject .com), our students can create screencast (video screen capture) tutorials for their classmates with their solutions. I have talked to students in Eric Marcos' classroom in Santa Monica, where he maintains a library of tutorials on a class website (www.mathtrain

.tv). One of Eric's young tutorial designers, age twelve, explained to me that she felt much more responsibility when she was challenged to design tutorials for her classmates. She said, "This is real work instead of homework." You can listen to her at www.mathtrain.tv. Take a look at her tutorial on factoring with prime numbers. More than five hundred people already have.

In too many classrooms, teachers do not have the right information at the right time to be their best. For example, I have watched classrooms where students take notes with a laptop, but the teacher has no way of knowing if everyone's notes in class are accurate. What generally happens is the bell rings, the students walk out, and many of them will be reinforcing incorrect concepts from inaccurate or incomplete notes (with or without a laptop).

What we could be doing in our classrooms is using free collaborative writing tools such as Google Docs where a team of official scribes can be writing together. In this way, it would be easy for the teacher to upload the collaborative notes for the whole class to review before the end of the period. This enables a group review for accuracy and completeness.

This process also provides instant feedback to the teacher about how well the class has organized the ideas and content. In my own work, I have gained immediate insight into the quality of my teaching with this tool after reading the notes from the official scribes with the class and listened to their classmates responses. There is nothing like real-time daily feedback for improvement. It is a humbling experience, but at the same time, a very exciting experience for me.

It is possible that collaboration is one of the most important 21st century skills. We need to prepare students who know how to manage their own work within a team setting and how to organize and manage global communications. In an interconnected world, our students will need to learn how to understand various points of view and how to work with people in different cultures. In this regard we need to globalize the curriculum.

> It is possible that collaboration is one of the most important 21st century skills. We need to prepare students who know how to manage their own work within a team setting and how to organize and manage global communications.

For example, if I ever returned to teaching high school American history, I would connect my students to a live debate about the origins of the American Revolution with students in England. We would probably use Skype, a free global communications tool that is blocked in too many U.S. school districts. I believe many of my students would be more motivated to prepare for the live debate than for a written test I correct. We know that teens and preteens are social by nature. As soon as many students wake up in the morning and come home from school in the afternoon, they jump on Facebook and MySpace. They have a basic need to connect with other people. We should take advantage of this natural communications need and channel it toward rigorous academic work.

An authentic debate (as opposed to dividing the class into the British and the colonists) would also lead to more understanding. My students would learn why the British do not celebrate July 4 and why busloads of English tourists visit Lexington, Massachusetts, and ask to see Buckman's Tavern. Empathy might be one of the most important skills in a globally linked planet.

A Culture of Learning

We are within reach of creating a culture of learning where our students own more of their own learning and where they are creating content that benefits their classmates, and even students around the world. This redefines the role of the learner and the teacher. While the teacher's knowledge remains essential, the traditional transfer method from the teacher to the students now evolves to the whole class working as a team. It becomes the teacher's role to build capacity for the students to be self-directed and interdependent.

If we are applying very expensive technology to continue the dependency of our students upon the structure of school to manage their learning for them, we are making a terrible strategic mistake. The opportunity before us is to redesign the culture of our schools to empower students to take more responsibility for managing their own learning and to work collaboratively with classmates and people around the world. Asking the right questions about the design of an empowering culture of teaching and learning is more important than bolting technology onto our industrial model of education. This is a once in a lifetime opportunity. Think big. We can do it.

References

Bauerlein, M. (2008). *The dumbest generation: How the digital age stupefies young Americans and jeopardizes our future (or, don't trust anyone under 30).* New York: Tarcher/Penguin.

Csikszentmihalyi, M. (1990). *Flow: The psychology of optimal experience.* New York: Harper and Row.

Friedman, T. (2005). *The world is flat.* New York: Farrar, Straus and Giroux.

Will Richardson

Will Richardson, MA, is known internationally for his work with educators and students to understand and implement instructional technologies—and, more specifically, the tools of the read/write Web—into schools, classrooms, and communities. A former public school educator for twenty-two years, Richardson's own blog (Weblogg-ed.com) is a leading resource for the creation and implementation of Web 2.0 technologies on the K–12 level. He is a leading voice for re-envisioning learning and teaching in the context of the fundamental changes these new technologies are bringing to all aspects of life. His critically acclaimed, best-selling book *Blogs, Wikis, Podcasts, and Other Powerful Web Tools for Classrooms* (2010), now in its third edition, has sold more than fifty thousand copies.

In this chapter, Richardson calls attention to the explosion of social network technologies. This powerful new landscape offers its share of problems, he says, but it is also rich with potential for learning. Richardson describes the rise of the virtual, global classroom; the challenge of the unrestricted learning it brings; its potentials and pitfalls; and how educators can make the shift to network literacy in order to improve the quality of students' learning experiences.

Chapter 13

Navigating Social Networks as Learning Tools

Will Richardson

Nelson Smith could not start a fire, even if his life depended on it. In fact, he could not even produce smoke. He had the perfect piece of yellow pine, a nice blob of lint from his clothes dryer, a sturdy spindle, and a perfectly strung bow to make it spin. But thirty minutes of pulling and pushing the bow back and forth produced little heat where the wood pieces ground together. The wood stayed cool even as his skin turned hot.

However, Nelson, a twelve-year-old from Victoria, British Columbia, Canada, with a passion for outdoor survival skills, had a plan. He wanted to master this crucial, yet basic, part of bushcraft, and he knew the perfect tool to make it happen: his mom's video camera.

"Hello," Nelson says in the opening frame of his video as viewers see one of his grass-stained bare feet holding down the block of yellow pine and his hands clutching the pieces of his set. "I'm trying my hardest here to make a bow-drill set . . ."

The next three minutes and forty-six seconds chronicle Nelson's frustration, breathing heavily as he shows his spindle technique, close-ups of the lukewarm wood after the attempt, and detailed descriptions of the assembly of the kit and the aggravation that ensued.

But here is the best part: at one point, in the middle of his demonstration, Nelson speaks directly to his audience. "I'm doing it wrong; I know I am," he says. "Please comment down below so you can teach me how to do it."

And his audience did just that.

"Shorten the spindle to be the distance from your pinky to your thumb when your hand is fully spread," said HedgeHogLeatherworks one day after Nelson posted his video plea to YouTube (Smith, 2009).

"First your drill needs to be on the outside of your bowstring, not on the inside as you show here," added BCNW1. "Also, the notch needs to be cut like a slice of pie [that] stops just short of the center (yours is off to the side)."

Finally, came a comment from hobbexp, a Swedish gentleman with his own YouTube video channel on bushcraft: "Make the [drill] a little shorter so you can hang over it more, to get more down force, don't forget to breathe!"

You guessed it; Nelson was creating fire in no time.

The Rise of the Virtual Global Classroom

We now officially live in a world where even twelve-year-olds can create their own global classrooms around the things about which they are most passionate. And even better, grown-ups can, too. This is a world of learning built on the connections that individuals create with one another, the personal networks that people build with far-flung, like-minded students and teachers, and the anytime, anywhere communities of practice that grow from them.

But this world is also filled with complexity and pitfalls that pose huge challenges for all educators. The safety of children's interactions online is paramount, to be sure, but the greater challenges get to the heart of teaching and learning in general: What should classrooms be when we can connect with other teachers and learners around the world? What is the best role for teachers when knowledge is distributed widely in these networks? And, most importantly, how

We now officially live in a world where even twelve-year-olds can create their own global classrooms around the things about which they are most passionate.

do we reframe our own personal learning experiences as educators and as people in light of these shifts?

How we as a society answer those questions may bring about a long-discussed transformation to a school system that, while now operating in the 21st century, still looks decidedly 20th (or even 19th) century in its form and structure. Or, it may not. One thing is certain: although schools may continue to fundamentally look and act as they have for more than one hundred years, the way individuals learn has already been forever changed. Instead of learning from others who have the credentials to "teach" in this new networked world, we learn with others whom we seek (and who seek us) on our own and with whom we often share nothing more than a passion for knowing. In this global community, we are at once all teachers and learners—changing roles as required, contributing, collaborating, and maybe even working together to re-create the world, regardless of where we are at any given moment.

These learning transactions require a shifted understanding of traditional literacies and the skills they employ, as well as new literacies and practices that learning in networks and online social communities demands. For educators, acquiring these *network literacies* is a crucial first step in developing new pedagogies and, in turn, new classrooms and curricula that prepare students for the future.

But at this moment, when the vast majority of connected kids are already flinging themselves headlong into the socially networked connections they can make online, the sobering reality is that most of them have no adults, neither teachers nor parents, in their lives who can help them see and employ the learning potential at hand. By and large, kids navigate these spaces on their own, with only their peers to guide them or an occasional warning from the old folks. They do not see these learning connections being modeled, nor are they being taught how to create, navigate, and grow these powerful, personal learning networks in safe, effective, and ethical ways.

Some kids are starting to figure it out on their own, and in that regard, Nelson's story is instructive on many levels. Take a moment to think of what he needed to understand about this new global classroom and the skills required to navigate it effectively. First, he knew that the Web is no longer a "read only" technology, that we now have a read/write relationship with other users that changes everything. Second, he knew that although there might not be anyone in his physical space who could provide answers about bushcraft, there were dozens (if not thousands) of others "out there" in cyberspace to answer questions about even the most esoteric subjects. Third, he knew enough of the basics of multimedia and Web technology to create the video and upload it for consumption. Finally, he did it all in a way that protected his privacy and identity—other than his bare feet and hands, and his screen name on YouTube, he revealed nothing about his identity. Captured in this movie of less than four minutes is a sophistication with the online world that most adults (and the vast majority of his peers) have not yet begun to come close to mastering.

What most of Nelson's peers are good at is staying connected to the friends and family that they see on a regular basis or those they have known in their physical lives for long periods of time. A 2008 MacArthur Foundation report found that kids are prolific at using online and mobile technologies in "friendship based" ways via texting or using MySpace or Facebook (Ito et al., 2008). But some young people are also beginning to use these tools and the vast array of other social technologies now available to develop "interest based" connections with other students—or even adults—whom they do not know offline yet but with whom they pursue real learning and collaborative creation around their passions. Those young people are, in effect, creating their own virtual classrooms, ones that look nothing like the spaces they inhabit during the school day where all of the desks are in rows.

In this way, the challenges these technologies present to traditional schooling are similar to the challenges the business, politics, music, and media industries face. The use of social networking technologies by political campaigns such as Barack Obama's changed the way Americans think about organizing and fundraising in campaigns both national and local. Businesses now put an emphasis on following and participating in the many conversations that take place online about their products. And in no other arena are the effects of these networks being felt more than in the media. Traditional newspaper models cannot survive in a world where readers are now writers (and photographers and videographers) and where people are able to share what they own easily with others. In almost every aspect of life, the ability to connect and communicate via the Web is changing long-held beliefs and habits, changes that education is finally beginning to feel as well.

The Challenge of Unrestricted Learning

In his book *Here Comes Everybody: The Power of Organizing Without Organizations* (2008), New York University professor and author Clay Shirky characterizes the moment of such change as a "tectonic shift," one that may be unprecedented in human history. And education cannot escape this moment of change:

> For any given organization, the important questions are "When will the change happen?" and "What will change?" The only two answers we can rule out are never and nothing. The ways in which any given institution will find its situation transformed will vary, but the various local changes are manifestations of a single deep source: newly capable groups are forming, and they are working without the managerial imperative and outside the previous strictures that bounded their effectiveness. These changes will transform the world everywhere groups of people come together to accomplish something, which is to say everywhere. (pp. 23–24)

As Nelson knows, learning—formal or informal—is no longer restricted to a particular place at a particular time. Individuals can learn anytime, anywhere, as long as they have access to the Web and, in turn, to other people with whom they can form groups. Learning is creative and collaborative, cross-cultural and conspicuous, and products are shared widely for others to learn with and from. No longer happening behind closed doors mainly for contrived purposes, the fruits of learning are now writ large, made transparent on the Web, for real audiences and real purposes. Learning networks bloom in the process.

No longer happening behind closed doors mainly for contrived purposes, the fruits of learning are now writ large, made transparent on the Web, for real audiences and real purposes. Learning networks bloom in the process.

All of this creates an interesting tipping point, according to Howard Gardner and his colleagues:

> Going forward, learning may be far more individualized, far more in the hands (and the minds) of the learner, and far more interactive than ever before. This constitutes a paradox: As the digital era progresses, learning may be at once more individual (contoured to a person's own style, proclivities, and interests) yet more social (involving networking, group work, the wisdom of crowds, etc.). How these seemingly contradictory directions are addressed impacts the future complexion of learning. (Weigel, James, & Gardner, 2009)

Those contradictions are at the heart of becoming a socially networked online learner, one who is able to follow his or her own personal passions in the context of diverse, global groups of people who share his or her interests. And from those contradictions rise a slew of important questions that are incumbent upon educators to answer for themselves and for their students: How do we find these people with whom we can learn? How do we make ourselves "findable" to them? How do we assess the people with whom we choose to interact? What roles do we as individuals play in our collaborative efforts to learn? How do we most effectively share the work we create? How do we maintain a healthy balance in our online and offline relationships? How do we make effective choices about our own privacy and that of the people to whom we are connected?

None of these questions are easily answered, and together they suggest a 21st century skillset, if not a new literacy altogether. The creation of and our participation in these learning networks requires a sophistication beyond the ability to find high school friends on Facebook. Teachers and their students must be well-versed in the process of sharing what they know, of finding others with whom to learn, of making sense of the huge stores of information and knowledge online, and of the operation of networks themselves.

The Potentials and Pitfalls of Sharing

Fundamental to this new skillset is fully understanding the potentials and pitfalls of sharing pieces of our work and pieces of ourselves online. Currently, approximately 80 percent of high school students in the United States engage in the act of publishing online, most of them through social networking sites such as Facebook and MySpace (Bernoff, 2009). These sites and others like them make easy work of publishing text, photos, and even audio and video to be shared with private groups or with the Internet public at large. At its heart, the read/write Web (or Web 2.0) is about the ease with which individuals can now publish. As a case in point, at this writing it would take more than four years of nonstop viewing to watch all of the videos uploaded to YouTube in one twenty-four-hour period (Lardinois, 2009). People are sharing at a pace and scale that literally boggles the mind. From a learning standpoint, the true power of this new Web comes in the second act, in the connections individuals create after they publish.

In this digital environment, a key characteristic of sharing is that the content is linkable, meaning others can take it and distribute it widely through hypertext. Every published artifact—be it a blog post, a YouTube video, or a wiki entry—has its own unique Web address. And it is that linkability that complicates the transaction and turns it into an exercise in participation. Linkability is the connective tissue upon which learning networks are built. Although the process of sharing is easy, the purposes and outcomes of that sharing are much more nuanced and complex. We write on blogs or post to YouTube not simply to communicate, but also to connect with an intention that others will interact, discuss, and perhaps collaborate with us. We do this writing transparently, in many cases under our real names, because we want to be part of a community of learners who we know and recognize and who know and recognize us. Although the bulk of what we share is relevant to our passions, we also share tidbits of our personal lives, creating a human face in a virtual world, all the while straddling the fence of privacy for ourselves and for our families. We are, in essence, creating our digital footprints, in many ways writing a new type of professional resume online, one that can be pulled together through a Google search. And we do this all knowing full well that we can never anticipate all of the audiences and readers that our work may find.

Without question, young people will be the subject of Google searches over and over again in their lives, and the results to those searches will play an integral role in their success. More importantly, however, is that future searchers, whether they are college admissions officers, potential employers, or future mates, will have an expectation of finding creative, collaborative, thoughtful, and ethical results to peruse. An empty Google search will beg the question, "What have you been doing with your life?" How well-prepared students are to answer that question will in large measure be determined by how well educators teach them to prepare for it.

Sharing in this way places an emphasis on the quality and consistency of the contribution. That is part of the way in which online reputations grow. If published content contains misinformation, shoddy research, illogical thinking, or if interactions lack empathy and respect, the writer's credibility suffers. The community of learners of which we become a part sets the expectations, and in education-related online networks, those standards are high. To reap the full learning benefits in these spaces, we must give as much as we take, and we must comport ourselves with a balanced dose of professionalism and personality.

Not to share means to cede the creation of this online reputation to others, and that could be devastating in students' lives. Part of this network literacy is a form of reputation management, the ability to monitor the conversation around online work. Knowing when others are writing or linking to the work that we share has multiple purposes; we can correct or clarify when others misread, and, most importantly, we can connect with those who find our work of interest. Becoming "findable" online by sharing is easy; recognizing those who find us and ensuring that they are appropriate and relevant takes a sophistication that must become an integral part of the K–12 curriculum. We must learn to "read" people, to regularly look for cues as to who they are, what their traditional credentials are, what connections they may have to others already in our networks, what their biases are, what the quality of their own sharing and contributions is, and much more. At the end of the process, we look for those with whom we can learn and trust in the virtual sense absent the typical physical space cues and interactions to which we are accustomed.

This process of sharing is all an integral part of what the National Council of Teachers of English (NCTE, 2008) describes as being able to "build relationships with others to pose and solve problems collaboratively and cross-culturally," one of the six skillsets that the organization articulated as requirements for 21st century readers and writers. In recognition of the massive amounts and forms of knowledge currently stored online, NCTE also suggests that students must be able to "manage, analyze and synthesize multiple streams of simultaneous information." This work, too, now occurs primarily in the context of networks.

Indeed, there is far too much information available for any one person to know. In the recent past, it was difficult to tap into the collective wisdom and knowledge of those who shared a passion or intelligence for any particular subject, but today those people are becoming more and more findable through their willingness to share their expertise on the Web. Through their blogs, their Twitter posts, the videos they share, or the podcasts they publish, we can begin to access and make sense of others' collective experiences and compare them with our own.

Managing all of that information is wholly different from managing the information streams most of us grew up with in the paper world. As the print world gives way to the digital age, the complexity of information increases. How do we find the most current reliable information? In many cases, we get that information not by mining Google but by mining our networks, perhaps by posting a question to Twitter when we need a resource or answer—thereby tapping into the wisdom of the community that many times provides more relevant and useful responses than the typical search engine—or writing a blog entry, or, as Nelson did, creating a video plea to his community. Our networks respond with answers and research, acting as a powerful human filter, raising the ratio of signal to noise in the information we access and process.

As suggested, what is new about this landscape of information is not only the people who inhabit it, but also the forms of information available. Consider Nelson's post as an example. At this moment, there are more than three thousand videos about bushcraft on YouTube, more than five thousand photos on Flickr, and more than ten thousand mentions of the word in blog posts. There is the Jack Mountain Bushcraft Podcast, among others, a handful of live-streamed amateur television shows on the topic at Ustream.tv, as well as bushcraft discussion groups, artwork, and even scholarly treatises on the subject. With acute editing skills, Nelson has access to more than enough material to create his own learning text around his passion. But here is the difference: whereas just a few years ago all of those materials could be looked upon as pieces of content, today Nelson can view all of them as potential connections, as entry points to new conversations, new teachers, and new learning.

This brings to bear important decisions we now must make when we find relevant learning online supplied by someone we can trust: Should we engage with the author of that content (or the one who supplied it)? If so, what is the most appropriate way to do so? For example, do we leave a comment on the author's blog, or do we write a post on our own blog regarding what we found? When do we email someone instead of comment? Do we create a video response? How do we disagree in appropriate ways? Unlike the paper days in which readers took a more passive stance toward consuming information, these communications require the reader to take on a much more active role, one who is capable of interactions in a variety of ways.

Even the way we organize the information we find takes on a dual role in light of participation with other learners. Accumulating handwritten notes in notebooks, on index cards, or in file folders may have seemed an adequate way of organizing thoughts not so long ago, but they pale in comparison to the digital tools now available. Online notes and captures are searchable, copyable, and, most importantly, shareable in ways that paper cannot be. We collect and save our research and artifacts online not only for ourselves, but also for others—if I find something that helps me understand the world more completely, I want you to find it as well. So I might save the best of those bushcraft artifacts to a social bookmarking site such as Delicious.com, where I can retrieve them with any device that allows me access to the Web, and, more importantly, where you can retrieve them as well. I organize these notes by assigning keywords, or *tags*, as I save them, using words that will help me find and retrieve the artifacts as needed, and using words that I think will allow you to find them too. We are participants in the process, constructing our personal, social taxonomies with one another in an effort to organize our information worlds more completely.

Similarly, because knowledge is now so widely distributed and accessible, we must participate more fully in making sense of it all. We are now the ones who must find and take disparate, related bits of knowledge and synthesize them into a greater understanding for ourselves; and in doing so, we create our own texts in the world. This knowledge work makes authors of all of us as we combine the most current, most relevant information we can for ourselves and, once again, for others. There is no better example than Wikipedia, which aspires to be "the sum of human knowledge online" (Wikimedia Foundation, 2006). Although the idea that anyone can contribute and edit anything on the pages of Wikipedia certainly lends itself to potential problems, the amazing resource that it has become is a testament to the potentials of this co-creation process on a large scale. Wikipedia makes clear the ways in which networks of connected, passionate souls can transform the knowledge world.

The Shift to Network Literacy

Becoming an online networked learner, however, requires more than the ability to navigate both people and information. The process takes a nuanced understanding of networks themselves, something that is difficult for young people (and some adults as well) to master. These online interactions we engage in must not simply affirm what we already know or support our current worldview. We must seek and embrace diversity in the connections, not in race, gender, or location so much as in including voices and viewpoints that are different from our own, people who are willing to respectfully challenge our opinions and assessments and be open for continuing debate or conversation (Downes, 2009). Not doing so could easily land us in an online echo chamber, which, although it may be a pleasant place to be, is not the most fertile learning environment. Similarly, we must ensure our networks are open to all, and at the same time, we must be able to discern those who may carry an agenda that may belie their sincerity to learn with us. In other words, to fully take advantage of what the Web makes possible, we must be network literate on many different levels.

For educators, the current challenge is how best to bring this new literacy to students so that every one of them can begin to leverage the amazing learning opportunities that the moment affords. Without question, that challenge is not so much about schools, curricula, or systems as it is about ourselves and our own abilities to connect and learn in these ways. At this crucial moment, we must be able to model for students our own connections outside of the physical spaces we inhabit, and we also must demonstrate our passion for learning transparently in our practice. We must become, in essence, network literate.

Unfortunately, many teachers find the path to network literacy a huge shift to undertake, for a wide variety of reasons. First, for many adults in general, the Web is an acquired taste, not simply a fundamental communication tool as many of our students see it. Many educators still live paper-based learning lives, and transitioning to digital technologies online or offline represents a huge shift in practice. Second, many schools have little or no access to technology in general, and a significant number of individuals are still without broadband access to the Web. Third, teachers complain of a lack of time not only to learn the tools, but also to create sound pedagogy around them. And the professional development opportunities they receive are primarily tool based, not based on connections or network building. Fourth, current assessment regimes make it difficult to integrate technology into the curriculum for fear of a lack of relevance. Finally, when it comes to social networking in general, most schools filter or completely block the tools out of fear, justified or not.

Because of these obstacles, the majority of schools are not rethinking their models in any significant way, and the stark differences between the ways we approach the learning process inside the walls as compared to online are pushing schools and classrooms toward a sense of irrelevance. These obstacles present a moment of huge disruption for the traditional model of education. As Tom Carroll, the president of the National Commission on Teaching and America's Future, suggests, in a networked world, schools can no longer see themselves as the "central learning hubs that they have been in the past." Instead, he says, "we must recognize that schools and classrooms are becoming nodes in networked learning communities" (Carroll, 2000).

How, then, do we begin to make this shift? Most simply, by becoming nodes ourselves. For anyone who has not experienced these passion-based learning connections, it is difficult to fully understand the pedagogical implications for curricula and classrooms. To be sure, at this moment, tens of thousands of teachers and no doubt hundreds of thousands of students around the world are employing social networking tools such as blogs and wikis in their classrooms. But close inspection of those implementations shows that the vast majority are little more than taking what has been done for years and years in the paper, analog curriculum and repurposing it into a digital format. In essence, we replaced a pen with a blog, and very rarely did the pedagogies change in the process. Why? Because the teachers leading those efforts are not networked learners themselves, ones who understand that the full potential of these tools is found not in the publishing of information, but rather in the resulting connections.

To change this disparity, we must look at adults in our classrooms as learners first and teachers second, and we must find ways to support rather than obstruct the creation and growth of global, personal learning networks among educators. These changes will require an investment in infrastructure and technology, a change in our learning worldview, and all sorts of other hugely complex shifts that will take many years to complete. From an individual teacher/learner standpoint, however, this work can and must begin now. At this moment, we as educators have a higher responsibility to understand these shifts and make them a part of our own practice so that we can more effectively model them and prepare our students for the technology-filled and network-driven future that we all will live in. For many of us, this will

> At this moment, we as educators have a higher responsibility to understand these shifts and make them a part of our own practice so that we can more effectively model them and prepare our students for the technology-filled and network-driven future that we all will live in.

require fundamentally changing what we do, not simply adding a layer of technology to it.

Make Technology a Part of Daily Practice

First, in a general sense, we must make technology a part of daily practice. We need to find comfort in digital environments, eschew paper when possible, and read and write online with fluency. We must move toward more mobile technologies, get comfortable with texting and instant messaging, and dabble in gaming environments online. In essence, we need to experience a steep "unlearning curve" that allows us to replace old habits of practice with newer, more interactive and collaborative ones. This may mean canceling the daily paper subscription and reading stories online (and participating in the conversations) or using cloud computing services such as Google Docs where we can create documents, presentations, and spreadsheets online securely for free and access them from any Internet connection. Or, it may mean treating the phone as a creation device, not simply a communication device, and experimenting with the capture of audio, video, and text. In whatever method we choose, we must embrace and become comfortable with the continuous changes that the Internet brings.

From a networked learning standpoint, however, the changes in our comfort zone may be even more difficult. First and foremost, we must be willing to accept, if not embrace, the ever-increasing "hypertransparent and hyperconnected" world in which we live (Seidman, 2007). Moving forward, the reality is that more and more of our lives and those of our students will be shared online, and we will be "econnected" ever more ubiquitously. That means that we must engage in the sharing process rather than avoid it, so that we can best understand the accompanying potentials and pitfalls. But we do so understanding, again, that sharing is not simply done to publish snippets of our personal or professional lives to communicate but to connect with others who may find those pieces interesting or relevant in their own learning. Long described as an isolated profession, teaching now has transparency: sharing lessons, reflections, or questions can move us into a real community of learners with others from far outside our physical spaces. And we do all of this in the context of our passions, whether it be bushcraft, mountain biking on a unicycle, or teaching Shakespeare. Grounding this work around the things we are most motivated to learn is a fundamental requirement for understanding it fully.

This sharing process can begin in small ways, perhaps by commenting on a blog post or contributing to a wiki. Sharing may grow into creating one's own blog, or publishing photos or videos online. All of this, however, we do with the knowledge that once we publish, we cannot take it back. And we do it using our real names, for if we truly want our networks to grow, we must be willing for others to find us online; the balance between network identity and privacy is struck by weighing the risk versus the reward. We want, in essence, to be googled well, so that we can become a part of other networks and grow our own, and so that we can model the creation of an appropriate online persona for our students. To that end, as we share, we monitor the effects of our sharing. With the distributed nature of the conversations on the Web, part of our own network literacy must be the ability to track the responses, citations, references, and links that are generated when others interact. We might use RSS (Real Simple Syndication), for example, to digitally subscribe to certain search results, bringing new conversations and reactions to us almost as they occur.

Further, we need to find comfort in co-creating content with others. The opportunities for collaboration online are almost endless, and we again need to understand the complexities of these interactions before we can fully prepare our students for a highly collaborative workplace. Whether the interactions are unit plans with other teachers or instructional videos with other bushcrafters, and whether the interactions are synchronous or time shifted, the process of identifying safe collaborators, negotiating the scope and pace, creating the products, and sharing those products widely is much more complex than it may seem.

Just as we look to others in our networks to help us filter information, give us feedback, and point us to the best, most interesting and relevant information, we must see ourselves as editors who contribute in this process as well. That means, as Donald Leu from the University of Connecticut suggests, that we must reframe the way we think about reading and writing: "Online reading and writing are so closely connected that it is not possible to separate them; we read online as authors and we write online as readers" (Leu, O'Byrne, Zawilinski, McVerry, & Everett-Cacopardo, 2009). Because of the expectation for active, participatory reading within our online networks, we must experience what it is like to read with the intent to share and to publish not as an end point but as a beginning to a continuing, distributed conversation. In other words, in networks, even the most basic of literacies shifts in important ways, ways that we must help students understand and leverage.

Model Balance

We must also find and model balance. With everything there is to know, and with the myriad of ways in which we can now engage others in learning around our passions, the pull of the Web can be powerful for young and old alike. Unfortunately, for many students, the Web has replaced the television as a babysitting tool, one that because of its interactive nature has a potentially addictive allure. Our own understanding of how best to balance online and offline relationships will speak volumes to students who have little context for what all of this means. It's important that we make transparent our own efforts to strike that balance by feeling free to discuss our own struggles and successes with our students, and encourage them to reflect on their own practice as well.

Schools need to support the efforts of educators to understand how online, virtual, social environments change personal learning practice, because good pedagogy around teaching with these technologies depends on it. Preparing students for a 21st century workplace cannot be done in an information literacy unit in the second half of eighth grade, nor can it be effective without getting technology into kids' hands. These new network literacies require a K–12 re-envisioning of curriculum where we teach even the youngest students in age-appropriate ways to assess information more carefully, collaborate with others, and share their work safely. Teachers must be able to do that for themselves first. Then, beginning in the earliest grades, they can make sound choices to include activities like creating podcasts, collaborating on wikis, even blogging with the intent of providing measured, appropriate ways that students can begin to understand the participatory and connective nature of the Web.

Make Network Literacy a Community Effort

Traditional professional development models are ineffective in these contexts because, again, this is not about tools. The mechanics of blogging, using a wiki, or creating a podcast are skills that can be learned in a two-hour workshop; in fact, the ease of the tools is one reason for the explosion of online publishing. Building networks around the work that we publish and share cannot be learned in "sit and git" trainings. As research from Stanford University and the National Staff Development Council suggests, effective professional development now "must be sustained, focused on important content, and embedded in the work of collaborative professional learning teams that support ongoing improvements in teachers' practice and student achievement" (Wei, Darling-Hammond, Andree, Richardson, & Orphanos, 2009). In other words, to make this shift, teachers and learners must immerse themselves in these networked environments over the long term, and they need educational leaders to be in there with them, participating, publishing, and collaborating with them.

These changes also require that schools bring parents and community members deeply into the conversation, helping them understand the ways in which our times look drastically different from recent history and explaining the new challenges of preparing students for the 21st century. A first step for schools is to become a node in the parents' learning network, modeling transparency and sharing, asking for input, and acting as a filter for reading and viewing that parents might find informative or provocative.

A New Landscape of Learning

This evolution to an anytime, anywhere networked landscape of learning will not be easy, for individuals or for schools. This "tectonic shift," as Shirky (2008, p. 21) describes it, is both vast and fast, and we are only at the beginning part of what promises to be a tumultuous process of change. It is change, however, that has significant implications for our students' futures. The 2009 *Horizon Report* (New

Medium Consortium, 2009), a collaboration between the New Media Consortium and the EDUCAUSE Learning Initiative, contextualizes the moment clearly:

> Increasingly, those who use technology in ways that expand their global connections are more likely to advance, while those who do not will find themselves on the sidelines. With the growing availability of tools to connect learners and scholars all over the world—online collaborative workspaces, social networking tools, mobiles, voice-over-IP, and more—teaching and scholarship are transcending traditional borders more and more all the time.

In the end, network literacy is all about our own ability to reach out to others to start our own fires, to attend to our own learning needs, and to navigate these new spaces with the same type of aplomb as Nelson Smith. This new networked space where we all can connect, create, and collaborate is one that is filled with amazing potentials for learning, many that promise to reshape the way we go about our lives both in and outside of school. How quickly we begin to understand those potentials, first for ourselves and then for our classrooms, will in no small way determine the preparedness of students to compete successfully in the world they will soon inherit.

References

Bernoff, J. (2009, August 25). *Social technology growth marches on in 2009, led by social network sites.* Accessed at http://blogs.forrester.com/ground-swell/2009/08/social-technology-growth-marches-on-in-2009-led-by-social-network-sites.html on December 17, 2009.

Carroll, T. G. (2000). If we didn't have the schools we have today, would we create the schools we have today? *Contemporary Issues in Technology and Teacher Education, 1*(1). Accessed at www.citejournal.org/vol1/iss1/currentissues/general/article1.htm on December 17, 2009.

Downes, S. (2009, February 24). *Connectivist dynamics in communities.* Accessed at http://halfanhour.blogspot.com/2009/02/connectivist-dynamics-in-communities.html on December 17, 2009.

Ito, M., Horst, H., Bittanti, M., Boyd, D., Herr-Stephenson, B., Lange, P. G., et al. (with Baumer, S., Cody, R., Mahendran, D., Martinez, K., Perkel, D., Sims, C., et al.). (2008, November). *Living and learning with new media: Summary of findings from the digital youth project.* Accessed at http://digitalyouth.ischool.berkeley.edu/files/report/digitalyouth-WhitePaper.pdf on December 17, 2009.

Lardinois, F. (2009, December 9). *Chad Hurley: YouTube needs to improve search—More live programming coming soon.* Accessed at www.readwriteweb.com/archives/chad_hurley_youtubes_revenue_is_up_-_operating_cost_down.php on December, 17, 2009.

Leu, D. J., O'Byrne, W. I., Zawilinski, L., McVerry, J. G., & Everett-Cacopardo, H. (2009). Comments on Greenhow, Robelia, and Hughes: Expanding the new literacies conversation. *Educational Researcher, 38*(4), 264–269. Accessed at www.aera.net/uploadedFiles/Publications/Journals/Educational_Researcher/3804/264-269_05EDR09.pdf on December 17, 2009.

National Council of Teachers of English. (2008, February 15). *The definition of 21st century literacies.* Accessed at www.ncte.org/governance/literacies on December 17, 2009.

New Media Consortium. (2009). *Horizon report.* Accessed at http://wp.nmc.org/horizon2009/chapters/trends/#00 on December 17, 2009.

Seidman, D. (2007). *How: Why how we do anything means everything—in business (and in life).* Hoboken, NJ: John Wiley & Sons.

Shirky, C. (2008). *Here comes everybody: The power of organizing without organizations.* New York: Penguin.

Smith, N. (2009, February 21). *Help with bowdrill set* [YouTube video]. Accessed at www.youtube.com/watch?v=JuFsDN8dsJU on December 17, 2009.

Wei, R. C., Darling-Hammond, L., Andree, A., Richardson, N., & Orphanos, S. (2009, February). *Professional learning in the learning profession: A status report on teacher development in the U.S. and abroad.* Dallas, TX: National Staff Development Council. Accessed at www.srnleads.org/resources/publications/pdf/nsdc_profdev_tech_report.pdf on December 17, 2009.

Weigel, M., James, C., & Gardner, H. (2009, March 3). Learning: Peering backward and looking forward in the digital era. *International Journal of Learning and Media, 1*(1), 1–18. Accessed at www.mitpressjournals.org/doi/full/10.1162/ijlm.2009.0005 on December 17, 2009.

Wikimedia Foundation. (2006, March 1). *English Wikipedia publishes millionth article.* Accessed at http://wikimediafoundation.org/wiki/Press_releases/English_Wikipedia_Publishes_Millionth_Article on December 17, 2009.

Douglas Reeves

Douglas Reeves, Ph.D., is founder of The Leadership and Learning Center. He has worked with education, business, non-profit, and government organizations throughout the world. Reeves is a frequent keynote speaker in the United States and abroad. The author of more than twenty books and many articles on leadership and organizational effectiveness, he has twice been selected for the Harvard Distinguished Authors Series. Reeves was named the 2006 Brock International Laureate for his contributions to education. He also received the Distinguished Service Award from the National Association of Secondary School Principals and the Parent's Choice Award for his writing for children and parents.

Reeves edited and contributed to the Solution Tree anthology *Ahead of the Curve* and contributed to the anthologies *On Common Ground* and *Change Wars.*

In this chapter, Reeves tackles the challenging problem of assessment. He argues that the new outcomes envisioned by advocates of 21st century skills can properly be measured only by abandoning standardized tests. He offers three criteria for determining how educators can know students are learning 21st century content and skills and shows how these might apply in practice.

Chapter 14

A Framework for Assessing 21st Century Skills

Douglas Reeves

How do we know students are learning? For most of the 20th century, the answer to that question was an idiosyncratic combination of subjective grades from classroom teachers and scores on standardized norm-referenced tests. From 1990 to 2010, norm-referenced tests were supplanted in elementary and secondary schools by standards-referenced tests, as their use exploded from twelve states in the early 1990s to fifty states in 2010. The use of tests linked to academic standards has also increased throughout Canada, the United Kingdom, Australia, and many other nations. Today, when someone asks, "How do we know students are learning?" the most common response is a test score that purports to show that students are "proficient" in meeting academic standards. Whereas in the previous era of norm-referenced tests, fewer than half the students could, by definition, be "above average," in the era of standards-referenced exams, all students can aspire to a combination of the knowledge, skills, and critical-thinking processes that combine to form the essential skills for 21st century learners.

Many thoughtful writers, such as Hargreaves and Shirley (2009), have suggested that standardized tests provide an insufficient answer to the question, "What is the evidence of student learning?" This chapter suggests that the question itself is flawed. Developing better tests of student learning in the 21st century is as futile as attempting to find a faster horse and buggy would have been in the 20th century. No amount of training or discipline would make the horse competitive with the automobile, airplane, or space shuttle. The nature of the horse makes such competition impossible. Similarly, the nature of testing—with its standardized conditions, secrecy, and individual results—is antithetical to the understanding, exploration, creativity, and sharing that are the hallmarks of a new framework for assessment.

Thus, teachers and school leaders need a different set of tools to determine whether or not students are learning in light of 21st century essential skills. In particular, we need practical ways to assess students in the following three ways:

1. In variable rather than standardized conditions

2. As teams rather than as individuals

3. With assessments that are public rather than secret

What Makes 21st Century Assessment Different?

The science of assessing human learning has a troubled history. In the classic *Mismeasure of Man* (1981), Stephen Jay Gould exposed the frauds of the 19th century, from the phrenologists who claimed to be able to infer intelligence from the shape of the head to the brain researchers of the day who claimed to measure cranial capacity with statistical precision and thus explained with scientific certainty the superiority of northern European males over the rest of the species. Equipped with another century of sophistication and social awareness, Richard Herrnstein and Charles Murray (1994) pleaded with readers of *The Bell Curve* not to shoot the messengers—they were simply interpreting the data, and, sadly enough, they reported that there were deeply ingrained differences in intelligence separating the races, which were reflected in educational and economic performance over the long term. Other scholars (Fraser, 1995; Gardner, 1995) have vigorously challenged both the statistical methodology and the conclusions of *The Bell Curve*.

Today, the terms *results* and *achievement* are almost invariably equated with the average performance of individual students on standardized tests. Some tests claim to assess 21st century skills because the instruments include constructed-response items (that is, students must write something rather than select a single response from four or five alternatives) and "authentic tasks" (that is, a context that might have applicability to the life and environment of the test taker). But it is not possible to reconcile the demands of 21st century skills with the realities of the traditional testing environment. Consider the contrast between what we expect of students and how we test them. The Partnership for 21st Century Skills offers both a compelling rationale and a useful framework for skills that are essential for students if they wish to enjoy lives that are free from want and fear, reminiscent of the clarion call enunciated by Franklin Roosevelt in his State of the Union message of 1941. The Partnership represents broad consensus among many stakeholders, including teachers, parents, employers, and policymakers. They note that while content knowledge remains a part of any education, the essentials also include global awareness, creativity and innovation, communication and collaboration, initiative and self-direction, and leadership and responsibility (see figure F.1 on page xv of the foreword of this volume for a complete list of the skills identified by the Partnership in their Framework for 21st Century Learning). But while the need for 21st century skills is clear, assessment practices lag far behind because they are bound by three destructive traditions: standardized conditions, secrecy of content, and individual results. Table 14.1 (page 308) contrasts these assessment parameters and the assumptions behind them.

Nonstandardized Instead of Standardized Conditions

The 20th century requirement for standardized conditions is based on the assumption that the purpose of the test is to compare one student to another. Therefore, all conditions—time, room environment, and the lead in the pencil (neither no. 1 nor no. 3 will do)—must all be the same. When we scientifically control the environment, then the only variation must be in the performance of the individual student. Under these conditions, students are rewarded for memorization and following established rules. Write within the lines, work within the

Table 14.1: Test Parameters and Assumptions

20th Century Test Parameter	20th Century Assumption	21st Century Test Parameter	21st Century Assumption
Standardized Conditions	The purpose of the test is to compare one student to another, so the only variation must be in the student, not in the conditions of the test. Students are rewarded for memorization and for following established rules.	Nonstandardized Conditions	The purpose of the test is to reflect the real world, so there is always variation and volatility. Students are rewarded for creativity and their reactions to the unexpected.
Secrecy of Content	Fairness means that no student knows in advance what is expected. Therefore, the more knowledge students acquire and recall, the less likely they will be surprised by anything on the test.	Openness of Content	Fairness means that students are partners in the assessment process. They not only are aware of the broad array of possible challenges on the test, but they have contributed some of these challenges themselves.
Individual Results	Success means beating other students. The leader is the one who is the boss and who knows the most. Teamwork sounds nice, but once students are taking the test, it's every person for him- or herself.	Combination of Individual and Team Results	Success is a reflection of individual and collaborative effort. The former without the latter is insufficient. The leader is the one who influences others with insight and support, not with authority.

time limits, and neither offer nor accept help from a classmate. Even if we assess something with a 21st century label, such as a constructed-response test item or a real-world task, every student will respond to the same item, and every scorer will use the same scoring guide. We will not let a contemporary label hinder us from our antiquated assumptions of stability, normality, and control. Therefore, even on these apparently new tasks, students are rewarded for following the formula: the same essay, the same graph, the same reasoning, and the same vocabulary. After all, the evaluation of the scorers rests upon their inter-rater reliability; that is, their agreement with one another. Consideration of creativity risks an inconsistent score, so it is better if the adults, like the students, stay within the lines.

Assessments with 21st century assumptions, however, are quite different. A standardized environment does not exist, and change and volatility are typical. Variation is neither good nor bad, but merely reflective of the complexity of the tasks and processes entailed in authentic assessment of 21st century skills. For example, some teams require more time for successful collaboration just as some individuals require more time for analysis of alternatives. The more challenging a task and the more variable the assessment environment, the less appropriate it is for time to be a standardized testing condition. Scorers of these assessments must be sufficiently sophisticated that they can recognize and reward creativity, critical thinking, and problem solving. Accordingly, they must be entrusted with the judgment to allow variability in the time, context, and processes for the assessment tasks.

Openness of Content Instead of Secrecy

The 20th century demand for secrecy is the result of a deep-seated sense of fairness. If one student knows the content of a test in advance and the other does not, then the former is cheating and has an unfair advantage. Secrecy is enshrined in test procedures and codified into law, making it a felony in some states for students or teachers to violate this sacred tenet of testing. In an environment of test secrecy, students are rewarded for maximum memorization.

The 21st century assessment, by contrast, values openness. Not only are test items openly available for study and consideration, but students themselves contribute to the creation of assessments. It is not cheating to know the questions in advance of the test; rather, it's the only thoughtful and responsible thing to do. Consider this the next time you board a commercial aircraft: the pilot in command of your aircraft had access to the Federal Aviation Administration's pilot test questions before he or she took the exam (Federal Aviation Administration, 2009). In one of the most high-stakes tests of the 21st century, we value openness, not secrecy. Applying this principle to student assessments, teachers who intend to pose two essay questions on a test should publish twenty or more such questions, giving students the opportunity for comprehensive study and preparation. Teachers should pool their potential test questions, making them widely available to all students. In fact, they should welcome contributions of test items from students, so that the test is no longer a mental fencing match between teacher and students, but a collaborative endeavor in which every student has a fair opportunity for academic success.

Both Individual and Team Results

The third characteristic of 20th century assessments, and the one most deeply ingrained in our educational tradition, is individual scores. Teamwork sounds fine in principle, but unfortunately, many people believe the most important purpose of assessment is to rank individuals and single out the best of the best. In my work with parents around the globe, this commitment to individualism appears to be strongly reinforced at home. When teachers attempt to support teamwork and collaborative effort, parents do not always express appreciation for the teacher's emphasis on this essential 21st century skill; they often express frustration that their own child's efforts were insufficiently recognized as superior when he or she was required to work in a team.

When these students enter the world of work, society, and life in the 21st century, their hyper-competitive habits of mind will be sadly out of place. Leadership will stem not from rank but from influence and service. Performance will be measured not by the success of the individual, but by the success of the team, perhaps a multinational team with members spanning the globe. The arrogance and individuality that brought early success will lead to a life that is professionally and personally unsatisfying. Because a preponderance of evidence has exposed the folly of the short-sighted and self-righteous pursuit of rewards based on individual merit, new reward structures will focus on teamwork and collaboration (Pfeffer & Sutton, 2006).

A Better Way: A New Framework for Assessing 21st Century Skills

Learning was the end goal in the 20th century. In the parlance of researchers, it was the dependent variable. Dependent variables are effects—test scores, for example; independent variables are causes—teaching, leadership, curriculum, demographic factors, and many other factors that influence the effects. Analyses of these variables can offer useful insights into a new framework for assessing 21st century skills. Think of this assessment framework as a constellation of stars. Individually, the stars may be bright and powerful, but they are only among the billions that illuminate the night sky. But stars in constellations have meaning because of their relationship to other stars and the interpretive framework that the viewer attaches to them. Similarly, 21st century skills will grow in complexity and number over time, but we can nevertheless put them into perspective with a framework that lends coherence to the skills.

Figure 14.1 (page 312) includes five essential core realms for the assessment of 21st century skills: learn, understand, create, explore, and share. This is not a comprehensive list of skills. In his foreword to this volume, Ken Kay has provided a much more extensive listing of 21st century skills. He also makes the point that these skills are not an alternative to academic content, but rather are integrally related to the need for students to learn and demonstrate proficiency in core academic standards. My framework is limited to these five core areas because they are adaptable to every academic level and subject. Moreover, the practical reality of the classroom is that teachers have ever-multiplying demands and fixed amounts of time. This framework offers a clear and consistent focus for every lesson that balances the need for learning and understanding of academic content with the need to create, explore, and share.

The circles surrounding the core of 21st century skills suggest the nonlinear, nonsequential nature of this new framework. They

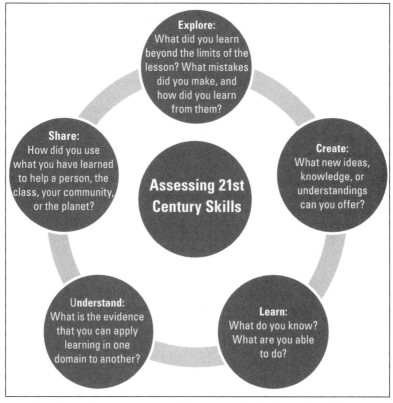

**Figure 14.1: A new framework for assessing 21st century skills—
a constellation of learning.**

also provide a sense of context: however elegant individual tests of learning may be, they are but a single star in the constellation. Teachers and school leaders can apply this framework to consider the gap between traditional assessments and the opportunities to create new challenges for students that respond to the demands of a new century. For example, most tests focus on the "learning" skill in the lower right of the framework. They typically consider the questions, "What do you know?" and "What are you able to do?" That assessment could be enhanced significantly by including the other elements of the framework and their associated questions:

- **Explore**—What did you learn beyond the limits of the lesson? What mistakes did you make, and how did you learn from them?

- **Create**—What new ideas, knowledge, or understandings can you offer?

- **Understand**—What is the evidence that you can apply learning in one domain to another?

- **Share**—How did you use what you have learned to help a person, the class, your community, or the planet?

Consider a brief example to illustrate how teachers apply the framework to transform a traditional test-based unit to one based on assessment that is far more engaging. Let's imagine a group of middle school social studies teachers who use this framework to create new assessments for a history lesson on the years before the Civil War. Their original three-week unit included readings, presentations, and test questions on the Underground Railroad, the rebellion by John Brown, and the presidential campaign of 1860. Because these specific historical facts are included in their state academic content standards, the teachers are obliged to address them in class. They use the framework to come up with assessments that go beyond traditional test questions to engage students in 21st century skills and to assess these skills.

First, the teachers decide to begin with a pre-assessment, challenging students to work first alone, then in pairs, and finally in groups to identify what they already know about the three historical events. Students then create a table displaying what they know as "historical fact," what they judge to be "conclusions based on facts," and "opinions and beliefs." For example, it is a historical fact that John Brown killed people at Harpers Ferry, but whether he was a freedom fighter or a terrorist is an opinion that must be subjected to critical review. From this activity, students would observe that collaboration quickly expands their knowledge base and personal insights.

In their next grade-level team meeting, the social studies teachers ask their colleagues in music, English, art, science, math, and technology what connections they might offer to deepen student understanding of these events. The music teacher suggests songs sung by slaves and slave owners, which offer starkly different descriptions of plantation life. The art teacher provides a searing image of John Brown that hangs in the Kansas State Capitol today. The technology teacher shares an electronic game based on the Underground Railroad that was created by a student for fun during the previous year. The English teacher suggests that U.S. Supreme Court decisions of the era, such as the Dred Scott decision confirming that slaves were property, are rich with literary and poetic allusions. By the end of the discussion, the social studies teachers have compiled an enrichment menu from which each student can choose a project to demonstrate his or her deeper understanding. For example, some students might explore the contrasts between art, music, and poetry created by slaves, abolitionists, and those sympathetic to slaveholders. Other students might explore the speeches of Abraham Lincoln and trace the development of his attitudes toward slaves and black people living in the north. Others might write a short play to speculate on what it might have meant for the country had Stephen Douglas been victorious over Abraham Lincoln in the presidential election of 1860.

Finally, the teachers consider other elements of the framework: creating, exploring, and sharing. Students and teachers collaborate to create new and challenging tasks. For example, one group of students might ask, "What would happen if the Lincoln-Douglas debates were broadcast today?" Their presentation might include the two debaters attempting to make their serious arguments, with interruptions and objections from other students mimicking various contemporary broadcasters. Another group might write and perform a spiritual, using the minor keys, rhythms, and language that members learned from studying the genre. Another group might expand on the interactive game mentioned previously by creating a much more complex web-based version that engages students in other schools who are studying the same topic.

Assessments that focus exclusively on what students know and do are worse than incomplete; omission of the other essential elements of the framework sends the clear message to teachers that 21st century skills don't count. Without a combination of critical thinking, problem solving, effective teamwork, and creativity, learning remains stagnant, more useful for passing a test than solving a real-world challenge. Sharing requires the deliberate application of learning to help others, a commitment that constrains the impulse to erect boundaries around knowledge. Later in this chapter, I will apply this framework to a real assessment—one that I thought was quite well designed. By exposing even well-designed assessments to the questions in this framework, teachers can take good assessments and make them more engaging, relevant, and responsive to the requirements of 21st century learning.

Consider the role that each element of this framework plays in the assessment of 21st century skills. I emphasize these not because other 21st century skills are unimportant, but because these particular skills have been identified by a variety of sources as particularly important for economic opportunity and social justice in the 21st century (Csikszentmihalyi, 2003; Hamel, 2009; Quelch & Jocz, 2007). I will first consider the deficiencies in even the best assessments, and then offer five essential realms for the assessment of 21st century skills.

Assessing Assessments

One of the more frequent criticisms of the 21st century skills movement is that it diminishes the importance of factual knowledge (Matthews, 2009), an allegation undone by any careful reading of the Partnership for 21st Century Skills' framework, which clearly places value on learning and testing for content knowledge and literacy skills. Students must continue to acquire knowledge, practice skills, and apply those skills at an expert level. Information acquisition, however, is a necessary but insufficient condition for assessing 21st century skills. Assessing learning provides us with important insights, not only about student progress, but also about the role of teaching (Darling-Hammond et al., 2008; Hattie, 2009; Schmoker, 2006) and leadership (Marzano, Waters, & McNulty, 2005; Reeves, 2008; White, 2009). Despite the depth and breadth of these inquiries—Hattie's tour de force includes data on more than eighty-three million students from more than eight hundred meta-analyses—this research fails to inform our judgment on four of the five realms of 21st century skills on which this chapter focuses, and this list is not close to a complete replication of the Partnership's framework.

It is easy to snipe at poorly worded test questions that are ambiguous, too easy, culturally distinctive, or otherwise ineptly phrased.

But what about thoughtfully constructed assessments that aspire to be relevant and require authentic performance? The argument about the limitations of learning assessment might be best made by using an example I created. Guided by insightful assessment advice from Wiggins (1998), Wiggins and McTighe (2005), Ainsworth and Viegut (2006), Stiggins (2007), and years of practical experience, I created a multipart performance assessment designed to engage students in a relevant task, require performance of multiple skills, and require work that was far beyond simply meeting standards or passing a multiple-choice test. I have personally used the assessment with middle school math students, and it has been distributed to more than fifty thousand teachers around the world, many of whom have also used it in their classrooms. In brief, the assessment, titled "Design Your Ideal School," includes the following performance tasks:

- Describe the ideal school. This task includes a written description and digital visual images.

- Create a plan for the ideal school. This task includes an accurate scale drawing using computer-assisted design (CAD) software and the calculation of area and perimeter of the structures and the land. Students use actual zoning and facility standards so that the footprint of the building conforms to requirements for outdoor recreational space and setbacks from other properties.

- Evaluate the model. This task requires the student to consider the physical space requirements of students and faculty and compare the ideal model to these actual needs.

- Estimate the cost. This task requires students to create a mathematical model to estimate the cost of their school using publicly available data on school construction.

- Modify and improve the plan. This task requires students to modify their plan, improving the description, scale model, and financial model based on feedback from fellow students, teachers, administrators, and policymakers (the typical challenge here is reducing the cost of the project while maintaining the quality of the building).

Each task is accompanied by a scoring guide in student-accessible language. Over the course of two weeks, students are able to demonstrate proficiency in many different standards that include mathematics, literacy, and social science. I took a good deal of satisfaction in the fact that this assessment was superior to so many worksheets, quizzes, and multiple-choice tests. I had never seen a state or system-level assessment with tasks that were this complex, relevant, and demanding. But does it meet the needs of my students in the 21st century? This assessment, as with other well-designed tasks, will determine the extent to which students have mastered essential content knowledge in writing and math. It's possible that some of the tasks move the depth of assessment from learning to understanding. While most students have been taught that the area of a rectangle is the product of length and width ($A = L \times W$), a better understanding of the concept is demonstrated when students combine the area of many different polygons (the rooms and hallways in the school) and compare that area to the available land (calculating the perimeter of the school requires students to create another series of invisible polygons to calculate the total land area). Moreover, students have a relevant reason for thinking about area: required recreation space for students and legally required distance from surrounding buildings.

What about creativity, exploration, and sharing? This assessment, which is better than many I have seen in middle school math classrooms, falls sadly short of the mark. The assessment provided only constricted focus on some math, writing, and social studies standards and only appeared to encourage creativity as a result of the differences in design. If a student had said, "Wait—I don't want to build a school, but I'm going to create a virtual learning community without any buildings at all," then my response to this creativity would probably have been a notation that the student failed to demonstrate proficiency in scale, area, and ratio by omitting the required accurate scale drawing of the school. What about exploration? While the assessment permits some limited exploration in tangential fields of inquiry—zoning requirements and school finance in particular—the boundaries of exploration are limited. What if a student wishes to change the venue from the local neighborhood to Bangladesh, and rather than build an impossibly expensive new school, the student wants to convert an abandoned warehouse into a school? The thought never occurred to me, nor did I model such intellectual leaps for my students. What about sharing? When Hargreaves (2009) talks about sharing, he refers to an inspiring vision and compelling moral purpose. But when students "shared" their results from this assessment, too often the objective was simply showing off. In sum, this is not a bad assessment—it is far more engaging, relevant, and challenging than the average worksheet in a middle school math class and dramatically more pedagogically sound than the typical standardized test. Nevertheless, that is damning with faint praise. Even this relatively good assessment falls far short of the mark for assessing 21st century skills. By publicly criticizing my own classroom assessment and teaching, I hope that I can encourage other veteran educators and leaders to examine their practice with the same critical eye.

Educational leaders cannot talk about the need for collaboration, problem solving, critical thinking, and creativity and at the same time leave teachers and school administrators fenced in by obsolete assessment mechanisms, policies, and assumptions. Consider the five essential realms of the new framework in light of the essential shifts that must be made in the design and administration of assessments. For each essential realm (learning, understanding, exploration, creativity, and sharing), I will explore the transformations required of assessments: from standardized to fluid conditions, from secrecy to openness, and from individual to collaborative assessments.

Learning

At the risk of redundancy, let us be clear: assessment of 21st century skills requires content knowledge. Students will continue to learn vocabulary, be able to perform calculations without electronic assistance, speak in complete sentences, and support their assertions with evidence. As Kay has made clear in his foreword to this volume, a commitment to content knowledge is not mutually exclusive with an expectation of 21st century skills. Rather, learning is the first step, not the end goal. But if we stop with learning, we have produced no more than a generation of *Jeopardy!* champions who can display their learning a fraction of a second faster than a competitor. We can and must do better. Typical demonstrations of learning depend upon the 20th century assessment parameters of standardization, secrecy, and individual scores. Progressing beyond learning requires a significant change in orientation, as table 14.2 (pages 320–321) illustrates. We change from standardized to fluid assessment conditions, from secret to open assessment protocols, and from individual scores to a combination of individual and team scores.

Understanding

While there are certainly some elements of assessment where secrecy will always be legally necessary (for example, patient privacy in the assessment of psychiatric diagnostics), most assessments of 21st century skills have a bias for openness. Students not only know the tasks in advance of the assessment, but they help to create them. Indeed, their ability to create relevant tasks and design challenging rubrics is an excellent way for teachers to assess their level of understanding. One of our best assessments of student understanding is their ability to explain their learning to others, an inherently collaborative act of learning.

Exploration

Colvin (2008), Hattie (2009), and Ericsson, Charness, Feltovich and Hoffman (2006) all converge in an understanding of the notion of "deliberate practice." Students do not achieve performance breakthroughs through another week of perfect scores on spelling tests or by reciting "the square of the hypotenuse is equal to the sum of the square of the other two sides," a statement that the brainless Scarecrow said after he earned his diploma in *The Wizard of Oz*. Rather, students gain most when they explore. We venture from learning and understanding to exploration when we ask more challenging questions: "When was Pythagoras wrong?" "Why was he wrong?" "What does my understanding of correct spelling on last week's word list tell us about language development and political conquest?" While I confess that for many years I failed to ask these questions, I can attest as someone who continues to teach students from a broad range of economic and educational backgrounds that they are eager to explore these questions and many more like them. Nelson (2009) makes clear that while society reveres the individual explorers (who, for example, remembers the name of the third person to walk on the surface of the moon), veneration of the individual is based on the inaccurate mythology of the solitary hero. Exploration is an inherently collaborative endeavor.

Table 14.2: Practical Implications for Assessing 21st Century Skills

21st Century Skill Dimension	Standardized ⇧ Fluid Conditions	Secrecy ⇧ Openness	Individual ⇧ Group Scores
Learning	Use of standardized tests to check for knowledge of isolated skills is limited. Conditions are deliberately varied to reflect real-world application.	Secrets are kept only when essential for legal protection (for example, names of patients in psychiatric case studies). In general, there is a strong bias for openness, including the use of student-generated assessments.	Use of individual tests for "survival skills" such as literacy; use of group assessments for application. Individual assessment records include both individual and group assessment results.
Understanding	Flexible assessment menus help students achieve both competence and understanding.	Complete transparency is the norm; questions and tasks are readily available to students, parents, and teachers.	Evidence of individual understanding is only part of the assessment. Using that understanding to help others learn is also an essential process, and therefore collaboration is imperative.
Exploration	Teachers help open the door to the zone of exploration that is beyond the comfort of standardized conditions.	The goal of exploration is unlocking secrets, not maintaining them.	Exploration requires partnership, support, feedback, and inspiration by the paths of other explorers.

21st Century Skill Dimension	Standardized ⇨ Fluid Conditions	Secrecy ⇨ Openness	Individual ⇨ Group Scores
Creativity	Deliberately nonstandard conditions, with variations in place, time, and conditions, are all part of the expectation of students.	There are no secrets. Students are coauthors of assessments, not recipients of them.	While some creative processes are solitary, creative pursuits take place in a context that requires communication, feedback, and hyperlinked applications, all of which require collaboration.
Sharing	The attitude changes from "don't share your work" to "how have you shared your work recently?"	Students are not merely consumers of education, but share their new insights, processes, and ideas with students and teachers in their classroom and around the globe.	Interactions between student and teacher change from two-way exchanges to contributions by the student to a learning network. The goal is not simply for the student to prove his or her value to the teacher, but for the student to make a contribution to the learning community.

Creativity

In 1913, Igor Stravinsky conducted the premiere of *La Sacre du Printemps* (*The Rite of Spring*), a ballet with orchestral accompaniment that is now part of the standard repertoire of every major orchestra. But what is now regarded as a major creative stroke was, at the time, received with virulent insults and shouts of disapproval. Stravinsky and Schoenberg, along with almost every one of their iconoclastic successors, used the same twelve-tone scale that Bach used in the 16th century. While Stravinsky was profoundly creative, he accepted the basic boundaries of classical music upon which he had been trained. A few late-20th century and 21st century composers trained in the traditional classical twelve-tone scale have asked, "Why twelve tones?" Some South American and African musicians use quarter tones, giving them a palette that is four times larger than that used by Western artists. Jazz composer Maria Schneider goes further, incorporating the almost infinite range of Brazilian rain-forest bird songs into her music.

In the context of assessment, the idea of a standardized test of creativity is preposterous. Indeed, teachers must pursue precisely the opposite by challenging students to consider the boundaries of what they are already doing and then imaging a response to the challenge that violates all of those boundaries. I asked students to design a school so that they could demonstrate proficiency in math scale, area, perimeter, measurement, calculation, and other academic standards. But what are the scale, area, and perimeter of Web 3.0, where my next group of students may design their school? In fact, there are some mathematical responses to such a question (Barabási, 2003), but I simply never considered them for a middle school class. Creativity also requires collaboration, despite the stereotype of the lonely artist dancing to the tune of a different drummer. Vasily Kandinsky, one of the founders of abstract painting, was influenced by other ground-breaking musicians, from Richard Wagner in the 19th century to Arnold Schoenberg in the 20th (Messer, 1997). Creativity, therefore, does not imply alienation from learning and understanding, but is founded upon those essential elements. Wagner (2008) reminds us to be wary of our enthusiasm for new frameworks of knowledge lest we forget our debt to Aristotle, who presciently suggested that observation was one of only five means of conceptual understanding.

How do teachers translate the imperative for creativity into practical action in the classroom?

First, our assessments must support rather than punish errors. Errors are evidence that the students are taking risks and engaging difficult material in a creative manner, not evidence of failure. Second, we must encourage rather than punish collaboration. Collaboration encourages multiple perspectives, alternative points of view, and feedback, all vital to the creative process. Third, we must transform the assessment relationship so that students are not merely the recipients of piecework, but the co-creators of assessments and reflective feedback.

Sharing

The final star in the assessment constellation—sharing—requires a shift in student perspective. Students are not merely consumers of education laboring for the next reward. Their success is measured not just in terms of tests passed, but by the ways in which they apply their learning to help others. They measure their significance not by how they have distinguished themselves, but by the impact that they had on their communities and the world. When I first conducted my school assessment, students thought success meant completing the assignment and earning good grades. Today, I have students heading to Madagascar, and they are very impatient to build that school.

Meeting the Opportunities and Demands

The challenges of 21st century assessment can be overwhelming, requiring time, risk taking, and political courage. Political leaders, including school board members, are often those who achieved their present success by virtue of their performance on 20th century assessments. Standardization, secrecy, and individual assessment served them well, and many of them expect their own children to succeed within that same framework. Therefore, it will require explicit changes in assessment policy and practice if we are to meet the opportunities and demands of the 21st century.

References

Ainsworth, L., & Viegut, D. (2006). *Common formative assessments: How to connect standards-based instruction and assessment.* Thousand Oaks, CA: Corwin Press.

Barabási, A.-L. (2003). *Linked: How everything is connected to everything else and what it means.* New York: Plume.

Colvin, G. (2008). *Talent is overrated: What really separates world-class performers from everybody else.* New York: Portfolio.

Csikszentmihalyi, M. (2003). *Good business: Leadership, flow, and the making of meaning.* New York: Viking.

Darling-Hammond, L., Barron, B., Pearson, P. D., Schoenfeld, A. H., Stage, E. K., Zimmerman, T. D., et al. (2008). *Powerful learning: What we know about teaching for understanding.* San Francisco: Jossey-Bass.

Ericsson, K. A., Charness, N., Feltovich, P. J., & Hoffman, R. R. (Eds.). (2006). *The Cambridge handbook of expertise and expert performance.* New York: Cambridge University Press.

Federal Aviation Administration. (2009). *Sample airmen knowledge test questions.* Accessed at www.faa.gov/training_testing/testing/airmen/test_questions/ on December 11, 2009.

Fraser, S. (1995). *The bell curve wars: Race, intelligence, and the future of America.* New York: Basic Books.

Gardner, H. (1995, Winter). Cracking open the IQ box. *The American Prospect, 6*(20), 71–80.

Gould, S. J. (1981). *The mismeasure of man.* New York: Norton.

Hamel, G. (2009, February). Moon shots for management. *Harvard Business Review, 87*(2), 91–98.

Hargreaves, A. (2009). The fourth way of change: Towards an age of inspiration and sustainability. In A. Hargreaves & M. Fullan (Eds.), *Change Wars* (pp. 11–43). Bloomington, IN: Solution Tree Press.

Hargreaves, A., & Shirley, D. (2009). *The fourth way: The inspiring future for educational change.* Thousand Oaks, CA: Corwin Press.

Hattie, J. (2009). *Visible learning: A synthesis of over 800 meta-analyses relating to achievement.* New York: Routledge.

Herrnstein, R. J., & Murray, C. (1994). *The bell curve: Intelligence and class structure in American life.* New York: Free Press.

Marzano, R. J., Waters, T., & McNulty, B. A. (2005). *School leadership that works: From research to results.* Alexandria, VA: Association for Supervision and Curriculum Development.

Matthews, J. (2009, January 5). The latest doomed pedagogical fad: 21st-century skills. *The Washington Post,* p. B2.

Messer, T. M. (1997). *Kandinsky.* New York: Harry N. Abrams.

Nelson, C. (2009). *Rocket men: The epic story of the first men on the moon.* New York: Viking Adult.

Pfeffer, J., & Sutton, R. I. (2006). *Hard facts, dangerous half-truths and total nonsense: Profiting from evidence-based management.* Boston: Harvard Business School Press.

Quelch, J. A., & Jocz, K. E. (2007). *Greater good: How good marketing makes for better democracy.* Boston: Harvard Business Press.

Reeves, D. B. (2008). *Reframing teacher leadership to improve your school.* Alexandria, VA: Association for Supervision and Curriculum Development.

Schmoker, M. (2006). *Results now: How we can achieve unprecedented improvements in teaching and learning.* Alexandria, VA: Association for Supervision and Curriculum Development.

Stiggins, R. J. (2007). *Introduction to student-involved assessment for learning* (5th ed.). Upper Saddle River, NJ: Prentice Hall.

Wagner, T. (2008). *The global achievement gap: Why even our best schools don't teach the new survival skills our children need—and what we can do about it.* New York: Basic Books.

Wiggins, G. (1998). *Educative assessment: Designing assessments to inform and improve student performance.* San Francisco: Jossey-Bass.

Wiggins, G. P., & McTighe, J. (2005). *Understanding by design.* Alexandria, VA: Association for Supervision and Curriculum Development.

White, S. (2009). *Leadership maps.* Englewood, CO: Lead + Learn Press.

Andy Hargreaves

Andy Hargreaves, Ph.D., is the Thomas More Brennan Chair in Education at the Lynch School of Education at Boston College. He has authored or edited more than twenty-five books, which have been translated into a dozen languages. His book *Teaching in the Knowledge Society: Education in the Age of Insecurity* (2003) received the Choice Outstanding Book Award from the American Libraries Association for Teaching and the American Educational Research Association Division B Outstanding Book Award. Hargreaves' current research is funded by the United Kingdom's Specialist Schools and Academies Trust and the National College for School Leadership and is concerned with organizations that perform beyond expectations in education, sport, business, and health. He edited *Change Wars* (2009), a volume in Solution Tree Press' Leading Edge™ series, with Michael Fullan, which received the 2009 National Staff Development Council (NSDC) Book of the Year award. His latest book *The Fourth Way* (2009) discusses the inspiring future of educational change.

Hargreaves concludes this volume by asking tough questions about the 21st century skills movement. He uses metaphor to illuminate the historic ways that change has occurred in education and will occur in the future. He categorizes the emphasis on 21st century skills as the Third Way. He lists positive and negative results from each of the prior ways and looks ahead to an even more desirable Fourth Way.

Afterword

Leadership, Change, and Beyond the 21st Century Skills Agenda

Andy Hargreaves

Whether men are from Mars or women from Venus is a matter of argument and assumption. One thing is clear, though: the 21st century skills agenda may be moving us all to another planet. Whether it will be swift Mercury or sustainable Earth, or a combination of the two, is the challenge before us.

In the 21st century, we are faced with four major change imperatives:

1. The aftermath of a global economic collapse has created the economic necessity of developing 21st century skills for an innovative and creative economy.

2. The spread of excessive affluence and economic inequality has reduced the quality of most people's lives and put the United States and the United Kingdom at the bottom of the developed world on international indicators of child well-being. This has given rise to a social justice imperative of developing better lives for those all over the world that extends beyond economically relevant skills alone to reduce inequalities (United Nations Children's Fund, 2007; Wilkinson & Pickett, 2009).

3. The impact of climate change threatens the very survival of our species and raises the necessity of producing both innovative technological solutions as well as changes in education about sustainable living in a world where there are now clear limits to growth (Giddens, 2009).

4. The generational renewal of the workforce—the replacement of the baby-boomer generation with Generations X and Y, whose approaches to life and leadership are swift, assertive, direct, team based, task centered, and technologically savvy, but also at risk of being hyperactively superficial—raises the imperative of producing a new cohort of skilled and responsible leaders who will be the stewards of the future (Howe & Strauss, 2000).

Before examining how these imperatives can be addressed in educational leadership and change, it is important to get some sense of the strengths and limitations of the direction of past reform efforts. These past efforts and their proposed solutions have not yet materialized as leaders face the challenges of the future.

Two Old Ways of Change: Venus and Mars

There have been four stages or "ways of change" in many developed countries since the 1960s (Hargreaves & Shirley, 2009). The characteristics of these stages can be likened to the mythical properties commonly attributed to the four planets of the inner solar system: Venus, Mars, Mercury, and Earth.

The First Way of Venus

The *First Way of Venus* has been described as the First Way of social reform (Giddens, 1999; Goodson, Moore, & Hargreaves, 2006). The welfare state defined the status quo from the end of World War II to the mid-1970s. Economist John Maynard Keynes and his followers presented investment in state services and welfare safety nets not just as a social good, but also as a benefit for the economy, as it developed the pools of talent that would fuel future prosperity. There was enormous confidence in the state's ability to solve social problems, fueled by a booming economy and spurred by the rising baby-boomer population.

In the latter years of this age, a rebellious and creative spirit entered public schools in the form of experimentation, innovation, and child-centered or progressive teaching. Teachers and other state professionals had great autonomy in the First Way of Venus. They enjoyed high levels of passive trust from an increasingly prosperous public and were left alone to get on with the job.

Teachers today are sometimes nostalgic for the freedom to develop curricula to meet the varying needs of their students as part of a mission to change the world. Others bemoan the loss of the same professional autonomy because they could teach their subjects just as they chose—irrespective of how much students benefited (Goodson, Moore, & Hargreaves, 2006). The First Way of Venus therefore suffered from huge variations in focus and quality. Teaching was improved largely intuitively and individually, through improvisation while on the job.

The First Way brought innovation, but it also brought inconsistency. Teachers from this period remember their principals as larger-than-life characters who left their stamp on the school,

> The First Way brought innovation, but it also brought inconsistency.

but not always in a good way. There was no leadership development or professional development to create widespread consistency of impact or effort. The profession was unregulated, and what little accountability existed was local only. Figure A.1 (page 330) depicts the First Way of Venus.

The First Way of Venus has left a legacy of the importance of innovation—a legacy that needs to be recovered. Within and between schools, this innovation occurred only in islands—a danger that is present within the current concept of charter schools. Leadership made the biggest difference to the success of innovation, but investing in good leadership was not a focus, as it should now be. It was a matter of luck or chance. We also need to recapture the First Way's trust in educators as professionals; at the same time, however, we need to bear in mind that this trust was often blind. In the 21st century, we cannot presume trust; it has to be earned. The First Way might have expressed some of the love and passion of Venus, but with all the inconsistency that resulted, love was obviously not enough.

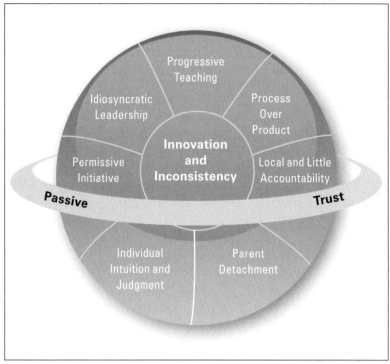

Figure A.1: The First Way of Venus.

The Second Way of Mars

A *Second Way of Mars*—more strident, aggressive, and competitive in nature, with an emphasis on markets and standardization—followed the First Way. With rising oil prices, long gas lines, and an economic recession, coupled with a maturing labor force in teaching that was becoming more expensive, people began to question whether the state was still the answer. During this time period, many Anglo-American nations placed schools in competitive systems of market choice for students and parents. The currency of this market was increasingly detailed standards linked to high-stakes tests that were widely publicized in league tables of performance and often combined with weakened levels of resourcing and accelerated timelines for implementation. This political strategy of educational change was subsequently adopted within the No Child Left Behind legislation in the United States.

Some benefits of this Mars-like way of force, competition, and conflict were evident in the emergence of clearer focus, greater consistency, and attention to all students, all with a stronger sense of urgency. But while achievement gains often occurred for a year or two, they soon reached a plateau. Parents had more choice, but only the affluent ones knew how to work the system to advance their interests and protect their privileges. The passive trust of the First Way of Venus was replaced by active mistrust between teachers and the public in the Second Way of Mars. Standards raised the bar, but shortfalls of professional support did not help students reach it. The costs were considerable to the quality, depth, and breadth of children's learning. The number of dropouts increased. Innovation declined, as did the caliber of teachers and leaders the profession could recruit and retain (New Commission on the Skills of the American Workforce, 2007; Nichols & Berliner, 2007; Oakes & Lipton, 2002).

In this Second Way, teachers bemoaned the "taking away of professional judgment and autonomy." They felt that "so much focus on meeting the standards set from the outside" meant they didn't "get to spend as much time thinking" about what was done in the classroom and enjoying it. Though some teachers were "still excited about teaching," they confessed that they couldn't "deal with the system . . . and [were] tired of fighting it" (Hargreaves, 2003, p. 91). Professional judgment was replaced by fidelity to prescribed methods. The Second Way of Mars precipitated a crisis of sinking professional motivation and lost classroom creativity.

Early in 2007, the prestigious New Commission on the Skills of the American Workforce pointed to America's declining educational performance compared to other nations. This was due to the relatively poor quality of the nation's teaching force, and to excesses of narrowly tested standardization that restricted the creativity and innovation necessary for a high-skill, high-wage workforce in a rapidly changing global economy.

In the Second Way, leadership was seen as overloaded, unattractive, and excessively exposed in the context of punitive accountability. Leadership had turned into line management. Teachers saw their leaders as managers who had forgotten how to lead. Their principals rotated in and out of schools with increasing frequency and seemed to have more attachment to implementing the district priorities or advancing their own careers than serving their own schools (Hargreaves, 2003). Figure A.2 depicts the Second Way of Mars.

A New Way of Change

A new way was needed that would focus on coherence and consistency, and retain the sense of urgency about learning and achievement for all students, but that would also restore professional energy and teacher quality, as well as develop the higher levels of creative learning and skill development essential for competitive economies and cohesive societies. In this *Third Way of Mercury*, 21st century skills would quickly gain prominence.

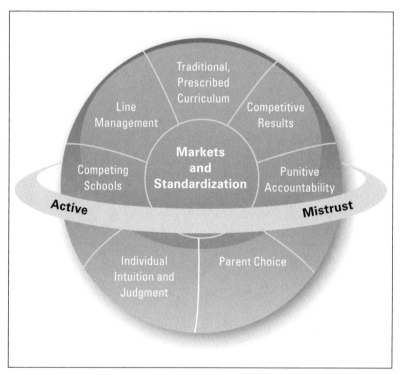

Figure A.2: The Second Way of Mars.

The Third Way of Mercury

The origins of the 21st century skills agenda stretch back to the late 1970s. In 1976, Daniel Bell invented the term *knowledge society* to describe a post-industrial world that would require an educated workforce capable of working in services, ideas, and communication. By the early 1990s, management guru Peter Drucker (1993) was anticipating a post-capitalist society where the basic economic resource of society would no longer be capital or labor, but instead knowledge, and where the leading groups of society would be "knowledge workers." In education, Phillip Schlechty (1990) was among the first to proclaim that the business of public education should shift to developing knowledge workers who would perform knowledge work. Meanwhile, former U.S. Secretary of Labor Robert Reich (2000) argued that, in a world of spiralling consumer choice, competitive companies needed the skills that could advance speed, novelty, cleverness, creation, invention, communication, and empathy with customer desires.

In the early years of the 21st century, leading international organizations began to take up the knowledge-economy cause. The Organisation for Economic Co-operation and Development (OECD) linked knowledge management to the challenges created by acceleration of change. This raised "profound questions for the knowledge students are being equipped with and ought to be equipped with" in the schools of tomorrow (OECD, 2001, p. 29). A world of just-in-time production and instant global communication requires people with ingenuity who can innovate and solve unanticipated problems swiftly and efficiently together (Homer-Dixon, 2000).

By 2003, I had discovered the pervasive negative effects of excessive competition and standardization in U.S. and Canadian schools, and was comparing these to a vision of a knowledge society that gave priority to the following:

- Deep cognitive learning, creativity, and ingenuity among students

- Research, inquiry, working in networks, and teams and pursuing continuous professional learning as teachers

- Problem solving, risk taking, trust in fellow professionals, the ability to cope with change, and commitment to continuous improvement as organizations

Teaching for the knowledge society, in other words, would promote creativity, flexibility, problem solving, ingenuity, collective (shared) intelligence, professional trust, risk taking, and continuous improvement (Hargreaves, 2003).

> Teaching for the knowledge society would promote creativity, flexibility, problem solving, ingenuity, collective (shared) intelligence, professional trust, risk taking, and continuous improvement.

The New Commission on the Skills of the American Workforce (2007) argues that America should have "a deep vein of creativity that is constantly renewing itself" (p. xvii). This requires "much more than a conventionally and unimaginatively tested curriculum focusing on basic skills and factual memorization." Instead, as well as strong skills in literacy and mathematics and core subjects, 21st century students must be comfortable with ideas and abstractions, good at both analysis and synthesis, creative and innovative, self-disciplined and well organized, able to learn very quickly, work well as a member of a team, and have the flexibility to adapt quickly to frequent changes in the labor market (pp. xviii–xix).

Tony Wagner (2008) identifies seven essential skills for adolescents and the modern economy that are rather reminiscent of the knowledge-economy skills listed earlier: critical thinking and problem solving, collaboration and leadership across networks, agility and adaptability, initiative and entrepreneurialism, effective communication, the ability to access and analyze information, and curiosity and imagination. Yong Zhao (2009) points out that many Asian competitors are already moving far faster in these directions than the United States.

The strategically influential Partnership for 21st Century Skills (2009) supports the work of these other organizations by emphasizing the essential skills that should be infused throughout the 21st curriculum: creativity and innovation; critical thinking and problem solving; communication and collaboration; information, media, and technological literacy; flexibility and adaptability; initiative and self direction; social and cross-cultural skills; productivity and accountability; and leadership and responsibility.

Twenty-first-century skills are part of a sort of Third Way of educational reform that is neither child centered and permissive, nor basic and standardized. Instead they are like the winged messenger of Mercury—characterized by speed and communication that suits a world of profit, trade, and commerce. This Third Way of Mercury promotes economically useful cross-curricular skills in learning; new patterns of professionalism, as well as professional interaction and networking among teachers; and more rapid and flexible ways of managing change in organizations. Figure A.3 depicts the Third Way of Mercury.

> Twenty-first-century skills are part of a sort of Third Way of educational reform that is neither child centered and permissive, nor basic and standardized.

The Third Way directly addresses three of the four 21st century imperatives outlined on pp. 327–328: (1) Its capacity to develop the

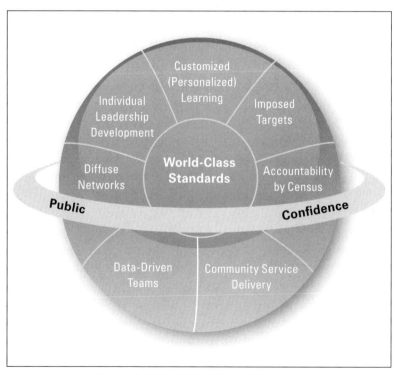

Figure A.3: The Third Way of Mercury.

skills and processes that accelerate innovation and knowledge circulation are vital for regenerating a floundering economy, (2) This culture of innovation and ingenuity may also be indispensible in dealing with the environmental challenges of climate change, (3) Engaging with the technical realities of the 21st century also appeals to students and their young teachers who have been born into this digital world. Economically, environmentally, and demographically, the 21st century skills agenda makes a good deal of sense. These developments are important and welcome; however, they are not without risk. In particular, the agenda harbors the following dangers:

1. It may overstate the advanced nature of the skills required in the new economy.

2. It does not really address the imperatives of social justice and increased equality.

3. In practice, it sometimes compromises 21st century ideals by maintaining Mars-like time-pressured performance goals related to standardized testing.

4. Its emphasis on speed and flexibility can lead to superficial engagements and interactions.

The dangers of the Third Way of Mercury. First, not all the work skills of the 21st century are 21st century skills. Matthew Crawford (2009) argues that many of today's middle-class workers are not dealing with complex problems at work using their judgment and discretion together. Instead, a great deal of white-collar work has been reduced to standardized operations. This is routine cubicle work, not advanced knowledge work. In other words, there are a lot more jobs like we see on NBC's *The Office* than those we see on the network's series *The Apprentice*. Brown and Lauder (2001) have pointed out that not all knowledge economies are like Finland with its high-skill, high-wage structure. Preparing cubicle workers to think critically and deal with complexity may sow the seeds of white-collar disaffection. It's not just people and their skills that need to change in the 21st century economy. The meaning of work has to be transformed as well.

Second, the 21st century skills agenda often (though not always) omits the knowledge, skills, and qualities that are beyond the world of business and sometimes directly opposed to it. Where in the 21st century skills agenda do we make sure that future business leaders will practice corporate integrity? How can we be sure that our teachers will teach that torture is always wrong, even in the name of democracy? Will attending to diversity just mean learning to get along with a range of others in the workplace, or will it also address the right of and necessity for different ethnic and religious groups to learn to live together? And where is the attention to ecological and organizational sustainability—to being prudent and thrifty in our lifestyles, buying smaller rather than bigger homes and vehicles, repairing rather than discarding broken items, sharing resources with our neighbours instead of guzzling greedily alone, avoiding working people to death, and so on? How can we be sure that 21st century skills will equip young people to fight for environmental sustainability, the eradication of poverty, and greater quality of life and social equality?

Interestingly, the OECD's (2008) international advocacy for 21st century skills addresses this second shortcoming of excluding the social agenda. It takes on much of this wider agenda compared to the Anglo-American nations when it describes the "core competencies and knowledge that OECD education systems aim to develop in students for the 21st century" (p. 11) as including ones that contribute to a happy life as well as to economic productivity. The question before all of us is whether we will define 21st century skills only as those skills relevant to the Third Way of Mercury's concern with speed, communication, and commerce, or whether it can and will also encompass the even broader and deeper concerns of quality of life, social justice, and sustainability.

For example, in 1996, the leadership of the U.S. Democratic Party signed a new declaration arguing for a political approach that could engage with a globalized economy, the end of the Cold War, and the collapse of the big institutions of industry and the state. They referred to this approach as the Third Way. Though Americans did not succeed in pushing this Third Way agenda forward—instead, the nation sank right back into the Second Way under No Child

Left Behind—Britain's new Labour Party government successfully broadened its base beyond the old working class and the unions. It sought to govern between and beyond the state and the market (Blair & Schröder, 1999; Giddens, 1999). England's Third Way emphasized responsibilities as well as rights, being tough on crime as well as the causes of it, maintaining social cohesion while stimulating a dynamic economy, and providing stronger support for state professionals at the same time as demanding more accountability from them. The Third Way was about developing the economy, but it was also about renewing the community and the social fabric of society. In the end, though, this larger Third Way went awry. The third and fourth dangers of the 21st century skills agenda illustrate why.

Third, in social policy and in education, the Third Way was undermined by persistence with too many negative aspects of the Second Way of Mars. In public education, a rebranded version of large-scale reform (LSR 2.0) has been even tighter in its imposition of ends than its Second Way predecessors, yet considerably more flexible in its orchestration of means (Barber, 2008; Fullan, 2006).

In LSR 2.0, government establishes a small number of specific goals, such as systemwide literacy and mathematics targets, and provides greater oversight in their prescription and pacing. Professional learning communities of inquiry in schools focus on test-score data, as do districts that then identify gaps and inconsistencies and design swift interventions accordingly. Collegial coaching and leadership supervision provide technical support to teachers while also ensuring they demonstrate fidelity to the reforms. League tables and school comparisons printed in newspapers and digital media inform the public about student achievement results, and parents in underperforming schools are given opportunities to transfer their children to schools with better results. Educators are encouraged to build lateral learning networks to generate professional motivation and drive change, and the public has access to information about teacher quality and student achievement levels. The government sponsors semiprivate alternatives such as charter schools or supplementary programs for students who are struggling in school. Politically imposed timelines for improvement are linked to short-term election cycles, and the failure of schools to meet these timelines leads to escalating amounts of intervention, so that, in general, intervention is inversely related to success.

Advocates of LSR 2.0 claim increased standards in measurable improvement, narrowed achievement gaps, enhanced professional quality and motivation, systemwide impact, and increased confidence in public education and the capacity of political leaders to manage it. Critics are more circumspect (see Hartley, 2007; Hargreaves & Shirley, 2009). They argue that the continuing overemphasis on tested and targeted basics marginalizes attention to arts, social studies, innovation, and creativity, which are essential for 21st century knowledge economies. There is also an inverse relationship between narrowly tested achievement and the development of the whole child and his or her overall well-being (Honoré, 2008; United Nations Children's Fund, 2007). The persistence of Second Way standardization both limits the economically relevant skills that schools can develop and ignores the other socially beneficial outcomes that exist beyond the economy. The intention to infuse 21st century skills into the curriculum is admirable, but if the skills are infused into an unchanged, Mars-like curriculum, then the aims of the new agenda will likely be thwarted.

This raises a challenge related to the fourth danger: speed. In 2005, Dennis Shirley and I inquired into and reported on a large school improvement network that had been established as a response to the plateau England's achievement results had reached under its LSR 2.0 strategy—the Raising Achievement Transforming Learning (RATL) project, initiated by the Specialist Schools and Academies Trust. The network was comprised of more than three hundred secondary schools that experienced a dip in student achievement scores over one or two years. Its approach was to promote improvement by schools, with schools, and for schools in peer-driven networks of lateral pressure and support, where participating schools were connected with each other and with self-chosen mentor schools, and then invited to conferences that supplied them with inspiration and technical support in analyzing achievement data, as well as a menu of short-, medium-, and long-term strategies for improving teaching, learning, and achievement results. The network's architecture emphasized transparency of participation and results, and most of its momentum and cohesion was basically lateral, rather than top-down (Hargreaves & Shirley, 2009).

The network was astonishingly innovative and, in terms of conventional outcomes, also highly successful. Two-thirds of network schools improved at double the rate of the national secondary school average in just two years. Pushing beyond and against the surrounding context of England's Third Way, the network elicited immense enthusiasm from educators. They were grateful for assistance in converting mountains of data into practical knowledge that they could act upon to improve student achievement, and they were appreciative of the concrete strategies they had gathered through conferences, visits with mentor schools, and on the Web portal. Here was a change network where energized educators could find and apply solutions in their own settings that produced demonstrable success.

Yet the network still had to allow for the pressing accountability processes of Third Way England, with its relentless pressure for ever-increasing and publicly displayed scores in examination results and standardized achievement tests. The consequence was what we call *addictive presentism* (Hargreaves & Shirley, 2009). This is when teachers' effervescent interactions often created a kind of hyperactive professionalism where they hurriedly and excitedly rushed around swapping successful short-term strategies with their mentors and each other in order to deliver the government's narrowly defined targets and purposes. The vast majority of strategies that teachers adopted were simple and short term, or "gimmicky and great" ones, as they put it, such as paying former students to mentor existing ones, establishing ways for students to access study strategies online from peers in other schools, and supplying bananas and water to hydrate the brain and raise potassium levels on test days. At conferences, school leaders engaged in interactions akin to speed dating in which they rotated in brief interactions of two or so minutes, swapped a successful strategy, and then exchanged business cards as they left. The ironic result was a new conservatism where collaborative interactions were pleasurable, but also hurried, uncritical, and narrow.

This kind of preoccupation with data-driven improvement too easily distracts teachers from deeper engagements with teaching and learning. An overwhelmingly short-term orientation leads to opportunistic strategies to improve results that secure only temporary success. What is missing here is a process by which educators can also develop and realize inspiring purposes of their own, or engage in deeper professional conversations about transforming teaching and learning. These consequences are not inevitable. As we continued our relationship with RATL and the network, it responded to our feedback, shifted its focus to longer-term transformations in teaching and learning, and developed specific strategies that still produced short-term improvements—but of the kind that supported and connected to these transformational goals, rather than diverting attention from them.

The risk of the Third Way of Mercury is that the age of instant information may combine with the political pressures of short-term election cycles to create a mercurial educational system of superficiality and unpredictability. But these risks are avoidable. It is not surprising that some of the most forward-looking educational systems in the world—like Singapore, Alberta, and Finland—have high degrees of political stability. Moreover, RATL demonstrated that it is possible to extend 21st century skills in learning, teaching, and change into the domain of broader transformation. Indeed, OECD's definition of such skills extends beyond economically related areas alone into the broader arena of personal development and public life.

We need an educational reform and leadership strategy that attends to the long term as well as the short term. This strategy must recognize that many business environments require not just speed and agility, but also the craft skills of cooking, carpentry, or even software development that take ten thousand hours or more of practice and persistence to hone to an expert level (Sennett, 2008). It must regard personalization of learning not only as a way of customizing existing learning in terms of how it is accessed (quicker or slower; online or offline; in school or at home; one pathway or another) but also as a way of transforming learning to connect it to personal interests, family and cultural knowledge, and future life projects. The Third Way of Mercury should be quick and agile and enable us to make urgent interventions when problems and needs are exposed, but it should avoid being driven by imposed targets and hurried meetings to make just-in-time adjustments to continuous flows of achievement statistics. And it can and should let go more readily of some of the controlling legacies of

> The risk of the Third Way of Mercury is that the age of instant information may combine with the political pressures of short-term election cycles to create a mercurial educational system of superficiality and unpredictability.

tested standardization that it has inherited. Alberta voted in 2009 to abandon one of its key standardized tests; and in its embrace of increasing innovation, England has not only abolished all but one of its standardized tests, but it has terminated its prescribed literacy strategy as well.

The Third Way of Mercury has part of the answer to the four imperatives, but not all of it. It offers immense promise compared to the preceding curriculum of excessive standardization and professional demoralization that characterized the Second Way of Mars. And it embraces creativity and professionalism without regressing to the incoherence and inconsistency of Venus. The 21st century skills agenda can be pushed harder into long-term transformation, like RATL; into a wider social agenda, like OECD; and into a creative and innovative world beyond the restrictions of standardized testing, like Alberta or England. Some of this can take place within the existing Third Way of Mercury, and some of it pushes into a Fourth Way beyond Mercury—the sustainable *Fourth Way of Earth*.

The Fourth Way of Earth

It's time to think about the future as well as the present, to care about our world as well as our work, to push for sustainability as well as success, and to commit ourselves to the common good of others as well as producing and consuming things for ourselves. Let's look at three examples of a Fourth Way of educational leadership and change that I have studied in partnership with colleagues.

> It's time to think about the future as well as the present, to care about our world as well as our work, to push for sustainability as well as success, and to commit ourselves to the common good of others as well as producing and consuming things for ourselves.

First is a report for OECD on the relationship between leadership and school improvement in Finland (Hargreaves, Halász, & Pont, 2008). Rebounding from an unemployment rate of almost 19 percent in 1992, Finland now tops the world on economic competitiveness and on the international PISA tests of pupil achievement. The secret of its astonishing recovery is Finland's inspiring mission of creativity and inclusiveness. This attracts and keeps highly qualified and publicly respected teachers on

whom the country's future depends. In cultures of trust, cooperation, and responsibility, these teachers design curricula together in
each municipality within broad national guidelines, and care for all
the children in their schools—not just those in their own grades and
classes. Schools also collaborate together for the benefit of the cities
and communities they serve.

Second is a study with Alan Boyle and Alma Harris of the London
Borough of Tower Hamlets. Unlike racially homogeneous Finland,
Tower Hamlets serves an immigrant population from poor parts of
the world like Bangladesh. In 1997, it was the worst school district
in England. Now, it performs at or above the national average on
primary school test scores and secondary school examination results.
Refusing to apply the punitive interventions or develop the market-like
academies that characterize England's Third Way reform strategy,
Tower Hamlets' inspiring district leaders have communicated high
expectations to and developed collaborative and trusting relationships
with leaders in their schools. District administrators are very present
in the schools. Relationships with people precede spreadsheets of
performance. Schools set ambitious performance targets together.
If one school falls behind, others rally round to help. Better teachers
are cultivated and kept as a result of positive partnerships with local
providers of teacher training. And droves of paid teaching assistants,
hired from the local community, work alongside classroom teachers,
easing the workload and developing active trust and committed engagement with parents and the community (Hargreaves & Shirley, 2009).

Third is a review of the Alberta Initiative for School Improvement
(AISI). AISI contributes significantly to the strong educational
performance of its province that almost matches that of Finland.
Created by the teachers' union and other partners with the government, AISI involves 90 percent of schools in self-initiated changes,
such as innovative teaching strategies, assessment for learning, and
engaging aboriginal parents in their children's schooling. Schools
select or design their own measures that extend far beyond test scores
to monitor progress. They are also being increasingly networked
with each other to promote peer learning, assistance, and success
(Hargreaves et al., 2009).

What do we learn from these examples that push us even further into a Fourth Way of educational change, and what does this mean for 21st century skills?

The Fourth Way of Earth begins with an inspiring and inclusive mission, not a vague embracing of "world-class standards" or a limiting of our sights to merely increasing test scores. The teaching and learning of the Fourth Way is deep and mindful, and so is the learning of professionals. This learning is often slow, not speedy; reflective and ruminative, not just fast and quick. Indeed, says psychologist Guy Claxton (1999), this kind of learning is essential for developing creative thought. Reflecting, slowing down, stopping—these are the mindful elements that foster creativity and breakthroughs (Honoré, 2004; MacDonald & Shirley, 2010).

Fourth Way schools act urgently in the present in order to protect and sustain the future. Their short-term targets are connected to long-term commitments, and schools share and own those targets— they are not politically imposed from elsewhere. As with the Finns, responsibility precedes accountability. Accountability remains, but not through a census of everyone. Effective industries test samples of their products—they don't test every last one. Exactly the same should be true of educators. While samples prudently elicit accurate quality controls, high-stakes and profligate censuses exert pressure, overfocus on what is tested, and often lead to opportunism and cheating.

The Fourth Way of Earth doesn't only build public confidence in education through improved results; it builds community with parents and others in relationships of active and engaged trust through extended school days, paid community appointments, and the kind of robust community organizing that President Obama has made famous (Obama, 2004).

In the Fourth Way, as in the Third, teachers and schools work together, but teachers work in thoughtful, evidence-informed communities that value both hard data and soft judgment, applied to deep and compelling questions of professional practice and innovation. They do not just hurry through meetings to produce just-in-time reactions to spreadsheets of test-score data. And schools do not only network with distant partners, as in charter networks, though that is an extremely valuable direction in itself. They also collaborate rather than compete with immediate neighbors, within and across district boundaries, in pursuit of a higher common good in a community where the strong help the weak.

Leadership here is not individual but systemic (Hopkins, 2007). Effective leaders help other schools. The system provides resources to replace their time when they and their key leaders assist their peers in this way. This distributes leadership around them and develops successors behind them. In the Fourth Way, leadership is sustainable as well as successful. Figure A.4 (page 346) depicts the Fourth Way of Earth.

Will 21st century skills stay only on Mercury, or can they also make it back to Earth? The Fourth Way of Earth meets all four of the change imperatives outlined earlier: economic, social, ecological, and generational. Like all reforms, the 21st century skills agenda will do best if it learns from the reforms that came before it and those that exist in systems elsewhere in the world. From the First Way of Venus, we can rekindle innovation and professional respect, but leave behind inconsistency. From the Second Way of Mars, it is important to retain the urgent and focused emphasis on achievement for all students, but to leave behind the narrowing of knowledge and loss of professional motivation that the excesses of tested standardization created.

The Third Way of Mercury contributes a focus on creativity, flexibility, lifelong learning, teamwork, and diversity to the 21st century skills agenda. Embracing the wider international definitions of 21st century skills from organizations like OECD, rather than being restricted to economically beneficial ones alone, will further expand these focuses. Turning to the Fourth Way of Earth and its concerns with inspiration and sustainability will help bring people together as leaders work together across schools, where the strong help the weak to serve a higher and sustainable purpose and to set and address short-term targets together that are directly connected to these inspiring long-term purposes. Outside the United States,

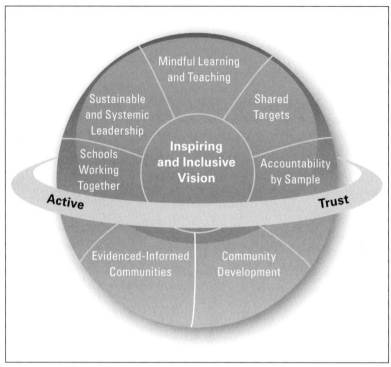

Figure A.4: The Fourth Way of Earth.

other nations have already attempted the Third Way, and we have much to learn from their findings of strengths and limitations. In other countries, we already have a sense of a wider agenda of 21st century skills that will not only enhance economic competitiveness (as in Finland), but also contribute to the social justice and quality of life that complement that competitiveness.

Twenty-first-century skills require 21st century schools. Mindful teaching and learning; increased innovation and curriculum flexibility; learning that is personally customized and also connected to students' wider life projects; evidence-informed rather than data-driven improvement; shared improvement targets; prudent accountability by samples on measures that match knowledge society objectives; energizing networks that connect schools to each other; and systemic leadership through which leaders assist weaker neighbors in the service of a greater common good—these are just some of the strategies that will give us the best 21st century schools that will develop the most challenging set of 21st century skills.

> Twenty-first-century skills require 21st century schools.

References

Barber, M. (2008). *Instruction to deliver: Fighting to transform Britain's public services.* London: Methuen.

Bell, D. (1976). *The coming of post-industrial society: A venture in social forecasting.* New York: Basic Books.

Blair, T., & Schröder, G. (1999). *The third way/die neue mitte.* London: Labor Party and SPD.

Brown, P., & Lauder, H. (2001). *Capitalism and social progress: The future of society in a global economy.* New York: Palgrave.

Claxton, G. (1999). *Hare brain, tortoise mind: How intelligence increases when you think less.* Hopewell, NJ: Ecco Press.

Crawford, M. (2009). *Shop class as soulcraft: An inquiry into the value of work.* New York: Penguin.

Drucker, P. F. (1993). *Post-capitalist society.* New York: HarperBusiness.

Fullan, M. (2006). *Turnaround leadership.* San Francisco: Jossey-Bass.

Giddens, A. (1999). *The third way: The renewal of social democracy.* Malden, MA: Polity Press.

Giddens, A. (2009). *The politics of climate change.* Malden, MA: Polity Press.

Goodson, I., Moore, S., & Hargreaves, A. (2006, February). Teacher nostalgia and the sustainability of reform: The generation and degeneration of teachers' missions, memory and meaning. *Educational Administration Quarterly, 42*(1), 42–61.

Hargreaves, A. (2003). *Teaching in the knowledge society: Education in the age of insecurity.* New York: Teachers College Press.

Hargreaves, A., Crocker, R., Davies, B., McEwen, L., Shirley, D., & Sumara, D. (2009). *The learning mosaic: A multiple perspective review of the Alberta Initiative for School Improvement.* Alberta Education, Edmonton, Alberta, Canada.

Hargreaves, A., Halász, G., & Pont, B. (2008). The Finnish approach to system leadership. In B. Pont, D. Nusche, & D. Hopkins (Eds.), *Improving school leadership: Case studies on system leadership* (Vol. 2; pp. 69–109). Paris: Organisation for Co-operation and Development.

Hargreaves, A., & Shirley, D. (2009). *The fourth way: The inspiring future for educational change.* Thousand Oaks, CA: Corwin Press.

Hartley, D. (2007, June). The emergence of distributed leadership in education: Why now? *British Journal of Educational Studies, 55*(2), 202–214.

Homer-Dixon, T. (2000). *The ingenuity gap: Facing the economic, environmental, and other challenges of an increasingly complex and unpredictable future.* New York: Knopf.

Honoré, C. (2008). *Under pressure: Rescuing childhood from the culture of hyper-parenting.* Canada: Knopf.

Honoré, C. (2004). *In praise of slowness: How a worldwide movement is challenging the cult of speed.* San Francisco: HarperSanFrancisco.

Hopkins, D. (2007). *Every school a great school: Realizing the potential of system leadership.* Columbus, OH: McGraw-Hill.

Howe, N., & Strauss, B. (2000). *Millennials rising: the next great generation.* New York: Vintage Books.

MacDonald, E., & Shirley, D. (2010). *The mindful teacher.* New York: Teachers College Press.

New Commission on the Skills of the American Workforce. (2007). *Tough choices or tough times: The report of the New Commission on the Skills of the American Workforce.* Washington, DC: National Center on Education and the Economy.

Nichols, S. L., & Berliner, D. C. (2007). *Collateral damage: How high-stakes testing corrupts America's schools.* Cambridge, MA: Harvard Education Publishing Group.

Oakes, J., & Lipton, M. (2002, December). Struggling for educational equity in diverse communities: School reform as social movement. *Journal of Educational Change, 3*(3–4), 383–406.

Obama, B. (2004). *Dreams from my father: A story of race and inheritance.* New York: Three Rivers Press.

Organisation for Co-operation and Development. (2001). *Schooling for tomorrow: What schools for the future?* Paris: Author.

Organisation for Co-operation and Development. (2008). *Innovating to learn, learning to innovate.* Paris: Author.

Partnership for 21st Century Skills. (2009). *Official website.* Accessed at www.21stcenturyskills.org/index.php on November 30, 2009.

Reich, R. B. (2000). *The future of success.* New York: Alfred A. Knopf.

Schlechty, P. C. (1990). *Schools for the 21st century: Leadership imperatives for educational reform.* San Francisco: Jossey-Bass.

Sennett, R. (2008). *The craftsman.* New Haven: Yale University Press.

Wagner, T. (2008). *The global achievement gap: Why even our best schools don't teach the new survival skills our children need—and what we can do about it.* New York: Basic Books.

United Nations Children's Fund. (2007). *Child poverty in perspective: An overview of child well-being in rich countries.* Florence, Italy: UNICEF Innocenti Research Centre.

Wilkinson, R., & Pickett, K. (2009). *The spirit level: Why more equal societies almost always do better.* London: Allen Lane.

Zhao, Y. (2009). *Catching up or leading the way: American education in the age of globalization.* Alexandria, VA: Association for Supervision and Curriculum Development.

Index

global work ethic, technology and
culture of schooling, 276, 278–282
good work, ethical mind type and, 19, 22
Google
social networks and, 291–292, 293
technology in daily practice, 299
technology use statistics, 243
as verb, 260
Google Docs
collaborative tasks and, 234, 281
technology in daily practice, 298
Gould (1981), 306
grading. *See also* testing
framework for assessments, 305
individual versus team results,
310–311
New Tech schools, 121
policies for 21st century demands, 40
gradual release of responsibility model,
231–239
Graham, Patricia, 27
Graham and Ferriter (2010), 87
graphics. *See also* visualization, as
innovation
graphic novel creation, 234, 237
innovation and, 250
syntheses and, 16
Great Britain, Key Stage 3 ICT Literacy
Assessment, 70. *See also* United
Kingdom
Greenwich Public Schools (2006), 187–188
group discriminations, respectful mind
type and, 19–20
group reports, constructive controversy
and, 204
guided instruction, gradual release of
responsibility model, 231–234
Guitar video, viewing statistics, 243

H

H1N1 virus, task example, 162–163
habits of mind
competitive habits, 310–311
elementary school example, 110–111
Hakkarainen, Palonen, Paavola, and
Lehtinen (2004), 266
Hargreaves (2003), 333–334
Hargreaves (2009), 318

Hargreaves, Halász, and Pont (2008),
342–343
Hargreaves and Shirley (2005), 339
Hargreaves and Shirley (2009), 339
Harris, Alma, 343
Hattie (2008), 88
Hattie (2009), 315
Henderson (2009), 197
Herbert et al. (2003), 154
Herrnstein and Murray (1994), 306
hierarchical workplace structures,
Framework for 21st Century Learning
and, xx–xxi
higher education. *See* postsecondary
education
Higher Education Academy (2009), 267
higher-order thinking skills
advances in assessment, 71
policies for 21st century demands,
34–35, 36
high-quality reasoning skills, need for
creative entrepreneurs, 213
high schools
cornerstone assessment tasks, 162–163
democratization of knowledge, 262
dropout rate, xviii, 246
Framework for 21st Century Learning,
xviii, 3
modeling and, 231
policies for 21st century demands,
46, 47
problem-based learning, 179–187
professional learning communities, 89
school building design, 128, 129,
132–136, 138–142, 144–145
sharing online, potentials and pitfalls
of, 291
technology and culture of schooling,
282
High Tech High
building design, 128, 138–142, 144
problem-based learning, 195
High Tech Middle
participatory learning, 264–265, 266
school building design, 140, 141
Hirschman (1970), 24–25
history education. *See also* social studies education
disciplined mind type, 12

On Excellence in Teaching
Edited by Robert Marzano
The world's best education researchers, theorists, and staff developers deliver a wide range of theories and strategies focused on effective instruction.
BKF278

Change Wars
Edited by Michael Fullan and Andy Hargreaves
In the third Leading Edge™ anthology, education luminaries from around the globe share their theories-in-action on how to achieve deep change.
BKF254

Ahead of the Curve: The Power of Assessment to Transform Teaching and Learning
Edited by Douglas Reeves
Leaders in education contribute their perspectives of effective assessment design and implementation, sending out a call for redirecting assessment to improve student achievement and inform instruction.
BKF232

On Common Ground: The Power of Professional Learning Communities
Edited by Richard DuFour, Robert Eaker, and Rebecca DuFour
Examine a colorful cross-section of educators' experiences with PLCs. This collection of insights from practitioners throughout North America highlights the benefits of a PLC.
BKF180